Understanding the European Union's External Relations

The European Union is one of the world's biggest economies. However, its role as an international actor is ambiguous and it is not always able to transform its political power into effective external policies. The development of an 'assertive' European Union challenges the image of an internal project aimed at economic integration and international relations theories based on unitary state actors.

The contributors explore a wide range of issues and policy areas in all three pillars of the Union – the European Community and its legislation, the Common Foreign and Security Policy, and Justice and Home Affairs. In doing so they unravel the dynamics that led to EU co-operation on external policies, the internal decision-making on external policies and the effects these policies have on other countries and the international arena.

This book systematically links the European Union's external relations to existing political theories, showing how existing theories need to be modified in order to deal with specific characteristics of the EU as an international actor. It will appeal to students and researchers of the EU as well as those with a general interest in political science discourse.

Michèle Knodt is Assistant Professor of Political Science at the University of Mannheim and director of a research project based at the Mannheim Centre for European Social Research. **Sebastiaan Princen** is working as a postdoctoral researcher at the Utrecht School of Governance at the University of Utrecht in the Netherlands.

Routledge/ECPR Studies in European Political Science
Edited by Jan W. van Deth
University of Mannheim, Germany on behalf of the European Consortium for Political Research

The Routledge/ECPR Studies in European Political Science series is published in association with the European Consortium for Political Research – the leading organization concerned with the growth and development of political science in Europe. The series presents high-quality edited volumes on topics at the leading edge of current interest in political science and related fields, with contributions from European scholars and others who have presented work at ECPR workshops or research groups.

Understanding the European Union's External Relations

Edited by Michèle Knodt and
Sebastiaan Princen

LONDON AND NEW YORK

First published 2003 by Routledge
11 New Fetter Lane, London EC4P 4EE

Simultaneously published in the USA and Canada
by Routledge
29 West 35th Street, New York, NY 10001

Routledge is an imprint of the Taylor and Francis Group

Typeset in Times New Roman by GreenGate Publishing Services,
Tonbridge, Kent

Printed and bound in Great Britain by MPG Books Ltd, Bodmin

British Library Cataloguing in Publication Data
A catalogue record for this book is available from the British Library

Library of Congress Cataloging in Publication Data
A catalog record for this book has been requested

ISBN 0-415-29697-8

Contents

viii *Contents*

Illustrations

Figures

Tables

Boxes

Notes on contributors

Marta A. Ballesteros is researcher at the Departamento de Ciencia Política y de la Administración, Facultad de Ciencias Políticas e Sociais, Universidad de Santiago de Compostela. Area of work or area of specialization: Fisheries management; Common Pool Resource management in the European Union. Publications: Losada, A., Ballesteros, M. A., and Mahou, X. M. (2000): 'A Información Agraria e Pesqueira na Voz de Galicia', in *Identidade Colectiva e Medios de Comunicación en Galicia 1977–1996*, Instituto Ramón Piñeiro, Santiago de Compostela; VVAA (2001) 'Ponencia Pesca' in Asociación Proyecto Galicia 2010 (ed.) Galicia 2010, Santiago de Compostela, chapter 10, 439–485.

Yves Buchet de Neuilly is Maître de conférence (Senior lecturer) at the University of Lille II, France. He is working on the institutionalization process of EU external action. Main publications: 'L'irrésistible ascension du Haut représentant pour la PESC. Une solution institutionnelle dans une pluralité d'espaces d'action européens' (2002), *Politique Européenne*, (8), 13–31; 'Des professionnels de l'innovation institutionnelle. La création d'une unité de planification de la politique et d'alerte rapide pour la PESC', in Didier Georgakakis (dir.), *Les Métiers de l'Europe Politique. Acteurs et Professionnalisations de la Construction Européenne* (2002), Strasbourg: Presses Universitaires de Strasbourg, 121–144; La Politique Étrangère et de Sécurité Commune. Dynamique d'un Système d'Action (1999), *Politix*, (46), 127–146.

Michèle Knodt is Assistant Professor at the Chair of Political Science II, Faculty of Social Sciences, University of Mannheim. In addition she is directing the research project 'Governance in an expanded multi-level system' at the Mannheim Centre for European Social Research (MZES) and is head of the Research Area 5 (International Embeddedness of European Governance) within Department B of the MZES. Her main research areas are the external relations of the EU and general questions of governance in the EU. Main publications: *Tiefenwirkung Europäischer Politik. Eigensinn oder Anpassung Regionalen Regierens?* (1998), Baden-Baden: Nomos; 'Europäisierung Regionalen Regierens: Mit Sinatra zum "autonomieorientierten Systemwechsel" im deutschen Bundesstaat?' (2002), in: *PVS*, 2/02, 211–234; (mit Markus

Jachtenfuchs, eds), *Regieren in Internationalen Institutionen* (2002), Opladen: Leske & Budrich.

Francesca Longo is Professor of EU Politics, Faculty of Political Science, University of Catania. Her main research areas: Theories of European Union, Internal security policy of European Union. Her latest publications: *The EU and the fight against organized crime: towards a common police and judicial approach* (ed.) (2002), Milan: Giuffrè; 'Italy', in M. Den Boer (ed.) *Organised Crime: A Catalyst in the Europeanisation of National Police and Prosecution Agencies?* (2002), Maastricht: EIPA; *Criminalità senza Frontiere. Le Istituzioni Internazionali di Lotta al Crimine Organizzato* (co-author) (1999). Catania: Bonanno Ed.

Ulrika Mörth is an Associate Professor in Political Science in the Department of Political Science, Stockholm University and also researches at the Stockholm Centre for Organizational Research (SCORE) at the same University in Sweden. Her main research area is European politics. Her publications include 'Europeanisation as interpretation, translation and editing of public policies', in *The Politics of Europeanisation: Theory and Analysis* (2002), Kevin Featherstone and Claudio Radaelli (eds), Oxford: OUP; 'Competing Frames in the European Commission – The Case of the Defence Industry/Equipment Issue' (2000), *The European Journal of Public Policy*, Vol. 7, No. 2; *Interdependens, konflikt och säkerhetspolitik – Sverige och den amerikanska teknikexportkontrollen* (1998), (co-author with Professor Bengt Sundelius), Stockholm: Nerenius & Santérus.

Dimitris Papadimitriou is a Research Fellow at the European Institute of the London School of Economics. He is the author of *Negotiating the New Europe* (2002), Ashgate, and has written in the areas of the EU's relations with the Balkans, administrative reform in Eastern Europe and EU enlargement. He has also published on Greece's relations with the EU.

Franck Petiteville is Maître de conférences de science politique (Senior lecturer) at the Université de Paris V–René Descartes Chercheur associé au CERI (Associate Researcher at the Centre d'Études des Relations Internationales, Paris). His research areas are the external economic relations of the EU, EU trade policy, regulation of globalization and WTO. Main recent publications: 'La Coopération Économique de l'Union Européenne, entre Globalisation et Politisation', *Revue Française de Science Politique*, vol. 51, no. 3, June 2001; 'L'Union Européenne, Acteur International Global? Un Agenda de Recherche', *Relations Internationales et Stratégiques*, no. 47, September 2002.

Sebastiaan Princen is working as a postdoctoral researcher at the Utrecht School of Governance, University of Utrecht (The Netherlands). He has studied the effects of trade measures on domestic regulatory standards in fields like environmental policy and consumer protection. His most recent publication is *EU Regulation and Transatlantic Trade* (2002), The Hague: Kluwer Law International.

Sten Rynning is Associate Professor at the Institute for Political Science, University of Southern Denmark. His research areas are the theories of Security and International Relations; Strategy and Civil-Military Relations; the EU's CFSP and ESDP; NATO and Transatlantic Relations. Main publications: *Changing Military Doctrine: Presidents and Military Power in Fifth Republic France, 1958–2000* (2002), New York: Praeger; 'Shaping Military Doctrine in France: Decision-Makers Between International Power and Domestic Interests', *Security Studies*, vol. 11, no. 1, 2002; 'Why Not NATO? Military Planning in the European Union', *Journal of Strategic Studies*, vol. 26, no. 1, 2003.

Helene Sjursen is Senior Researcher at ARENA, University of Oslo. Her research areas are the European foreign and security policy and EU enlargement. Main publications: *The United States, Western Europe and the Polish Crisis. International Relations in the Second Cold War* (2002), Basingstoke: Palgrave; 'Why Expand? The Question of Legitimacy and Justification in the EU's Enlargement Policy', *Journal of Common Market Studies*, vol. 40, no. 3, 2002: 491–513; (co-ed. with John Peterson) *A Common Foreign Policy for Europe? Competing Visions of the CFSP* (1998), London: Routledge.

Alasdair R. Young is a lecturer in the Department of Politics at the University of Glasgow. His teaching and research focus on the interaction between trade and regulatory policies and politics, with particular reference to the European Union. His most recent publications are *Extending European Cooperation: The European Union and the 'New' International Trade Agenda* (2002), Manchester University Press; and (with Helen Wallace) *Regulatory Politics in the Enlarging European Union: Weighing Civic and Producer Interests* (2000), Manchester University Press.

Series editor's preface

Travelling in Europe is easy nowadays. On high-speed trains from London to Cologne via Brussels, or from Turin to Paris via Geneva, borders are passed virtually unnoticed. In Porto the Euro is as common as it is in Utrecht and the same rules regulate many aspects of economic and social processes in many countries. Growing European unification means increasing competence of the EU as well as a further weakening of the member states. In just a few decades the European nation-state seems to have lost its relevance. 'Europe' has taken the place of the old national entities, as any traveller will notice right away.

As usual, common-sense notions should not be taken for granted. While the internal economic, political, social, and geographical borders are indeed closed down rapidly, the external position of the EU is less clear. Ever since the debacle of the plan for a European Defence Community in the early 1950s, the development of joint external positions and policies has been difficult. The development of a common market and the disappearance of borders, then, seem to be mainly restricted to internal European processes. These parallel processes of internal collaboration and external differentiation result in the paradoxical situation that the EU – one of the strongest economic blocks in the world – plays a rather minor role in international politics; be it forced interventions in Afghanistan or redefining UN-environmental policies.

In order to understand the external relations of the EU, detailed knowledge about the interdependencies of national, international, and European policy-making processes is required. The painstaking practice of collecting and interpreting information about such complex and complicated matters as the implementation of the Treaty of Nice, the arming of the Eurofighter, the negotiations with central-European membership candidates, or the management of world fishery disputes is but one of the aims of the contributions to this volume. As a second task, the authors all aim to examine the available theoretical approaches and to develop additional research strategies. Are existing approaches – which still rely on the concept of the nation-state – useful for understanding the external relations of the EU? The contributors to this volume differ clearly in their study designs, selected material, and the scope of their analyses, but they all cope with claims about the uniqueness of the EU as the crucial explanatory factor for its external relations. The three major parts of this volume address the central aspects of this project: co-operation and fragmentation in the EU, the challenges of multiple-levels and areas, and the relevance of EU-policies for the rest of the world.

Before specific treatments of these three themes are presented, Michèle Knodt and Sebastiaan Princen offer an overview of the main approaches and contested conclusions in this area (Introduction). The first part of the volume consists of three contributions mainly addressed to theoretical issues. Sten Rynning observes the rise of new tensions as a consequence of the introduction of defence co-operation in Europe (Chapter 1). As Helene Sjursen shows, understanding common institutions and capabilities in defence and security requires the enlargement of 'realist' approaches with deliberative strategies (Chapter 2). Alasdair R. Young pays attention to the Treaty of Nice as the most significant change in the formal foreign economic policy institutions in Europe (Chapter 3). The next three contributions focus on the consequences of fragmented policy-making processes. Ulrika Mörth starts this second part with a discussion of the technology gap between the EU and the USA (Chapter 4). Dealing with a very different situation, Yves Buchet de Neuilly examines the distinction between tough political declarations and the 'empty shell' of economic sanctions against Serbia (Chapter 5). Dimitris Papadimitriou discusses the various obstacles in the early association negotiations between the EU and Poland, Hungary, and Czechoslovakia (Chapter 6). The third part of the volume addresses the EU's opportunities to promote European ideas. Franck Petiteville defends the idea that EU economic co-operation is an attempt to export European values through 'soft diplomacy' (Chapter 7). In a remarkable comparison of European, US, and Canadian regulations Sebastiaan Princen shows how EU-policies induced a shift in US and Canadian regulatory standards (Chapter 8), while Francesca Longo reveals that the EU exports policy models that target transnational crime and influences national police and law-enforcement systems outside the EU (Chapter 9). In the last contribution to this part Marta A. Ballesteros discusses the crucial role of the EU in world fishery controversies and their management (Chapter 10). Finally, Sebastiaan Princen and Michèle Knodt return to the central questions of this volume – the EU's external relations and the merits of available approaches and explanations – in their extensive concluding chapter (Chapter 11).

Understanding the EU's external relations is not easy. The many policy areas are multifaceted and highly complicated. Institutional, historical, economic, and political factors for different states as well as for the international community have to be analysed in order to understand the challenges and opportunities for the EU. Beside, various theoretical approaches offer controversial analytical strategies and are still focused on nation-states. The unique character of this volume is that it offers a critical assessment of available approaches on the basis of careful empirical analyses. It promotes our understanding of the EU and European integration. The traveller between London and Cologne might be grateful for the disappearance of borders in Europe; in the long run it will be the strengthening of its common external position that will be decisive for the success of the EU.

Jan W. van Deth, Series Editor
Mannheim, September 2002

Preface

The development of an increasingly important and 'assertive' EU in the world arena, coupled with the EU's distinct and in many ways unique characteristics, poses interesting puzzles, not only for policy-makers but also for students of European integration and international relations. It challenges the image of the EU as a predominantly internal project aimed at economic integration, as well as theories of international relations based on unitary state actors as the main units of analysis. As a result, the EU's external relations have proven to be a fertile area of investigation for political scientists. At the same time, it has proven difficult to formulate adequate theories of the EU as an international actor. Whereas the EU's distinctive features have received ample attention, the attempts to link the EU's role and character to more general theories of international relations are still at their earliest stages.

Our book aims to contribute to the understanding of the EU's external relations in two ways. First, the book will link issues in the EU's external relations to existing political science theories. Second, the book will cover the EU's external relations in all three pillars. It will thus bring together debates from the literature on the CFSP and first pillar policies, as well as include a discussion of external policies under the third pillar (Justice and Home Affairs). Moreover, a number of chapters will deal explicitly with issues that fall under more than one pillar and focus on 'multi-pillar' processes.

This book resulted from our workshop 'Understanding the EU's International Presence', held at the ECPR Joint Sessions of Workshops, March 2001 in Grenoble. We would like to thank all participants of the workshop for their fruitful discussion on the papers. Among them, we owe a special thanks to the contributors to this book for their first-rate co-operation. In addition we would like to thank Sebastian Brünger and Rebecca Steffenson for technical help and language editing. We would also like to thank the Mannheim Centre for European Social Research (MZES) for their financial support in editing this volume.

Michèle Knodt and Sebastiaan Princen
Mannheim and Utrecht, January 2003

Acknowledgements

The authors and publishers would like to thank Ashgate Publishers for granting permission to reproduce Chapter 4, originally published in *Threat Politics*, edited by Johan Eriksson (2001).

Introduction

Puzzles and prospects in theorizing the EU's external relations

Michèle Knodt and Sebastiaan Princen

The evolving role of the EU in the international arena

Over the last years of deepening European integration, the role of the European Union as an international actor has become more obvious. Although at times the EU seems to be 'a silent global player'[1] rather than an openly assertive one (Rummel 1990), the EU shows an increasing and expanding presence in world affairs. Nevertheless, the active international role of the EU stays problematic.

The European Union's role in the international arena has always been ambiguous: on the one hand, the EU represents one of world's largest economies, which (potentially) gives it considerable political clout. On the other hand, the EU lacks a number of attributes that have traditionally been associated with actors in the international arena. Most conspicuously, as a regional co-operation scheme between sovereign states, the EU lacks the kind of centralized authority that 'traditional' nation-states usually possess.

Still, the EU has never been able to confine itself to internal matters. From the beginning, the process of European integration has had significant external ramifications, if only for the sheer size of the European market and the importance of the EU's trade relations with third countries. Since the EU has always been a predominantly economic union, it has been able to assume the greatest role in policies that are now associated with Pillar I, that is in issues that are covered directly by the EC Treaty. External trade policies have been conducted at the EC level since the 1960s, and the EC has become a member of several international organizations and a party to a number of international treaties (often alongside its member states).

In Pillar I, the EU has some exclusive powers (for instance in external trade policies), as well as a number of powers it shares with its member states (for instance in the field of external environmental policies). In all these policy areas, EU institutions, such as the European Commission and the European Parliament, play an important role, although to a varying extent according to the issue at hand. As a result, the EU member states have relinquished part of their sovereignty over Pillar I issues, giving a much greater role to European-level representation.

At the same time, policies under Pillars II and III (foreign and security policies, and justice and home affairs, respectively) have remained firmly intergovernmental. Even though they have been brought under the umbrella of 'the' European Union and the European Commission has often actively sought to gain a foothold in these areas, the formal role of EU-level institutions in them is limited. Decision-making and implementation remain completely under the member states' remit, even if they try to act together as 'the EU'. As a consequence, the EU has developed a unique set of institutions that differ not only from those found in 'traditional' states and international organizations, but also among themselves depending on the issue or policy area at hand.

The development of an increasingly important and assertive EU in the world arena, coupled with the EU's distinct and in many ways unique characteristics, poses interesting puzzles, not only for policy-makers but also for students of European integration and international relations. Scholars have grappled with the way in which the EU can best be conceptualized and how the EU's external conduct can best be explained. Thus, the scientific occupation with the topic has been as heterogeneous as the EU's involvement in external policies itself.

Shortcomings of the existing literature on the EU's external relations

An overview of the literature on the EU's external relations (see Conzelmann and Knodt 1999) reveals a clear separation according to pillars and a concentration on Pillar II, as well as an approach that is either descriptive or limited in its theoretical focus, and struggling with the special character of the EU.

Separation by pillars and focus on Pillar II

First of all, the literature is clearly divided by research on each pillar of the EU. In addition, much of the relevant literature tends to focus on developments in Pillar II, that is, on the EU's Common Foreign and Security Policy (CFSP).[2] This literature tends to discuss the shortcomings of the CFSP in the face of crisis, its poor external representation and the largely symbolic institutional reforms in the Amsterdam Treaty.[3] The focus on Pillar II poses the danger of neglecting some equally important dimensions of the external activities of the Union, namely those dealt with within Pillar I.

Theoretical focus in studies on Pillar II

A large part of the literature on the CFSP is more descriptive than theoretically guided research with sometimes very useful thick descriptions on the emerging CFSP as well as the common defence policy.[4] Often, however, the authors succumb to the seductive political rhetoric of the Council and the Commission's official documents. There, a common foreign policy is presented as 'self-evident' and more over as 'imperative'.[5] Two concepts are central to the discussion. First, 'the coercion to act', which refers to the argument that Europe has to face challenges that can only be coped with in a common foreign policy. Second, 'the logic of development', which describes the history of the CFSP as a natural process towards an ever closer co-operation.

The notion that the EU is 'forced to act' is based on three assumptions. The first is the realist assumption of the international system as an anarchic world where the struggle for interests and power is a potential threat for a political community. Second, as a result of the size of the challenges and the limited power of the individual states, the Europeans are forced to bundle up their power. Third, the world is divided into 'the others' and 'we Europeans'. The others are anonymously appearing as a challenge or threat. This vagueness of the others makes it easier to create a common identity. Thus, all elements to legitimize a European CFSP are available: the evidence of a need to act, the argument for why it is necessary to act, and the construction of the identity of the actors.

This argumentation is found in most of the official Council and Commission documents, most of the times in an explicit way (cf. European Commission 1999: 59), but also in political scientists' explanations of the CFSP. Thus, Stanley Hoffmann states that 'new threats were arising, or being perceived, by the Europeans' (Hoffmann 2000: 191) and describes how the Europeans react towards them. Similarly, Ginsberg argues that, in the period between 1972 and 1985, EC foreign policy actions were increasingly driven by responses to global economic interdependence and an emerging sense of an EC mission in world politics (Ginsberg 1989: 4).

The second concept of the 'logic of development' suggests an inevitable development in the direction of a CFSP. The argument is concentrated, first, on the message that the concept of the CFSP has always existed: at regular intervals, European states launched new initiatives to work together, which sometimes failed, but in the early years of the 1990s started to succeed.[6] A more detailed historical analysis would show that the intervals described were not turning inevitably into a kind of dynamic and that the label of a European foreign and security policy has covered different contents. The second implicit message is that the development of a European foreign and security policy is a question of competence. It begins with a constitutional step: shifting foreign and security competence from the member states and the establishment of common institutions, which should ensure efficient common actions. The new institutions are then provided with strategies and resources. The quality of these institutions is not at the centre of the discussion, which is focused on whether, from a subjective point of view, the EU carried out the 'right' policy. This could be observed in the Kosovo case, where the visible outcome of the common policy, the flood of refugees, made the European observer expect common European action to solve the problem. Compared to these expectations, the criticism on the CFSP is harsh and leads rapidly to the judgement that the effectiveness of the EU leaves much to be desired. This view found its entrance into the political science literature under the heading of the 'capability-expectation gap' (Hill 1993, 1998) and turned into a questionable scientific measure as well as part of the dynamic of the CFSP development. Both concepts are not satisfactory from a political scientist's point of view. Too vague are the mechanisms of explanation as well as the explanandum of the analyses, and too veiled are the theoretical concepts of the work.

Theoretical focus in studies on Pillar I

While with respect to Pillar II there is an ample discussion on the interconnection and co-operation between the CFSP, NATO and the OSCE, the discussion on the EU's relations with international organizations relevant to Pillar I policies (such as the WTO, the OECD and some branches of the UN) tends to receive less attention in the political science work. The available literature is often written by lawyers, which may account for the high salience of the topic of representation and membership of the EU in these organizations (cf. Sack 1995). If at all, the political science literature focuses on the intergovernmental perspective on European preference-formation at the international level, as well as the question of political consequences for the EC polity and the relations between supranational institutions and member states.[7]

The analysis on Pillar I also presents us with another limitation in the EU's external relations literature. Most authors working on the external economic relations of the EU are using a multi-level game framework which is based on the 'two-level games' approach presented by Putnam in the late 1980s and early 1990s (Putnam 1988). According to his approach, domestic groups pursue 'their interests by pressuring the government to adopt favorable policies, and politicians are seeking power by constructing coalitions among those groups' (Putnam 1988: 430). On the international level national governments try 'to maximize their own ability to satisfy domestic pressures, while minimizing the adverse consequences of foreign developments' (Putnam 1988: 430). Putnam assumes that, in international negotiations on international co-operation, domestic actors put pressure on national governments to gain leverage on the international level. Moreover, national governments use international negotiations to meet or escape domestic constraints. Both levels are simultaneously involved in negotiations, and cannot be treated separately as a two-step process but as a reciprocal process of influence.

Multi-level games, as Putnam describes them, focus exclusively on negotiations between governments at the international level. Negotiations are carried out by rational actors, which have to take into account the interests of domestic actors. Hence, it can be argued that Putnam's two-level games fit into Moravcsik's liberal intergovernmentalist approach (Moravcsik 1993, 1998). In this approach, the levels are clearly distinct from each other.

Most authors modelling multi-level interactions between the EU and the international level are analysing these multi-level games based on Putnam's assumption. Authors such as Edwards (1990), Patterson (1997), Collinson (1999), Moyer (1993), Deutsch (1999) and von Schöppenthau (1999) started from Putnam's two-level games and extended them to three-level games.

They did so by dividing the second, the international, level into an EU and an international level. The authors focus especially on the fact that negotiations are taking place simultaneously at all the three levels. Thus, interactions are influencing negotiations on each of those levels. However, all of these attempts are limited to bargaining situations, trying to explain the outcome of the negotiation by analysing actors' preferences and the type of negotiation situation.

Combining three-level games with an historical institutionalist approach, Alasdair R. Young (2000: 94) is one of the first authors who tries to go beyond a purely rationalist analysis of these multi-level games. In his work, the European level is constructed as an interface between the multi-lateral and the national level: on the one hand is the level of aggregation and formulation of the interests and positions of member states and on the other hand is an institution that is passing over multi-lateral agreements to the member states. This dual character as an 'international institution' and an 'international actor' is influencing the shape and content of member state positions, as well as the implications of multi-laterally agreed regimes for European and national rules. Analytically, he treats the *acquis communautaire* as an institution that is framing the interaction between member states and the European level. Member state preferences in respect of co-operation and their negotiation power are shaped by extra-EU and intra-EU interdependence (Young 1999, 2000; and Young in this volume).

The special character of the EU

Studies analysing the EU's external relations from a theoretical perspective have to come to terms with the ambiguous *sui generis* nature of the EU/EC, as the previous section has already indicated.[8] The discussion about what status the EC may gain in international organizations and international negotiations often makes a tacit assumption that the EU/EC can be understood as some kind of proto-state, bound to develop a more state-like character in international relations in the future.[9] Seen that way, the question of how to treat the EU/EC analytically and legally constitutes a temporary rather than general difficulty.

These characteristics of the existing literature have consequences for the structure and content of this volume. It is the separation by pillars, the concentration on the CFSP, the descriptive nature of texts, the legitimizing rhetoric and the theoretical limitation on multi-level games displayed by most publications which we want to overcome. Thus, this volume is going to discuss to what extent existing theories can help us to analyse the external relations of the EU and how we can deal with the special character of this entity just described above.

Challenges and approaches in theorizing the EU's external policies

The EU challenges existing theories of international relations that are based on unitary state actors as the main units of analysis (cf. White 1999). As we have seen, scholars have taken different positions on how to conceptualize the EU as an international actor. From one perspective, we have a strong community working on the implicit (sometimes also explicit) assumption that the EU is becoming a state-like actor. As we have shown, part of this community already treats the EU as a unitary actor, judging its policy-making by state-like criteria.

From another perspective, it can be argued that the EU is a unique entity, or an entity *sui generis* (cf. Jachtenfuchs and Kohler-Koch 1996) as it is often called.

The question is: why do some authors describe and categorize the EU as unique and what are the main characteristics of this entity?

The specific character of the EU

There are two developments that require an alternative conception, which is particularly relevant when it comes to the analysis of the EU's external relations. First, we can observe a tendency of blurring boundaries and transnationalization. The evolving nature of international negotiations shows that the clear territorial boundaries between national and international politics that developed with the rise of modern nation-states cannot be maintained. The same is true of the boundaries between national, European and international politics. Governmental space and the scope of unsolved problems are increasingly diverging to the point that the division between policy-making within the state and the environment is vanishing and the functional capacity of the nation-state is questioned (Albert and Brock 1995; Neyer 1995). Applied to European integration, different authors in Beate Kohler-Koch's (1998a) publication *Regieren in entgrenzten Räumen* (Governance in Political Space without Boundaries) deliver a vivid analysis of this process. Kohler-Koch assumes that interaction beyond the national borders, together with the functional differentiation of society, is leading to a functionally (instead of territorially) defined construction of political space and the drawing of new functional boundaries (Kohler-Koch 1998b). As a result, political competencies are shifted and sometimes superimposed across the varying levels.

Second, the discussion on multi-level governance within the EU has shown the complexity of European governance. By the end of the 1980s/beginning of the 1990s, acknowledgement of the so-called third (regional) level and the involvement of sub-national actors in the complex system of European decision-making drew attention to policy-making across the levels (Marks 1993; Jachtenfuchs and Kohler-Koch 1996; Kohler-Koch *et al.* 1998; Knodt 1998; Conzelmann and Knodt 2002). This development led to the conception of the 'system of governance' approach for analysing the EU instead of looking at policy-making on separate levels (Kohler-Koch and Knodt 1997). Referring to Sharkansky (1981), Kohler-Koch and Knodt compared this dichotomy with a marble cake as opposed to a layer cake (Kohler-Koch and Knodt 1997: 3).

The very nature of the European multi-level system – comprising both supranational institutions and member states acting together – gives way to a different kind of governance. The joint exercise of sovereignty in the EU has two consequences: it enlarges the territorial scope for political action 'beyond the nation-state' and it incorporates the member states into a complex transnational, multi-level system of decision-making. Being a member of the EU has the consequence that political institutions, that is governing agents, have lost their exclusive privilege of authoritative allocation (Kohler-Koch and Knodt 1997: 3f). This phenomenon could be described by Rosenau's concept of 'penetrated systems' (Rosenau 1969), that is where external actors do not just influence but have a share in political decisions. The concept could be applied to governance in the

European multi-level system. In acting beyond territorial borders, actors allocate authoritative norms and rules for the European political space. Thus, for governance in the European multi-level system the notion of an 'interpenetrated system of action' (Grote *et al.* 1996) has been used, which helps to analyse the linkage of formerly separated levels.

Following this logic, the core characteristics of a European system of governance could be described as follows.

1   A polycentric system, where various centres of decision-making exist that are formally independent of each other (Ostrom *et al.* 1961; Ostrom 1999). The hierarchical centre of the system is replaced by functional networks (Kohler-Koch 1999).

2   A system split into multiple, overlapping arenas characterized by loose coupling (Benz 2000: 152f; Frey and Eichenberger 1999; Hooghe and Marks 2001). These interlocking arenas include different actors, whose interests diverge. Thus, individual interests serve as the constitutive logic of the polity: 'Governing has to reconcile the competing preferences of self-interested individuals in an institutionalised system of peaceful conflict resolution. The legitimate right to have "voice" is not confined to members of a given community, but is extended to all who are "affected" by a policy' (Kohler-Koch 1999: 22f), that is those who hold certain rights or interests.

3   The organizing principle of political relations within the European system is based on consociation, which helps actors to manage heterogeneity within political communities. Combined with individual interests as the legitimate political unit of action, the governance of the EU could be categorized as 'network governance' (Kohler-Koch 1999: 23). Policy-making is consensus oriented and gives priority to problem-solving strategies rather than bargaining (Scharpf 1999).

4   Consensual policy-making relies heavily on interaction and communication between its entities (Knodt 2000). Thus accumulation of knowledge, collective learning and the exchange of ideas and concepts are significant.

The question will then be: does this *sui generis* character defy existing categories and theories and require completely new or distinct approaches? Taken to its extreme, does this position imply that most existing theories are largely irrelevant or useless in relation to the EU's external relations, and that it is necessary to develop a new set of concepts and theoretical notions specifically geared to understanding the EU?

In addition, most of the theories applied to the EU are using a concept of actors as traditional states or at least unitary actors. Thus, the question has to be, how can we deal theoretically with the EU without falling into the trap of conceptionalizing the EU as unique, or as a state-like actor?

Consequences for theorizing the EU's external relations

Three general arguments can be made against treating the EU as an entity *sui generis*. First, each of the traditional actors in world politics also has unique characteristics and can be argued to be *sui generis*. For example, the role and internal political structure of the United States are quite distinct from those of other states, but this has not inhibited the formulation and application of more general theories that apply to both the US and other states.

Second, even if the EU exhibits certain new or distinct characteristics, it may be useful to analyse them in terms of existing theories or to examine how they relate to the characteristics of traditional states in international relations. An analysis in terms of established theories may make certain seemingly unique characteristics look less particular. At the same time, it may also highlight the ways in which the EU does actually differ from traditional states and thereby contribute to a clearer understanding of what exactly differentiates the EU from traditional states and international organizations.

Third, using existing theories to analyse the EU's external relations will also maximize the contribution to theory formation and testing. Only by applying existing theories to the EU's external relations is it possible to criticize those theories and modify them where appropriate. It is exactly in this process that the EU's external relations are likely to make the greatest contribution to international relations theory, and political science more generally.

The EU's external relations may challenge existing theories in two ways.

1   By requiring the reformulation of existing theories to take into account the EU's specific characteristics.
2   By being a laboratory for developing theories about new phenomena that can be observed more widely in the international arena but present themselves most clearly in the context of the EU.

The second way offers the most promising new avenues for political science theories. For instance, the EU arguably offers the clearest example of a multi-level governance system, and most studies of this phenomenon have focused on the EU. At the same time, elements of multi-level governance can be discerned in international relations more generally, and are by no means confined to the European Union. As a consequence, studies of the EU can develop new insights that can later be applied to other international systems.

Conversely, the EU's external relations may modify our understanding of traditional states by highlighting dynamics that until recently received little attention. For instance, although the EU's decision-making processes involving both the European and the member state levels may seem to be unique to the EU, they may point to similar national–subnational dynamics in federal states, such as the US and Canada. These dynamics are not new, but a focus on the EU's decision-making processes may make them more salient and offer a useful framework for analysing them.

In addition the arguments we have made on the characteristics of the EU could lead us to another consequence. We should think about shifting our research focus and questions on our conception of policy-making in the EU (with respect to external relations) away from approaches which focus on the characteristics of actors. Rather, we should place processes at the centre of our research, a point that will be discussed in more detail in our conclusions.

Understanding the EU's external relations: puzzles and prospects

The specific characteristics of EU policy-making in respect to its external relations, described in the previous sections, give rise to three claims for uniqueness that would require special theories for understanding the EU's external relations. These claims relate to: the degree of external co-operation, the internal decision-making about external policies, and the effects that the EU's external policies have.

The decision to co-operate

First, the EU differs in the degree to which its member states co-operate externally. As was shown above, the EU's external competencies differ considerably between policy areas. Even in the most 'Europeanized' policy areas, some issues have and others have not been transferred to the EU level. For instance, external trade policies have always been the clearest example of exclusive European competence in external relations. However, in 1994, after the European Commission had negotiated the series of agreements that led to the creation of the World Trade Organization, the European Court of Justice ruled in its 1/94 decision that some forms of trade in services and intellectual property did not fall under the exclusive EU competence, and that those parts of the GATS and TRIPS agreement had to be ratified by the EU as well as the individual member states (ECJ 1994). Meanwhile, with the Nice Treaty, parts of the GATS and TRIPS agreement have moved into exclusive competence of the EU. In other areas, the EU's external competencies are still less clear. As a result, and unlike in traditional states, the boundaries of the EU's external conduct and competencies are unclear, often hotly contested, and continually moving as shown by the WTO example, which may strongly affect the scope and character of the EU's international conduct. The decision to co-operate externally is addressed in Part I of this volume.

The contributions in Chapters 1, 2 and 3 deal with a number of questions: Why and under which conditions does the EU co-operate externally? Can we differentiate between different degrees of co-operation? What effect does the degree of co-operation have on future EU and member state behaviour? Are there differences between the different Pillars? Could there be any kind of cross-fertilization from bringing together research on the different Pillars? As a result, do we have to characterize the EU as an incomplete actor when it comes to co-operation in the international arena?

Three contributions elaborate on these questions with regard to Pillars I and II. Sten Rynning and Helene Sjursen are taking a look at the setting up of the EU's

Common Foreign and Security Policy from different theoretical approaches. While Rynning is taking a neo-classical realist approach, Sjursen bases her analysis on an 'interpretative' institutionalist approach. Alasdair Young focuses on policies under Pillar I, combining a multi-level game with an institutionalist approach.

Internal decision-making on external policies

Second, once the EU is acting externally, its internal decision-making processes about external affairs differ from those in traditional states. The EU's distinctiveness in this regard is arguably most pronounced in two characteristics: its *multi-level* character, and its *multi-pillar* character. The EU's decision-making processes involve actors at different levels and in different arenas. In many areas, both European-level actors and member states play a role, as well as actors that simultaneously operate at more than one level (such as certain interest groups). In general, the role played by EU member states is incomparably larger than that played by subnational units in any 'traditional' state.

As was discussed above, the EU also operates under different institutional configurations depending on the pillar under which an issue is handled. This is a complication for theories in itself, but it is compounded by the fact that several issues fall partly under one and partly under another pillar. For instance, economic sanctions require a political decision under Pillar II and implementing decisions under Pillar I. Likewise, external justice affairs have partly been dealt with under Pillar III and partly under Pillar II. Thus in addition, we have to cope with cross-pillar or multi-pillar issues in our analyses.

Both the multi-level and the multi-pillar characteristics add a degree of complexity to the EU's decision-making processes. Besides, they cause a degree of incoherence that has often been lamented by commentators and which arguably gives the EU the character of a fragmented actor. In terms of political science theory, they complicate the use of theories that were developed for other kinds of actors.

The issues of multi-level and multi-pillar decision-making are especially dealt with in the contributions that form Part II of this volume. The questions relevant here are: what does the multi-level and multi-pillar character mean for the decision-making system of the EU? How does it affect the policies within the EU? How does it affect the roles of the actors? What does the choice of the arena mean for the outcome of negotiations on an issue? What consequences can negotiations on the same issue on different levels have?

Ulrika Mörth's contribution focuses on the issue of defence equipment, which combines military and foreign policy as well as technological and economic aspects. She shows how, through a process of 'framing', it is decided within which EU arena the issue will be negotiated and which role the different actors within the European multi-level system can play.

In his contribution, Yves Buchet de Neuilly deals with the cross-pillar issue of sanctions. Examining the sanctions against Serbia, he analyses the different outcomes of decisions within the framework of the two pillars.

A similar disparity between the statements before negotiations and the outcomes of those negotiations is found by Dimitris Papadimitriou in relations between the EU and the Central and East European Countries (CEECs). In his analysis, he takes a close look at the parallel negotiations on various levels that led to the association agreements between the EU and the CEECs.

The effect of the EU's external policies

Third, and finally, if the EU is said to be a distinctive actor, this should also be reflected in the effects it has on other actors or the international system as a whole. Thus, the EU's external policies may differ in fundamental ways from those of 'traditional' states and international organizations. In this volume, we look at this issue from the perspective of 'exporting models'. Key questions are: how is the EU carrying out a kind of institutional policy at the international level and within international organizations? Does the EU succeed in exporting its models of problem-solving and its norms and values to other countries and the international arena? What factors are crucial for effective institutional policy-making and exporting models, norms and values to external arenas? And, is there a difference between the EU and 'traditional' nation-states in carrying out this kind of institutional policy?

Four contributions in Part III of this volume examine these effects, showing us that we should look not only at the internal changes within the EU through external representation but also on the changes in the external arenas caused by the appearance of the EU as an actor. Franck Petiteville analyses the instrument of what he calls 'soft diplomacy', asking how the EU is exporting European values by the use of economic co-operation. Sebastiaan Princen also examines attempts to export values, but this time focusing on trade measures in transatlantic relations. Using the example of Justice and Home Affairs, Francesca Longo shows how the EU is exporting its model of police and judicial co-operation to CEECs, Russia and the Mediterranean countries. In her work on the EU's external fisheries policies, Marta Ballesteros shows how the involvement of the EU in policy-making within different internal and external arenas is affecting the management of fisheries.

Examining the three claims

The differences, if any, between the EU and 'traditional' states and international organizations may have important implications for the applicability of existing theories in international relations and political science, as they contradict several assumptions that underlie them. Still, it is not at all certain whether these differences do indeed undermine existing approaches, or whether these approaches are also useful in the context of the EU's external relations.

This book aims critically to analyse the three claims for a distinctive EU theory discerned above by bringing together a number of theoretical and empirical studies that seek to apply and explore the boundaries of existing international relations and political science theories in the context of the EU's external policies.

In selecting the contributions for this volume, we therefore chose not only theoretical articles but also empirical studies which apply theoretical concepts and can tell us more about difficulties in that application.

In the end, we aim to answer three questions.

1   To what extent is the EU a unique or distinct actor in the international arena?
2   To what extent can the EU's external conduct be explained by existing theories in political science?
3   What does this imply about the future of political science theory?

In answering these questions, we will follow the distinction made above between three claims for a distinctive EU theory: the decision to co-operate (Part I), the multi-level and multi-pillar characteristics of the internal decision-making processes about external policies (Part II), and the effects the EU has on other actors and the international system as a whole (Part III). Moreover, we will discern several ways in which the EU may challenge and thereby contribute to existing theories in political science.

Notes

1   The notion of a silent global player reflects upon events such as the building of the new airport of Sarajevo, where the EU served as a main sponsor, but where US Foreign Minister Madeleine Albright chaired the opening in the glare of publicity.
2   See among others the recent works by Regelsberger *et al.* (1997), Peterson and Sjursen (1998), Hill and Smith (2000), White (2001).
3   See the detailed discussion by Cameron (1998).
4   See Regelsberger *et al.* (1997), Holland (1997), Dembinski (2000), Schwarz (2000), Howorth (2000), Algieri and Emmanouilidis (2000), Duke (2001), Müller-Brandeck-Bocquet (2002).
5   For this and the following argument see Kohler-Koch *et al.* (2002).
6   See as an example Piening (1997: ch 2).
7   See Piening (1997), Rhodes (1998); Meunier and Nicolaïdis (1999), Meunier (2000).
8   For a discussion of current literature on EU foreign policy studies according the distinction between *sui generis* or comparative phenomenon see Tonra (2000). For a treatment of the EU foreign policy as *sui generis*, see Bretherton and Vogler (1999).
9   As observed by Allen and Smith, '[al]though there are few who would explicitly argue that the EC is on the verge of emerging as a "European state", it is the ideal type of a state-based foreign policy which lies behind much contemporary analysis of Western Europe's international status' (Allen and Smith 1990: 19).

References

Albert, M. and Brock, L. (1995) 'Entgrenzung der Staatenwelt. Zur Analyse weltgesellschaftlicher Entwicklungstendenzen', *Zeitschrift für Internationale Beziehungen*, 2, 2: 259–285.

Algieri, F. and Emmanouilidis, J. A. (2000) 'Setting Signals for Euorpean Foreign and Security Policy. Discussing Differentiation and Flexibility', *CAP Working-Paper*, October.

Allen, D. and Smith M. (1990) 'Western Europe's Presence in the Contemporary International Arena', *Review of International Studies,* 16: 19–37.

Benz, A. (2000) 'Entflechtung als Folge von Verflechtung: Theoretische Überlegungen zur Entwicklung des europäischen Mehrebenensystems', in E. Grande and M. Jachtenfuchs (eds) *Wie problemlösungsfähig ist die EU? Regieren im europäischen Mehrebenensystem,* Baden-Baden: Nomos: 141–164.

Bretherton, C. and Vogler, J. (1999): *The European Union as a Global Actor,* London: Routledge.

Cameron, F. (1998) 'The European Union as a Global Actor: Far from Pushing its Political Weight Around', in C. Rhodes (ed.) *The European Union in the World Community,* Boulder: Lynne Rienner Publishers: 19–43.

Collinson, S. (1999) '"Issue-Systems," "Multi-level Games" and the Analysis of the EU's External Commercial and Associated Policies: A Research Agenda', *Journal of European Public Policy,* 6, 2: 206–224.

Conzelmann, T. and Knodt, M. (1999) 'Understanding Multilevel Complexity: The European Community's Role in International Organisations and International Treaties', Paper for presentation at the 6th Biennial Conference of ECSA/USA, Pittsburgh, PA, 2–5 June 1999.

Conzelmann, T. and Knodt, M. (eds) (2002) 'Regionales Europa – Europäisierte Regionen', *Mannheimer Jahrbuch zur Europäischen Sozialforschung* 2001/2002, Bd. 6, Frankfurt/M.: Campus.

Dembinski, M. (2000) 'Perspektiven der Europäischen Sicherheits- und Verteidigungspolitik', *HSFK-Report,* 11.

Deutsch, K. G. (1999) 'The Politics of Freer Trade in Europe. Three-Level Games in the Common Commercial Policy of the EU 1985–1997', Hamburg: Lit.

Duke, S. (2001) 'Autonomy tamed: CESDP's Evolution and Role in European Security?', Paper presented at the AEI-conference 'EU as an international actor', Mannheim.

ECJ (1994) 'Opinion 1/94', *European Court Reports,* I–5267.

Edwards, G. (1990) 'The Relevance of Theory to Group-to-group Dialogue', in G. Edwards and E. Regelsberger (eds) *Europe's Global Links. The European Community and Inter-Regional Cooperation*: 201–218.

European Commission (1999) *Der Vertrag von Amsterdam,* Leitfaden, Luxemburg: Amt für amtliche Veröffentlichungen der Europäischen Gemeinschaften.

Frey, B. and Eichenberger, R. (1999) *The New Democratic Federalism for Europe. Functional, Overlapping, and Competing Jurisdictions,* Cheltenham: Edward Elgar.

Ginsberg, R. H. (1989) *Foreign Policy Actions of the European Community: The Politics of Scale,* Boulder: Lynne Rienner.

Grote, J., Knodt, M. and Larat, F. (1996) 'Convergence et Variation des Styles Régionaux de Politique dans le Cadre des Politiques Communautaires'. Arbeitspapier des Mannheimer Zentrums für Europäische Sozialforschung (MZES), AB III, Nr. 17, Mannheim.

Hill, C. (1993) 'The Capability-Expectations Gap, or Conceptualizing Europe's International Role', *Journal of Common Market Studies,* 31, 3: 305–328.

Hill, C. (1998) 'Closing the Capabilities-Expectations Gap?' in J. Peterson and H. Sjursen (eds) *A Common Foreign Policy for Europe? Competing Visions of the CFSP,* London: Routledge, 18–38.

Hill, C. and Smith, K. E. (eds) (2000) *European Foreign Policy: Key Documents,* London: Routledge.

Hoffmann, S. (2000) 'Towards a Common European Foreign and Security Policy?', *Journal of Common Market Studies,* 38, 2: 189–198.

Holland, M. (eds) (1997) *Common Foreign and Security Policy: The Record and Reforms,* London: Pinter.

Howorth, J. (2000) 'The Common European Security and Defence Policy: Nice was the easy bit: now for the real problems', Paper delivered to the Fifth ECSA-World Conference, Brussels, 14–15 December.

Hooghe, L. and Marks, G. (2001) 'Types of Multilevel Governance', *European Integration online Papers (EIoP),* 5, 11, available HTTP: <http://eiop.or.at/eiop/texte/2001-011a.htm>

Jachtenfuchs, M and Kohler-Koch, B. (1996) Regieren im dynamischen Mehrebenensystem, in M. Jachtenfuchs and B. Kohler-Koch (eds) *Europäische Integration,* Opladen: Leske und Budrich, 15–44.

Knodt, M. (1998) *Tiefenwirkung europäischer Politik. Eigensinn oder Anpassung regionalen Regierens?,* Baden-Baden: Nomos Verlag.

Knodt, M. (2000) 'Europäisierung à la Sinatra. Deutsche Länder im europäischen Mehrebenensystem', in B. Kohler-Koch and M. Knodt (eds) *Deutschland zwischen Europäisierung und Selbstbehauptung,* Mannheimer Jahrbuch zur Europäischen Sozialforschung 2000, Bd. 5, Frankfurt/M: Campus: 237–264.

Kohler-Koch, B. (ed.) (1998a) *Regieren in entgrenzten Räumen,* Politische Vierteljahresschrift, Sonderheft 29, Opladen: Westdeutscher Verlag.

Kohler-Koch, B. (1998b) 'Effizienz und Demokratie: Probleme des Regierens in entgrenzten Räumen', in B. Kohler-Koch (ed.) *Regieren in entgrenzten Räumen,* Politische Vierteljahresschrift, Sonderheft 29, Opladen: Westdeutscher Verlag: 11–25.

Kohler-Koch, B. (1999) 'Evolution and Transformation', in B. Kohler-Koch and R. Eising (eds) *The Transformation of Governance in the European Union,* London: Routledge: 14–35.

Kohler-Koch, B. *et al.* (1998) *Interaktive Politik in Europa: Regionen im Netzwerk der Integration,* Opladen: Leske und Budrich.

Kohler-Koch, B., Conzelmann, T. and Knodt, M. (2002) *Europäische Integration – Europäisches Regieren,* Studienbrief, Fernuniversität Hagen.

Kohler-Koch, B. and Knodt, M. (1997) 'Multi-Level Governance: the Joy of Theorizing and the Anguish of Empirical Research', Beitrag für den ECPR Workshop on 'Regional Integration and Multi-Level Governance', der Joint Sessions of Workshops, Bern, Switzerland, 27 February to 4 March 1997.

Marks, G. (1993) 'Structural Policy and Multi-level Governance in the EC', in A. Cafruny G.G. Rosenthal (ed.) *The State of the European Community. The Maastricht Debates and Beyond,* 2nd edn: S. 391–410.

Meunier, S. (2000) 'What Single Voice? European Institutions and EU-US Trade Negotiations', *International Organization,* 10, 1: 103–135.

Meunier, S. and Nicolaïdis, K. (1999) 'Who Speaks for Europe? The delegation of Trade Authority in the EU', *Journal of Common Market Studies,* 37, 3: 477–501.

Moravcsik, A. (1993) Preferences and Power in the European Community: A Liberal Intergovernmental Approach', *Journal of Common Market Studies,* 31, 4: 473–524.

Moravcsik, A. (1998) *The Choice for Europe: Social Purpose and State Power from Messina to Maastricht*, Ithaca: Cornell University Press.

Moyer, H. W. (1993) 'The European Community in the GATT Uruguay Round: Preserving the Common Agriculture Policy at all Cost', in W. Avery (ed.) *World Agriculture and the GATT*, Vol. 7 of International Political Economy Yearbook, Boulder: Lynne Rienner: 95–119.

Müller-Brandeck-Bocquet, G. (ed.) (2002) *Europäische Außenpolitik: GASP- und ESVP-Konzeptionen ausgewählter EU-Mitgliedstaaten*, Baden-Baden: Nomos-Verlag.

Neyer, J. (1995) 'Globaler Markt und territorialer Staat. Konturen eines wachsenden Antagonismus', in *Zeitschrift für Internationale Beziehungen*, 2, 2: 287–315.

Ostrom, V. (1999) 'Polycentricity (Part I and II)', in M. McGinnis (ed.) *Polycentricity and Local Public Economies. Readings from the Workshop in Political Theory and Policy Analysis*, Ann Arbor: University of Michigan Press: 52–74.

Ostrom, V., Tiebout, C. and Warren, R. (1961) 'The Organization of Government in Metropolitan Areas: A Theoretical Inquiry', *American Political Science Review*, 55: 831–842.

Patterson, L.A. (1997) 'Agricultural Policy Reform in the European Community: A Three-Level Game Analysis', *International Organization*, 51, 1: 135–165.

Peterson, J. and Sjursen, H. (1998) *A Common Foreign Policy for Europe? Competing Visions of the CFSP*, London: Routledge.

Piening, C. (1997) 'Global Europe. The European Union' in *World Affairs,* Boulder: Lynne Rienner Publishers.

Putnam, R. D. (1988) 'Diplomacy and Domestic Politics: The Logic of Two-level Games', in *International Organization,* 42: 427–60.

Regelsberger, E., Shoutheete de Tervarent, P. de and Wessels, W. (ed.) (1997) *Foreign Policy of the European Union. From EPC to CFSP and Beyond,* Boulder: Lynne Rienner Publishers.

Rhodes, C. (ed.) (1998) *The European Union in the World Community,* Boulder: Lynne Rienner Publishers.

Rosenau, J. N. (1969) 'Pre-Theories and Theories of Foreign Policy', in B. Farrell (ed.) *Approaches to Comparative and International Politics*, 2nd edn, Evanston: S. 27–92.

Rummel, R. (1990) *The Evolution of an International Actor. Western Europe's New Assertiveness*, Boulder: Westview Press.

Sack, J. (1995) The European Community's Membership of International Organisations, *Common Market Law Review*, 32: 1227–1256.

Scharpf, F. (1999) *Governing in Europe. Effective and Democratic?*, Oxford: Oxford University Press.

Schwarz, K.-D. (2000) 'Europäische Sicherheits- und Verteidigungspolitik: Auf dem Weg zur Realisierung?', *SWP-working-paper*, AP 3127, April.

Schöppenthau, P. von (1999) *Die Europäische Union als Akteur der internationalen Handelspolitik: die Textilverhandlungen der GATT-Uruguay-Runde*, Wiesbaden: Deutscher Universitäts-Verlag.

Sharkansky, I. (1981) 'Intergovernmental relations', in P.C. Nystrom and W. H. Starbuck (eds) *Handbook of Organizational Design*, Oxford: Oxford University Press, 1: 456–470.

Tonra, B. (2000) 'Mapping EU Foreign Policy Studies', in *Journal of European Public Policy*, 7, 1: 163–69.

White, B. (1999) 'The European Challenge to Foreign Policy Analysis', *European Journal of International Relations*, 5, 1: 37–66.

White, B. (2001) *Understanding European Foreign Policy*, Palgrave: London.

Young, A. R. (1999) 'Beyond the Final Frontier? Integrating Another Level of Governance', Paper to the ECSA Sixth Biennial International Conference, Pittsburgh, 2–5 June 1999.

Young, A. R. (2000): The Adaptation of European Foreign Economic Policy: From Rome to Seattle, *Journal of Common Market Studies*, 38, 1: 93–116.

Part I

The development of the EU's external role

Between co-operation and fragmentation

1 A fragmented external role

The EU, defence policy, and New Atlanticism

Sten Rynning

The principled decision to craft an EU Security and Defence Policy (ESDP) in 1999 raises a number of fundamental questions about the political nature of the Union itself. The ESDP can be seen as an example of states seeking to form an alliance, in order to increase their weight in armed conflict. However, the depth of EU centralized decision-making authority and EU policy breadth, make the label 'alliance' inadequate. We are then left with two basic options. We may see the ESDP as a linear consequence of past integration and think of the EU as an incipient strategic actor – an emerging pole in international politics. Conversely, one could argue that the ESDP is one of several factors that push the EU in a novel direction, effectively breaking the past trajectory of a seemingly 'ever closer union' and pointing to a more fragmented organization of European political authority.

This chapter questions whether the EU is a new strategic actor in the making, or whether a fundamental break is occurring with the past idea of 'one' community. The question is not whether the EU is already a strategic actor, because it is clearly not. Neither is it the aim of this chapter to rank centralized and hierarchical governance higher than other political models: this is a normative question better left for other contexts. The question is, rather, whether viewing the EU as a strategic actor helps us understand its dynamics. This analysis will search for answers by focusing on the key dimensions of a strategic actor, the extent to which the political centre is endowed with a vision of itself, its purpose, and finally whether it is supported by institutions capable of mobilizing defence resources.

The argument is that the EU is not a strategic actor in the making. Rather, the introduction of defence co-operation exposes a number of underlying tensions that likely will lead to a break with past patterns of integration and necessitate new institutional arrangements. The EU will become a more capable 'civilian actor' building on the vision of peaceful co-existence that is part of the EU's foundation. However, defence policy and the use of military means for coercion – peacemaking, intervention, and war – will not be rooted in the EU. Instead, we are likely to witness the development of a new 'concert' among the willing and capable – here labelled 'New Atlanticism' – that will attract notable attention among the old great powers of Western Europe (Great Britain, France, and Germany) along with the US. This development is contingent: it demands of the EU the recognition that 'flexible co-operation' must be applied to the defence domain, and it demands of the US a willingness to promote, via NATO, a more capable European security and defence pillar. The analysis concludes that these scenarios are likely, and that they invite scholars and observers to assess the nature and scope of a new turning point in the history of European integration.

High politics and grand strategy

How do we assess the impact of the ESDP on the EU? Realist theory offers itself as a useful tool because it deals primarily with the high politics inherent in the ESDP. It focuses on enduring questions of order (Kissinger 1994: 806): what are the basic units; what are their means of interaction; and what are the goals on behalf of which they interact?

Realist theory generally does not foresee a qualitative transformation of international politics and has tended to focus on the limitations rather than the potentials of European integration (see for example Wivel 2000: 99). A motley crew of constructivist scholars has therefore challenged the fundamental validity of realism, arguing that the EU is either representative of a fundamental transformation in international relations or, alternatively, a phenomenon of international relations so heavily dominated by ideas, as opposed to material power, that realism is reputed. These critics tend to use Waltz's (1979) abstract *Theory of International Politics* as a baseline for comparison (Katzenstein 1996; Wendt 1999) and argue that the realist model, 'based solely on material conceptions of actors' interests' (Risse *et al.* 1999: 148), cannot cope with 'ideas'.

Two problems are evident. First, neo-realism is a theory of the international system, not policy,[1] and second, realists who do analyse foreign policy – that is neo-classical realists – naturally accept that ideational and material factors interact.[2] Moreover, the jury is still out on the issue of whether the EU is an important anomaly in the history of international relations.[3] As long as the EU is significantly influenced by states acting autonomously of the EU itself, there is no reason to discard realist theory a priori. Realists have historically demonstrated how states block integration beyond the nation-state, harness economic gains from co-operation and struggle to establish political primacy within common institutions (Hoffmann 1995; Taylor 1983; Milward 1992; Pedersen 1998). Realists also believe that Europe's future is intimately tied up with the poles of power that emerge on the basis of collective histories and political leadership (Calleo 2001).

We may take our analytical clue from here: vision and material power are the key dimensions of a strategic actor. In the vocabulary of Fareed Zakaria's (1998: 38) 'state-centred realism', states will expand political interests abroad when central decision-makers perceive a relative increase in state power. State power has two dimensions. First, decision-makers must define the scope of state responsibility – define a vision for the state – and they must to some extent be autonomous from other social forces in the pursuit of this vision. Second, states must have a central policy-making apparatus capable of articulating and implementing policy, and they must be able to mobilize resources for policy. These dimensions combine into a spectrum where at one end we find states that are cohesive, autonomous, and wealthy, and at the opposite end states that are divided, society-penetrated and poor (Zakaria 1998: 39).[4]

Will the EU find itself at the poor end of the spectrum because states will bicker about ESDP prerogatives, or will the ESDP to the contrary put the EU on a path to become more autonomous and coherent? An answer will emerge from a consideration of (a) the ability of EU leaders to articulate a coherent vision and (b) the ability of the EU institutions to produce policy and mobilize resources. These two questions will be dealt with in the sections below.

First, it may be worth noting that we are dealing with more than just a spectrum running from strong autonomy to dependency. I label these opposites 'strategic actor' and 'community'. The former is capable of coercing the environment to respect its ideas, the latter focuses on the task of maintaining cohesion within.[5] In addition, centralized institutions may conceivably combine with abstract visions to produce an actor rich in means but with poorly defined and therefore fragile policies. This possibility I label 'civilian actor' because it is incapable of generating the policy cohesion necessary to exert violence – to coerce – in a specific conflict. It is conversely conceivable that fragmented institutions co-exist with strong visions. In this case we are dealing with a 'directorate' that will emerge whenever the context (i.e. an external crisis) calls attention to the area of common vision, after which the capable and willing will act on behalf of the larger community. The combined image of EU futures is presented in Table 1.1.

Turning now to political vision and institutional power, we are capable of tracing the trajectory of the EU and the impact of the ESDP. Many people will argue that Europe has traditionally centralized, but that it has been split between two visions of 'Europe puissance' and 'civilian power Europe'. An analysis of current developments indicates that the EU is following a new path and that a 'directorate' is the more likely scenario.

Political visions of Europe

The EU convention outlining a founding treaty, which EU heads of state and government will negotiate in 2004, has provoked a debate on the purpose and destiny of European co-operation. German Foreign Minister Joska Fischer ignited the debate in May 2000 when he outlined his vision of a federal Europe building on a

Table 1.1 EU futures

Vision ＼ Resources	Centralization	Fragmentation
Specific	Strategic actor	Directorate
Abstract	Civilian actor	Community

core of proactive states. Federalism was soon opposed by intergovernmental co-operation based on the 'democratic nation-state', first by French President Chirac in June 2000, then by British Prime Minister Blair in October 2000. Hovering above the political fray, the High Representative for the Common Foreign and Security Policy (CFSP), Javier Solana (2001), has argued that 'The Common European Security and Defence Policy (ESDP) is part of the wider project of building Europe's political identity'. While recognizing that the ESDP will not be easy, 'It demands a reorientation of national militaries and wiser spending. It requires new expenditure. And it necessitates a look at other imaginative solutions'. But Solana is optimistic. He argues that, 'All of these steps are underway'.

Observers may not share this optimism. Even in a favourable setting of regional stability, EU governments tend to get bogged down by treaty bickering that provides for, at best, incremental solutions. In the current setting, stability is far from given. This is particularly the case when one considers two external developments: first, the EU is about to enlarge its membership to include up to 27 countries, although 24 is the likely number in the short run; second, the US is waging a global security campaign against sources of terrorism.

Realist theory normally points out that 'external threats' generate internal cohesion. States band together to provide for their security and wellbeing. However, enlargement is not commonly recognized as a 'threat' in the European Union. Some countries, such as France and Spain, have vested interests in the smaller Union and have historically fought to secure 'deepening' before 'widening'. But a significant number of EU countries are strongly supportive of enlargement and believe that a bigger Union will reinforce their European visions. If game theory has taught us that institutionalization is more likely when group membership is held constant over time (Axelrod 1984), then game theory also tells us that the EU's current 'opening' – in terms of membership and practical policy – will weaken political cohesion. Enlargement may therefore be a cause of political division rather than a factor of internal unity.

The same condition applies to the US security campaign launched in the wake of the terrorist attacks of 11 September 2001. All European countries support the campaign against terrorism but they respond differently when it comes to policy detail and the extent to which the US should gain political and military support for operations in the Middle and the Far East. Some EU countries are drawn closer to the US, while some remain at a distance. The EU has responded to terrorism by outlining a strong package of anti-terrorist measures, but a symptom of the EU's 'low-intensity' role is that these measures fall within the third pillar of the EU (Justice and Home Affairs) and the EU has not responded to terrorism through its second pillar (the ESDP). In short, terrorism has reinforced the difficulties of generating a joint EU security and defence vision.

The impact of these events is underscored by an inquiry into the history of European security policy in the 1990s and notably the development of a 'low-intensity' security role standing in stark contrast to the US focus on global competitors and 'high-intensity' warfare. Recent events demonstrate that this supposed division of labour, while once appearing to rest on solid ground, is frail.

In the mid-1990s, European unity as a 'vision' was encouraged by an aloof American policy and the intractable difficulty of intervening in the Balkan wars while also building an institutional architecture in Western and Central Europe. A political vision took root in Paris, London, and Berlin. Europe – in one shape or another – needed to organize itself in order to deal with a range of new security tasks that notably the US was not interested in handling. Britain and France, along with the Netherlands, therefore spearheaded a Rapid Reaction Force that intervened in Bosnia ahead of the Dayton peace talks in 1995. Later, in 1998, Britain and France joined forces in the St Malo agreement that became the turning point in the creation of the ESDP (Cogan 2001: 99). The two countries agreed that if the US does not want to become engaged, the EU must be able to act autonomously. This ambition of European conflict resolution had an instinctive appeal to most EU members (EU Presidency 1999a, 1999b). Germany lacked a national defence policy, for obvious historical reasons, and demonstrated its engagement in mediation during the Kosovo conflict of 1999. The small and neutral EU countries have traditionally supported policies that reinforce the general principles of international order – as opposed to power politics – and they, like Britain, saw in the ESDP an opportunity to maintain the American engagement in European security. Enhancing EU crisis management capacities and US leadership vis-à-vis European great powers were thus mutually supporting goals.

For its part, the US focused on its global security posture. An 'hegemonic impulse' is present throughout the 1990s, beginning with the new world order in the wake of the 1991 Gulf War and the 1992 Pentagon 'Planning Guidance' that urged post-Cold War dominance. But this impulse, however constant, has also given birth to policies that waver between 'off-shore balancing' and 'continental engagement'. Continental engagement is visible in the continued presence of 100,000 US troops deployed in Europe and US investment in NATO as 'a means of maintaining and lengthening America's grip on the foreign and military policies of European states' (Waltz 2000: 20). In contrast, the balancing position is visible not only in the erratic engagement alongside Europeans in the Balkan conflicts, revealing an aversion to missions of 'nation-building',[6] but also in the policy of discouraging the defence dimension of the EU from developing too far. As Deputy Secretary of State Strobe Talbott declared in the fall of 1999, the US does not want a European defence capability 'that comes into being first *within* NATO but then grows *out* of NATO and finally grows *away from* NATO' (Talbott 1999).

Through the 1990s, then, a transatlantic consensus emerged around the axis of high and low intensity operations. In the words of Pentagon analyst James Thomas (2000), the US prefers 'high-intensity offensive' operations and is increasingly willing to let other allies undertake 'long-term peace-support operations'. Few political leaders have explicitly emphasized this division of labour for fear of promoting a complete Atlantic de-coupling, but through the 1990s it became increasingly clear that the Euro-Atlantic area was in need of a new security deal based on precisely this division. The US does not handle 'nation-building' operations, while the Europeans realize their 1992 Petersberg ambition to handle crisis management – up to the level of 'peacemaking' – and thus give impetus to their political identity.

Differences in national outlook within Europe presented an obstacle to the realization of the Petersberg agenda, but this fact, as noted by some observers (Heisbourg *et al.* 2000: 21), 'is not particularly novel, and is of limited helpfulness'. In light of the Kosovo intervention and the fact that 'half of NATO's European members were participating in combat operations', they conclude that 'differences between the two ends of the spectrum are narrowing' and furthermore that 'the centre of gravity of the spectrum is moving to greater, not lesser, acceptance of participation in operations involving the use of military force'.

However, the combined impact of enlargement and the campaign against terrorism has cast doubt on this optimistic conclusion. Kosovo may be revelatory of a European willingness to participate in conflicts that are becoming rare because they are fought on the periphery of Europe, thus fairly close to European territories, and moreover to participate in conflicts where defeat, essentially, was not an option. US leadership and its commitment to defending the credibility of NATO (more than the fate of Kosovars) ensured a very favourable context for this supposedly unprecedented European enthusiasm for combat operations. In fact, the European reaction to the American campaign in Afghanistan reveals a different but familiar image of European states dealing mostly bilaterally with the US in the defence domain, and of Europeans warning against a prolonged military campaign and its extension to, for instance, Iraq. Europe seems split once again between states who 'abhor the idea of power' and big countries like Britain and France who 'have the habit of power' but who are 'historically antagonistic' (Védrine 1997: 181). While Britain and France indeed did give birth to the ESDP in late 1998, one is well advised not to overlook the distinctiveness of their ulterior motives: respectively an 'Atlantic' and an 'autonomous' Europe (cf. Howorth 2000). Combined, the disunity in this core of Western Europe along with a stringent US focus on global terrorism will incite most European states to balance between 'ordinary great national power' and 'self-indulgence in self-absorption,' as Stanley Hoffmann once noted in relation to a united Germany (1995: 298).

Institutions, policy and resources

Why bother to analyse EU policy and resources if the underlying political cohesion is absent? Indeed, why even question that cohesion is a problem? If Ole Wæver (2000: 270) is right, then it may be 'a condition for European stability that the major powers think *differently* about Europe'. As long as national visions do not collide, each country can live with its comforting, if vain, vision of Europe. Europe will thus be impotent but stable.

We should nevertheless go further into the matter because the EU countries, cognizant of their visionary muddle, strive to build institutions that can articulate and implement policies. These policies relate to a set of liberal values, concerning human rights and democracy, and should operate while the member states juggle with the deeper vision. This balancing act is inherently challenging because difficult external crises and deep-rooted internal political dissent simultaneously challenge EU policy. In consequence, the EU has repeatedly built up expectations but failed to produce the necessary policy capabilities (cf. Hill 1994, 1998). European weakness, not strength, drew the US into Bosnian crisis management and the Dayton Peace Accord.[7] 'When confronted with the crisis caused by Yugoslavia's dissolution, the West used the United Nations to pursue a course of shameless diplomatic compromise mixed with inadequate military responses and well-intentioned but counterproductive humanitarianism' (Weiss 1999: 135). Does the ESDP represent a new departure or old wine in new bottles? In light of the conclusion reached earlier, that a common vision is absent, the question is really related to the lower level of Table 1.1 (p.21). In other words, will the EU become a 'community' akin to the view of Ole Wæver, or will it gain enough institutional coherence to become a 'civilian actor'? Empirical evidence indicates that an actor, albeit civilian, is in the making. Three aspects should be emphasized.

First of all, the EU is building a set of institutions that is much more stringent and capable than previously. This achievement is a direct result of the St Malo initiative and the ESDP process. As noted, St Malo brought together the main proponents of Atlanticism and Europeanism and therefore undid the deadlock of the Amsterdam Treaty of June 1997. This treaty brought crisis management operations, notably including their military dimension, into the EU (hitherto they were in the WEU) but also failed to provide an appropriate institutional infrastructure. Atlanticist and neutral countries refused institutional strengthening as long as it appeared that NATO thus would be challenged and the EU might become a 'strategic actor'.[8] Following St Malo and the Kosovo war, the EU decided first in Cologne in June 1999 and then in Helsinki the following December to build the necessary institutions to provide continuity and coherence.

The Council of Ministers now relies on two pillars in the ESDP, one bureaucratic, the other political (cf. EU Presidency 2000b; Rynning 2001). The bureaucratic pillar, headed by the High Representative for the CFSP (a post created in Amsterdam), received a new component in the shape of a Military Staff composed of approximately 130 officers tasked with 'early warning, situation assessment and strategic planning for Petersberg tasks'.[9] The political pillar was substantially modified. Access to the Ministers' meeting is gained through the familiar Committee of Permanent Representatives (COREPER), but underneath COREPER we find first a new Political and Security Committee (PSC) (composed of national representatives) that must draw up policy options, supervise CFSP operations and co-ordinate with NATO. The PSC will in turn draw on the expertise of another new institution, the Military Committee, composed of national Chiefs of Staff and their representatives,[10] which is the highest military body of the EU.

Second, the EU has come far, from a historical perspective, in planning military capabilities that will sustain the ESDP. The development of these capabilities is attached to the quantitative goal defined in Helsinki, December 1999: the EU must be able to project up to 60,000 troops (along with 400 ships and 100 aircraft) into a zone of conflict for up to one year. Capability or force planning has now become an integral part of the EU, beginning with the Helsinki announcement that the EU 'will develop a method of consultation' through which the Helsinki goals can be met, 'with a regular review of progress made' (EU Presidency 1999b: annex IV). The regular review so far consists of a Capabilities Commitment Conference, November 2000, where a first catalogue of national force contributions was assembled, as well as a Capabilities Improvement Conference, November 2001, where major investment areas were identified. Currently, the member states are not planning another such major conference but intend instead to focus on achieving new investments and thus military capabilities. Current efforts are focusing on the establishment of various 'Action Groups' composed of countries willing to invest in a certain capability. In line with the Helsinki ambition to respect 'Member States' political will', these groups are co-ordinated but not centrally directed or distributed.

This capability process has potential although one should not overlook inherent difficulties. Budgets illustrate one major difficulty: EU members are spending only half as much on defence as the US, and, even more revealing, less than one third on research and development (R&D), and approximately 35–40 per cent less on acquisitions. Lean budgets significantly increase the need for procurement co-operation. Revealingly, the force catalogue assembled at the November 2000 capabilities conference dealt with existing forces only (cf. Yost 2000). The process of managing new investments has only just begun – in the aforementioned Action Groups – and has so far yielded promises but no capabilities. In addition, the Helsinki figure of 60,000 is an 'input' figure. Should the EU actually wish to deploy 60,000 combat troops it would have to calculate with a triple force in order to allow for troop rotation. Thus, a total of 180,000 troops (cf. de Wijk 2000) – a daunting figure for the economically pressed EU ministers of defence – would be needed.

A third concern is EU-NATO co-operation. NATO assets (i.e. physical resources such as headquarters) and capabilities (i.e. services such as lift) – some of which are common, some national – have the potential to reinforce EU action, and the Atlantic Alliance has since the mid-1990s sought to define the way in which assets and capabilities could be transferred to the 'European pillar' (Lutz 2001). The current agreement, the so-called Berlin Plus Agreement, dates from NATO's Washington summit (April 1999) and contains four points (NATO 1999):

1   the EU will have 'assured access' to NATO planning capabilities;
2   the EU must 'presume' the availability of NATO capabilities and assets;
3   NATO's Deputy SACEUR must prepare a number of European command options;
4   NATO's defence planning should be adapted to reinforce EU force planning.

This agreement remains applicable even though first Turkey and then Greece have blocked its practical implementation for reasons of regional politics. Still, the Berlin Plus Agreement builds on work of previous years, such as in 1996 when NATO's command structure was made more flexible to accommodate the European pillar (the Berlin agreement), and subsequently in November 1996 when the WEU asked for and was granted the right to contribute to NATO's defence planning process. WEU 'Petersberg profiles' were thus transferred to NATO's Ministerial Guidance in mid-1997, signalling a minor change to NATO's very elaborate process but a major rapprochement between the two organizations. Modalities for EU-NATO co-operation are elaborately defined within the ESDP and involve regular and formalized meetings at political as well as technical-military levels.

Hubert Védrine (1996: 635) once noted in the Bosnian context that bombing only works when all major external powers agree on a peace plan, that is the political purpose of using force. The EU may be approaching a condition where it is not unreasonable to expect that the ESDP process will regularly produce modest doses of such agreement. The EU lacks a unifying vision in strategic affairs but it has gained an institutional infrastructure, access to improving military capabilities and a pragmatic relationship to NATO in its effort to define specific policies. In relation to the past absence of institutions and capabilities and an inflamed relationship to NATO, this is an achievement that probably will lead to the realization of most of the Petersberg ambition. In short, the EU may become a 'civilian actor' with an ability to back diplomacy with peacekeeping forces.

New Atlanticism

I argued in the introduction that the ESDP would produce a rupture in the EU trajectory toward an ever-closer union. Yet, the discussion so far indicates that the ESDP will reinforce a long-standing and widespread ambition to develop the EU into a unique 'civilian actor' promoting peace and conflict resolution. However, this image of continuity is only partially an accurate reflection of security trends. We must in fact combine two scenarios from Table 1.1 (p.21): the EU as a 'civilian actor' and a parallel defence 'directorate'. This combination is labelled 'New Atlanticism'.

The engine of New Atlanticism is the tension arising from the meeting of the two analytical dimensions above. There is an increasing ability to articulate policies but also the absence of a unifying political vision. The external role within the EU's reach, the 'civilian actor', will not satisfy a number of Western European countries. Some will fear that the EU's inability to undertake coercive military operations at the high end of the Petersberg scale (i.e. peacemaking operations) will precipitate a sharp decline in the American engagement in European security. To be sure, the US will handle the conflicts it deems relevant to its national interests, but the US will not invest in Western European security organizations that prove incapable of producing added military weight. Thus, some states will be eager to develop high-end capabilities in order to tie the US to Europe. Other states will pursue the same capabilities for the reason that they wish to influence developments within the EU and ultimately produce a greater European voice in all aspects of world politics. Those who develop high-end capabilities will be able to take part in the informal directorate, although the directorate's political strength will depend on the degree to which these ulterior motives can be reconciled on a case-by-case basis.

Table 1.2 New Atlanticism

Resources Vision	Centralization	Fragmentation
Specific	US +	ESDP directorate
Abstract	EU civilian actor	

Table 1.2 outlines the contours of New Atlanticism. The EU will become a civilian actor capable of early political and economic engagements in external conflicts, and capable of deploying peacekeeping forces once a conflict has flared but settled down. The EU, in short, will be an actor in the early and late phases of conflict management. The US is the strategic actor par excellence with a specific vision of itself and considerable resources, including military force, to back policy in all phases of conflict management and war. The ESDP directorate will be mobilized only in particular contexts, on a case-by-case basis. In this informal setting almost free of institutional constraints, mobilization will indicate that those participating will share a vision of what must be done. Hence, we can speak of 'specific', if momentary visions. Resources will be allocated by participating states and the collective armour is therefore best characterized as 'fragmented' rather than 'centralized'. All in all, New Atlanticism is an appropriate label because the 'directorate' will become the operational bridge between US strategy (global and high intensity) and EU security policy (regional and low intensity).

Can this bridging directorate develop within current political arrangements (i.e. EU and NATO structures)? Formally, the answer is yes. NATO has already made its European component separable through the flexible command structure and the Berlin Plus Agreement to let this pillar draw on common assets and capabilities. Naturally, most of these belong not to NATO but to the US and assistance will be granted only on a case-by-case basis. Still, within this political context the NATO structure is capable of supporting a directorate. The same is the case for the EU. Article 17 of the Nice Treaty (European Union 2000) introduces the overall ambition of elaborating a policy that includes 'all questions relating to the security of the Union, including the progressive framing of a common defence policy'. However, further down in Article 17.4 we find the following:

> The provisions of this article shall not prevent the development of closer co-operation between two or more Member States on a bilateral level, in the framework of the Western European Union (WEU) and NATO, provided such co-operation does not run counter to or impede that provided for in this Title.
>
> (European Union 2000)

There is, then, no formal objection to the development of a directorate, as long as it does not actually undermine the EU.

However, from a practical political perspective we must raise the question of whether the 'willing' will also be 'capable'? There are two answers to this question.

First, those who are willing to work with the US in high intensity operations will be able to do so with fairly modest investments. These countries will not have to invest in all the technology and hardware of the American-driven Revolution in Military Affairs (RMA) but may focus on a number of key technologies and skills that allow them to insert themselves in niche operations. European states could choose to focus on electronic surveillance, air-to-ground attack, or special operations, to mention just a few possibilities. Their operational significance will then be as much political as military, but the political significance may be desirable for both parties. Niche specialization can take place on a bilateral level, which is to say in a dialogue between the US and the country in question, and also within NATO where the defence planning process consists of a 'bilateral' dialogue between each ally and NATO as such.[11]

The second answer reveals deeper problems. If the European pillar is to act 'autonomously' of the US, and if only a limited number of European countries are willing to act, as the directorate scenario presupposes, then the countries may find that they have either too few capabilities or simply the wrong capabilities. They will have too few capabilities if the coalition is small and the operation major. They will have the wrong capabilities if they have invested narrowly in overlapping or commonly-owned equipment or services. The latter scenario is a real possibility because European governments with no prospect of increasing defence budgets will have to co-ordinate their investments in order to avoid redundancies. In short, they will have to specialize. In consequence, narrow coalitions therefore risk lacking certain capabilities.

This leads to the question of whether the coalition or directorate will not have to be, by and large, the size of the EU for it to be capable. In this case, we could simply be content to distinguish between the US operating with niche allies (hence the 'US +' label in Table 1.2) and the EU (which remains locked into a collective civilian role). This leads to some concluding remarks in defence of New Atlanticism.

The split between political visions within the EU remains valid and the EU is already preparing to allow flexible coalitions of the willing to move ahead of the rest of the Union. The further application of this principle will enhance New Atlanticism, even if it remains a fact that a directorate will have to tailor its missions to its capabilities and simultaneously respect the engagement of the EU, which is likely to come early in conflicts. The autonomy of the directorate vis-à-vis the EU is therefore circumscribed. Still, we witness emerging flexible co-operation in the ESDP. In some ways, flexibility began in 1993 when Denmark was allowed to exercise a defence opt-out in the Maastricht Treaty. Moreover, the current ESDP is open to outside participation, particularly from non-EU NATO members and EU applicant countries, in ESDP 'preparation' and 'implementation' (although not 'decision-making') (EU Presidency 2000a: appendix 1 to annex 1; EU Presidency 2000b: annex VI to annex VI). The EU may choose to apply the principle of 'enhanced co-operation' to the defence area, which is currently not the case, in order to tighten the relationship between an informal avant-garde (directorate) and the EU proper.[12] However, such an 'enhanced co-operation' clause may not be necessary – because a parallel track is already feasible (cf. the Nice Treaty) – nor desirable to the extent that the EU would want to insulate itself from the political responsibility of a crisis gone wrong. In short, the EU construction is likely to include a mechanism that enables parallel co-operation and simultaneously disengages the EU from automatic political responsibility in case the directorate's operation goes awry.

Conclusion

Sometimes political leaders and observers of European affairs discuss blindly, but with vigour, the current and unfolding institutional shape of the EU. This article has addressed a key question within this debate, namely whether the inclusion of 'high politics' in the shape of ESDP will transform the institutional foundations of the EU. Logically, the EU could either become a more coherent actor, akin to the strategic actor ideal type, or become reshaped, more fragmented perhaps and certainly different in institutional form. The analysis concludes that the simple opposition between 'unity and fragmentation' explains little of the ESDP's impact on the EU. The analysis focused on a distinction between political vision and institutional capacity – both dimensions being drawn from neo-classical realism. It outlined four scenarios and concluded that three will come into play in the future. This amalgam was labelled 'New Atlanticism' to capture at one time the continued strengthening of the European pillar and the continued attachment of this pillar to the US.

The EU will become a 'civilian actor' promoting liberal values of reconciliation and dialogue. The US will operate as a 'strategic actor' on a global scale but with the support of selective European allies that offer specialized military services and political support. In between, as a new transatlantic bridge, a directorate will develop. It will be informal (not institutionalized) and its membership will vary from case to case, although France, Britain, and Germany are bound to play decisive roles. The directorate will be able to handle military coercion close to Europe, alleviating pressure on the EU, which is too large and diverse to act forcefully. It will also alleviate pressure on the US, which is not interested in becoming involved in a range of minor conflicts.

The gestation of New Atlanticism may prove difficult, and it may not be durable. Still, a directorate with firm roots in Western Europe appears a likely response to the very diverse (the EU) and the global (the US). A directorate weakened by continuing debates over the purpose of 'autonomy' – vis-à-vis the US, the EU, Russia, and so on – is certainly a likely prospect. But a directorate will also bring us back to the Western European origins of integration and thus be reflective of the symbiosis between historical continuity and change.

Notes

1 The real argument with Kenneth Waltz must be one of whether the EU is developing into simply another state, a development which Waltz's neo-realism can accommodate, or whether the EU is becoming a post-modern, neo-medieval type of polity that falls outside the neo-realist universe.

2 For an overview see Rose (1998). The idea, stripped to its core, is to add state motivation to state capabilities. This comes out very clearly in the analysis of Schweller (1998) and is rooted in the classical realist discussion of varying foreign policy goals: 'power, glory, and idea' in the words of Raymond Aron ([1966], 1984: ch 3). For an introduction and critical discussion see Donnelly (2000).

3 Analysing the meeting between ideas and material factors is difficult, and it is not obvious, judging from the theory's track record, that constructivism is a powerful perspective. To Andrew Moravscik (1999: 670), constructivists work on their proper meta-theory but 'contribute far less to our empirical and theoretical understanding of European integration' because they fail to 'place their claims at any real risk of empirical disconfirmation'. Mark Pollack (no date) likewise notes that he can think of two constructivist studies 'that pose testable hypotheses and come away with *negative* findings, i.e. results that show no clear effect of EU institutions on actor identities and preferences, at least for some actors in some issue-areas'. Finally, John Duffield (2001: 109), who is critical of realism, notes that shifts in beliefs or identities are difficult to establish with 'any degree of confidence', and that their causes are equally difficult to discern.

4 Zakaria's vision of a strong and wealthy state resembles – not coincidentally – that which underpins the realist analysis of 'grand strategy' (cf. Posen 1984; Rosecrance and Stein 1993).

5 It should be emphasized that 'strategic' here, with reference to the literature of strategic studies, refers to an actor capable of using military force in its external action. Some people use the concept of 'strategy' to refer to rational-instrumental behaviour, as when an actor applies means to obtain a goal, and 'communities' – as I define them here – can thus be thought of as strategic. However, as noted, 'strategic' in this analysis refers to action involving military means as an instrument of coercion (whether applied or threatened).

6 These operations were consequently circumscribed in May 1994 by a strict set of rules, in a Presidential Decision Directive (PDD 25: see White House 1994), that guide the US deployment of forces. This circumscribed approach to low intensity operations was also reiterated in the 1999 national security strategy (White House 1999: 19–20). In fact, since the mid-1990s, the US has focused on using military force primarily for strategic purposes (forward deterrence, major conflicts), while low intensity conflict planning is limited to specific operational roles (embargoes, raids, shows of force, disaster relief) that deliberately are very loosely connected to the rebuilding of local government. See the Pentagon's 'Doctrine for Joint Operations' (1995).

7 Richard Holbrooke (1998: 68) recalls stating to a surprised President Clinton in June 1995: 'NATO has already approved the withdrawal plan. While you have the power to stop it, it has a high degree of automaticity built into it, especially since we have committed ourselves publicly to assisting NATO troops if the UN decides to withdraw.'

8 France and Germany proposed the integration of the WEU in the EU in December 1996 and later received support from Belgium, Spain, Italy, and Luxembourg. However, the spring of 1997 revealed opposition from Great Britain, Denmark, Ireland, Austria, Sweden, and Finland.

9 The Military Staff is divided into five sections: (a) politics and planning, (b) intelligence, (c) operations and exercises, (d) logistics and resources, and (e) communication and information. Cf. Jensen (2000: 11).

10 Most national representatives in the EU Military Committee are double-hatted and thus also sit in NATO. France is a notable exception.

11 NATO's defence planning process naturally contains many collective elements, including the strategic Ministerial Guidance that outlines the package of scenarios and threats according to which military authorities plan. The bilateral aspect is visible, however, in the review process when 'NATO' confronts each ally, on the basis of a Defence Planning Questionnaire, with its plans and priorities. In other words, two or more allies are never examined collectively.

12 The EU currently allows enhanced co-operation – taking place among at least eight EU members and being open to all – to take place in foreign and security policy but not in defence or military policy (European Union 2000, Article 27.b). Likewise, the Amsterdam Treaty stipulates that 'joint action' can take place following a majority vote in the Council of Ministers, providing that it happens within the framework of a 'common strategy' elaborated among the heads of government and state in the European Council. However, such a majority vote is prohibited in relation to defence policy (European Union 1997: Article 23.2).

References

Aron, R. (1984) *Paix et Guerre entre les Nations*, Paris: Calmann-Lévy.

Axelrod, R. (1984) *The Evolution of Co-operation*, New York: Basic Books.

Calleo, D. P. (2001) *Rethinking Europe's Future*, Princeton: Princeton University Press.

Cogan, C. S. (2001) *The Third Option: The Emancipation of European Defence, 1989–2000*, Westport: Praeger.

de Wijk, R. (2000) 'Convergence Criteria: Measuring Input or Output?', *European Foreign Affairs Review*, 5, 3: 397–417.

Donnelly, J. (2000) *Realism and International Relations*, Cambridge: Cambridge University Press.

Duffield, J. S. (2001) 'Transatlantic Relations after the Cold War: Theory, Evidence, and the Future', *International Studies Perspectives*, 2, 1: 93–115.

EU Presidency (1999a) *Presidency Conclusions: Cologne European Council, 3 and 4 June 1999*, Http://ue.eu.int/Newsroom/related.asp?max=1&bid=76&grp=1799&lang=1.

EU Presidency (1999b) *Presidency Conclusions: Helsinki European Council, 10 and 11 December*, Http://ue.eu.int/Newsroom/related.asp?max=1&bid=76&grp=2186&lang=1.

EU Presidency (2000a) *Presidency Conclusions, Santa Maria da Feira European Council, 19 and 20 June*, Http://ue.eu.int/Newsroom/LoadDoc.asp?BID=76&DID=62050&LANG=1.

EU Presidency (2000b) *Presidency Report on the European Security and Defence Policy*, Http://ue.eu.int/Newsroom/related.asp?max=1&bid=76&grp=3018&lang=1.

European Union (1997) *Treaty of Amsterdam* http://europa.eu.int/eurlex/en/treaties/dat/eu_cons_treaty_en.pdf

European Union (2000) *Treaty of Nice*, http://europa.eu.int/eur-lex/en/treaties/dat/nice_treaty_en.pdf.

Heisbourg, F. *et al.* (2000) 'European Defence: Making it Work', *Chaillot Papers*, 42, Paris.

Hill, C. (1994) 'The Capability-Expectations Gap, or Conceptualizing Europe's International Role', in S. Bulmer and A. Scott (eds) *Economic and Political Integration in Europe: Internal Dynamics and Global Context*, Oxford: Blackwell: 103–126.

Hill, C. (1998) 'Closing the Capabilities-Expectations Gap?', in J. Peterson and H. Sjursen (eds) *A Common Foreign Policy for Europe? Competing Visions of the CFSP*, London: Routledge: 18–38.

Hoffmann, S. (1995) *The European Sisyphus: Essays on Europe, 1964–1994*, Boulder: Westview Press.

Holbrooke, R. (1998) *To End a War*, New York: Random House.

Howorth, J. (2000) 'Britain, France and the European Defence Initiative', *Survival*, 42, 2: 33–55.

Jensen, F. P. (2000) *Opbygningen af en fælles europæisk sikkerheds-og forsvarspolitik: de institutionelle implikationer i EU*, Copenhagen: Danish Institute for International Affairs.

Katzenstein, P. J. (ed.) (1996) *The Culture of National Security: Norms and Identity in World Politics*, New York: Columbia University Press.

Kissinger, H. (1994) *Diplomacy*, New York: Simon and Schuster.

Lutz, R. A. (2001) *Military Capabilities for a European Defence*, Copenhagen: Danish Institute of International Affairs.

Milward, A. S. (1992) *The European Rescue of the Nation-State*, London: Routledge.

Moravscik, A. (1999) 'Is Something Rotten in the State of Denmark? Constructivism and European Integration', *Journal of European Public Policy*, 6, 4: 669–681.

NATO (1999) *Washington Summit Communiqué, 24 April*, Http://www.nato.int/docu/pr/ 1999/p99-064e.htm.

Pedersen, T. (1998) *Germany, France, and the Integration of Europe: A Realist Interpretation*, London: Pinter.

Pentagon (1995) *Joint Pub 3–0: Doctrine for Joint Operations, 1 February 1995*, Washington D.C., www.defenselink.mil/pubs.

Pollack, M. (no date) 'The New Institutionalism, Hypothesis Testing, and the Question of Methods', Http://jsis.artsci.washington.edu/programs/europe/Institutionsp/ Pollack2.htm.

Posen, B. (1984) *The Sources of Military Doctrine: France, Britain, and Germany Between the World Wars*, Ithaca: Cornell University Press.

Risse, T., Engelmann-Martin D., Knopf, H.J. and Roscher, K. (1999) 'To Euro or Not to Euro? The EMU and Identity Politics in the European Union', *European Journal of International Affairs*, 5, 2: 147–187.

Rose, G. (1998) 'Neoclassical Realism and Theories of Foreign Policy', *World Politics*, 51, 1: 144–172.

Rosecrance, R. and Stein A. (1993) *The Domestic Bases of Grand Strategy*, Ithaca: Cornell University Press.

Rynning, S. (2001) 'Det europæiske forsvar efter Nice', *Politologiske Studier*, 4, 1: 50–55.

Schweller, R. L. (1998) *Deadly Imbalances: Tripolarity and Hitler's Strategy of World Conquest*, New York: Columbia University Press.

Solana, J. (2001) 'European Defence: the Task Ahead', *European Voice*, 24 October 2001, http://ue.eu.int/solana/list.asp?BID=108.

Talbott, S. (1999) 'America's Stake in a Strong Europe', Remarks at a conference on the future of NATO, *The Royal Institute of International Affairs*, London, 7 October, www.riia.org/conferences/strobe.zip.

Taylor, P. (1983) *The Limits of European Integration*, London: Croom Helm.

Thomas, J. P. (2000) 'The Military Challenges of Transatlantic Coalitions', *Aldephi Paper* 333.

Védrine, H. (1996) *Les Mondes de François Mitterrand*, Paris: Fayard.

Védrine, H. (1997) 'France: le Piano ou le Tabouret?', *Le Débat*, 95: 165–182.

Wæver, O. (2000) 'The EU as a Security Actor: Reflections from a Pessimistic Constructivist on Post-sovereign Security Orders', in M. Kelstrup and M. C. Williams (eds) *International Relations Theory and the Politics of European Integration*, London: Routledge: 250–294

Waltz, K. N. (1979) *Theory of International Politics*, New York: McGraw-Hill.

Waltz, K. N. (2000) 'Structural Realism after the Cold War', *International Security*, 25, 1: 5–41.

Weiss, T. G. (1999) *Military-Civilian Interactions: Intervening in Humanitarian Crises*, Lanham: Rowman and Littlefield.

Wendt, A. (1999) *Social Theory of International Politics*, Cambridge: Cambridge University Press.

White House (1994) *Reforming Multilateral Peace Operations*, Washington D.C., May www.whitehouse.gov/textonly/WH/EOP/NSC/html/documents/NSCDoc1.html

White House (1999) *A National Security Strategy for a New Century*, Washington D.C., December.

Wivel, A. (2000) 'The Integration Spiral: International Security and European Integration, 1945–1999', Ph.D. dissertation, University of Copenhagen.

Yost, D. (2000) 'The NATO Capabilities Gap and the European Union', *Survival*, 42, 4: 97–128.

Zakaria, F. (1998) *From Wealth to Power: The Unusual Origins of America's World Role*, Princeton: Princeton University Press.

2 Understanding the common foreign and security policy

Analytical building blocks

Helene Sjursen

Many people have considered it unrealistic to expect member states to build a common foreign, security and defence policy, as integrating in this area of so-called 'high politics' has been described as synonymous with 'surrendering sovereignty' altogether. It is true that throughout the history of European integration there have been attempts at establishing a common external policy but, when put to the test, national perspectives have seemed to prevail over such efforts. Nonetheless, at the end of the 1990s, several decisive moves were taken in this direction.

The important turning point came in the autumn of 1998, when Britain under the leadership of Tony Blair declared its support for a more independent security role for the EU and thus abandoned its position as defender of the political independence of the WEU. With the Franco-British 'St Malo declaration' work on strengthening the EU's security and defence capacity was given new life.[1] The St Malo declaration was followed by systematic discussion amongst the member states of the EU on the practical shaping of co-operation in security and defence. The question then arises of how we can make sense of these developments. Were these late-1990s efforts to strengthen the Common Foreign and Security Policy (CFSP) and build common institutional structures and shared capabilities in security and defence only a passing phenomenon, dependent on a particular and temporary state of affairs and thus likely to remain at the planning stage rather than to be fully implemented? Or can we consider these developments as evidence of a more lasting trend? And if so, what is the glue that keeps this policy together?

No doubt both internal and external factors influence development of the EU's foreign and security policy. Identification of the most important factors does however depend on what kind of process we consider the EU to be. This in turn depends on what kind of driving forces we see as most influential in the development of foreign, security and defence co-operation. In this chapter it will be suggested that if we rely exclusively on a realist approach, where political processes within the EU are defined as processes of bargaining between self-interested actors, we risk underestimating the longer-term changes involved in political processes within the second pillar. We need an alternative analytical perspective, in addition to – not instead of – the realist one. If nothing else then this perspective can at least measure if there is something more to the CFSP than a coalition of interest, which by definition is likely to be temporary. This perspective will be referred to as a deliberative perspective.

The distinction between the realist and the deliberative perspective should be seen as analytical. They are not empirical descriptions of reality. Thus, they provide different concepts allowing us to analyse different dimensions of foreign policy co-operation in the EU. If one restricts oneself to one of these perspectives, important dimensions of the EU's foreign policy are likely to be ignored, because we lack the concepts necessary to capture them. The first part of this chapter will look at the realist perspective and at what kind of 'story' it would tell of the prospects for a common foreign and security policy; any limitations to this story are also discussed. The second part of the chapter turns to the deliberative perspective and asks in what ways this might supplement a realist analysis.

Co-operation as interest-driven

From the perspective of the first analytical model, policy is seen as driven by material self-interest. In the classical realist literature, interests are defined in terms of power (Morgenthau 1946). The international system is seen to be composed of sovereign states that act on the basis of self-interest, without reference to common norms, identities or values. The international system is defined as anarchical; in other words, there is no overarching authority to identify common rules. Order is considered to be maintained as a result of a balance of power rather than as a result of a common authority as is the case in domestic politics. What counts in the end is power, measured in material terms as economic or military capabilities, not an assessment of whether or not actions are normatively right or 'good'. International institutions such as the CFSP are not attributed any independent role in this perspective. Co-operation will only be possible if national interests coincide for example because states face a common external threat, as they did during the Cold War. When their interests cease to coincide, one would also expect co-operation to disintegrate. Thus, in the case of the EU, if or when other groups of states emerge as more attractive allies in terms of serving the national interest, loyalty to the EU would disappear.

Many studies of the CFSP, although not always explicitly theoretical, implicitly rely on the basic assumptions of this perspective. These are studies that primarily focus on describing the EU's foreign policy behaviour and assessing the EU's performance in the international system. They assess the CFSP on the basis of its policy output and, more often than not, the EU seems to come up short in these assessments (Pijpers 1991; Ifestos 1987; Hoffmann 2000). Sometimes these analyses contain a prescriptive element as well, indicating what needs to be done with the explicit or implicit aim in mind of making the CFSP an 'effective' instrument, which would then be able to provide utility for the participant states (Kintis 1997). Two issues are often in focus in these analyses: the institutional structure or decision-making system, and the instruments or capabilities of the EU's foreign policy. The CFSP is often criticized for having a slow decision-making system and for being incapable of acting decisively, in particular in situations of international crises, such as Kosovo, Bosnia or the Gulf wars. The institutional structure suffers from the need for consensus between member states on all decisions. This takes time and may lead to timid results. There are also broader problems of coherence both vertically and horizontally. The problem of vertical coherence has to do with ensuring that the foreign, security and defence policies of individual member states 'mesh' with the other states (Smith, K. 2001: 173). The problem of horizontal coherence has to do with the extent to which the various external activities of the EU are logically connected or mutually reinforcing each other. This problem is to a great extent the result of the compartmentalization of the EU's external relations in two different decision-making pillars. Most observers suggest that the nomination of a high representative for the CFSP has not helped this, and the new committees and institutions established as a result of the strengthening of defence and security do not promise to make coherence much better. These characteristics of the CFSP make it difficult to respond effectively to crisis-situations and reduce the effectiveness of the EU's external policy: the policy output is often unsatisfactory.

A second issue in focus is the EU's capabilities/policy-instruments. The CFSP is often seen to be incapable of letting words be followed by action. Thus, in the 1990s the CFSP was criticized for failing to take the lead in European politics at the end of the Cold War. This role was filled by the US, it is argued, not the EU and its new Common Foreign and Security Policy (Allen 1998; Kintis 1997). An often-quoted historical example of the same problem is the Venice Declaration of 1980 where the EU officially recognized the Palestinians' right to self-determination (Ifestos 1987). This happened at a time when the US was far from accepting such a principle. Yet, it was not followed up with concrete policy initiatives. The US was still seen as the actor that determined the policy-agenda in the Middle East and any symbolic value of the EU declaration was not considered. This is what the development of capabilities in security and defence should resolve. However, scepticism is often expressed as to whether or not the EU will live up to its headline goals, and even if it does, whether or not this will be enough in terms of ensuring that it has sufficient 'muscle' to follow words with action.

The difficulties of the EU in building strong common institutions in foreign policy and in developing policy-instruments that allow them to 'effectively' pursue collective goals can easily be explained with the help of the realist perspective. In fact, a realist perspective would lead us to expect such limitations to co-operation in security and defence, as no state will voluntarily agree to a policy that challenges its national interest. From this perspective, the institutional structures of the CFSP can only be seen to reflect the interests of its member states. Institutions cannot be expected to put limits on the foreign policy initiatives of the member states, to shape their interests or to bring them to stick to common policies if these collide with their own interest. It is also logical from such a perspective to dismiss the CFSP as irrelevant and simply to conclude that the EU does not have a foreign and security policy.

However, several empirical observations suggest there is something else going on inside the second pillar of the EU in parallel with these apparent 'policy-failures' and that in fact EU membership has modified the unlimited effects of states' self-interest, even within the area of 'high politics'. Furthermore, it is clearly documented that the EU has considerable impact on the international system, despite the fact that its foreign policy is often defined as almost 'non-existent'. These observations are more difficult for realists to explain. It is in fact difficult for the realist perspective to explain why the CFSP occasionally succeeds, why member states sometimes comply with common positions even if there is no evident gain for them in doing so, or why most member states seem to acknowledge that there will be no return to the pre-Maastricht situation of European Political Co-operation (EPC). It becomes difficult from this perspective to understand the criticisms that emerge towards member states when they act unilaterally, as for example Germany did on the issue of the recognition of the former Yugoslav republics Croatia and Slovenia as sovereign states in 1991–1992. If one expects that the CFSP will not create any ties on member states and that states at all times will act according to their own interest, this kind of independent action should neither be perceived as surprising nor unacceptable, but rather as legitimate and logical. Finally, it is difficult to explain why the member states keep spending time and resources on seeking a consensus and building common institutions if the output can only be expected to be limited.

Before discussing whether an alternative theoretical perspective can help answer these questions it is useful to look more closely at some of the empirical observations of change.

Elements of transformation or change

Several authors note a change in the way European states formulate their foreign policy as well as increasing institutional constraints on national foreign policy-making as a result of participation in the CFSP. Hill and Wallace (1996) observe that the preparation of foreign policy now takes place in the context of European consultation and that, as a result, 'Officials and Ministers who sit together on planes and round tables in Brussels or in each others' capitals begin to judge "rationality" from within a different framework' (Hill and Wallace 1996: 12). This is similar to the so-called 'co-ordination reflex' first referred to by Simon Nuttall (1992), which has brought the member states of the EU to develop the habit of automatically consulting with their partners before defining their own national positions. According to Tonra a former participant in the CFSP process noted a '… habit of thinking in terms of consensus' that went beyond formalized diplomatic consultation and another stressed that '… where there is ever any new foreign policy initiative in the making, the first reflex is European. The question is now "what will our European partners say – what is the opinion in Europe"' (Tonra 2001). Elsewhere Hill has noted tendencies according to which European foreign policy is formulated within a system of multi-level governance, or a *logic of diversity*. He argues here that the emergence of a system of European external relations has had a considerable impact on national foreign policies. Even though the system is still composed of states, he considers the behaviour of these states to be constrained by increasing institutionalization at the European level. Furthermore, the interests of other EU states as well as the EU as a whole are increasingly taken into consideration when states formulate their own foreign policies: 'the limits set by the logic of diversity on European actorness are just as firm as those set by the *acquis* politique on unilateralism' (Hill 1998: 37).

A further indication of change in the way European states formulate their foreign policy is what Allen (1998) has referred to as the process of 'Brusselsization' of European foreign policy. Although foreign and security policy remains formally in the control of the nation-state and has not been transferred in any substantial way to the European Commission, it has in practice become more difficult for the foreign ministries of the member states to control the foreign policy process. National representatives increasingly make foreign policy in Brussels. This gradual transfer of decision-making from national capitals to Brussels has developed in parallel with efforts in the Treaties of Maastricht and Amsterdam to increase cohesion between the first and the second pillar. One consequence has been that rivalries have developed between the political directors (who traditionally deal with the CFSP) and the permanent representatives, and later also between representatives of the Commission and the high representative. The important point however is that this tendency towards Brusselsization suggests that centrifugal forces within the EU are quite strong and that the foreign policies of member states undergo important changes as a result of membership in the EU and participation in the CFSP.

Jolyon Howorth has stressed similar developments in what he calls 'Brussels-based intergovernmentalism'. He expects that the tendency to locate national co-ordinating committees such as the Political and Security Committee in Brussels will lead to a new balance within the intergovernmental framework, between national capitals and their Brussels-based permanent representatives. The most likely outcome in his view is that the member states will develop a collective ethos of their own and generate trans-european perspectives on CFSP and CESDP (Howorth 2000). This process also has implications for the administrative structures and procedures in national foreign ministries. Smith (2000) highlights three important changes here. The first is the establishment of new officials who are permanently devoted to political co-operation. He highlights in particular the 'European correspondents' who prepare meetings for the political directors and liaise with their counterparts in other EU states. The second and third ones are the expansion of most national diplomatic services and the reorganization of national foreign ministries towards the EU. Between 1972 and 1978 seven out of nine EU member states increased their missions in third countries (Hill and Wallace 1979) and in order to improve their participation in the CFSP member states made structural changes within their national bureaucracies. Denmark for example reorganized its foreign ministry from a functional division between economic and political to a geographical dimension for this reason (Smith 2000: 623).

There is also a documented change in the content of foreign policy of member states as a result of participation in the CFSP. In the case of the Netherlands, Pijpers notes that:

Although a certain amount of individual leeway remained possible, while from the formal point of view national sovereignty is still largely preserved, in practice Dutch foreign policy gradually had to abandon many of its peculiar traits, due to the nature of intensive European consultations on South Africa, the Middle East, Central America and Eastern Europe.

(Pijpers 1996: 252)

A similar change is noted by Torreblanca in the case of Spain. He writes that ten years after EU membership

... Spanish foreign policy had acquired a clear EU profile: all the positions Spain had adopted in areas such as disarmament and non-proliferation, multilateral trade and investment, international financial co-operation, human rights and democratization, peace-keeping and global warming, could only be understood in the framework of Spanish membership of the EU. Clearly, in all these matters, Spanish preferences and interests were pre-determined by its participation in the EU.

(Torreblanca 2001: 11–12)

Likewise, the ability of the norms of the CFSP to penetrate into core areas of national foreign policy and provoke changes is illustrated by Sweden's and Finland's reinterpretations of their status as neutral states.

With regard to the international impact of the CFSP Hazel Smith (2002) shows that the EU has developed sophisticated and influential policies towards a number of states and regions in the world. The example of Norway is also telling. The strengthening of the CFSP has had important effects for almost all dimensions of Norway's foreign relations and the Norwegian Ministry of Foreign Affairs spends an increasingly large proportion of its time and resources on the CFSP (Sjursen 2000). The interest of the other Nordic states in co-ordination and co-operation within the Nordic Council has been seriously reduced after their entry into the EU and the dynamics of interaction within NATO are changing as a result of an increasingly more cohesive European bloc, leaving Norway increasingly marginalized (Utenriksdepartementet 2001). Norwegian authorities are also concerned that Norway's non-participation in the CFSP will reduce its ability to protect its own interests in its relations with larger neighbours such as Russia, where difficult questions regarding environmental safety, immigration and disputes of resources in the Barents Sea are almost permanently on the agenda (*Aftenposten*, 20 June 2002: 9). In order to compensate for this situation, Norwegian governments, regardless of their position on Norwegian membership in the EU, increasingly align their foreign policy stances with the CFSP. Furthermore, Norway has developed a foreign policy strategy that consists in seeking to make itself an 'interesting partner' for the EU, amongst other things by taking on mediating tasks for example in the Middle East, on Sri Lanka and in Central America. In the same vein Norway has also committed troops both to the EU's military force and to the EU's international police force and it has worked ardently and consistently to ensure European NATO-members' participation within the EU's new security and defence structures. Finally, several reorganizations in the ministry of foreign affairs have also been prompted in attempts to increase the efficiency of Norway's input into the foreign policy of the EU.

Several of the above observations point to national foreign and security policies as being formulated in interaction with European partners within the CFSP. What seems to characterize this interaction is a consideration for the perspective and interests of the other. A norm of consultation has developed and the expectation that individual interests must be curbed and occasionally give way to common positions seems to be increasingly accepted. The CFSP seems to have a transformatory capacity vis-à-vis national foreign policies. How should we make sense of this? How can we explain the emergence of the 'centrifugal forces' within the CFSP? Why do member states seem increasingly to take into account the common interest and not only the national interest when formulating policies?

Can an improved, more sophisticated version of realism do the job?

More sophisticated versions of classical realism

The classical power politics perspective has been further elaborated upon and modified into the neo-realist and neo-liberal perspectives on international relations. A central difference with the power-based theories is that from the neo-realist and neo-liberal perspectives the different strategies of negotiation, the calculations of actors, also contribute to explain the outcome in international politics. In the older, or 'classical realist' perspectives, the focus is mostly on the power resources of actors. Amongst themselves, neo-realists and neo-liberals disagree on the likelihood of co-operation. Both perspectives accept that the anarchical nature of the international system puts particular constraints on co-operation. Yet neo-realists consider international anarchy to represent a greater hindrance to inter-state co-ordination than do neo-liberal institutionalists. The two perspectives also disagree on whether or not states have a common interest in co-operating: the neo-liberal institutionalists consider states to be mostly interested in relative gains, whereas the neo-realists stress states' interest in maximizing their absolute gains. Nonetheless, when it comes to their basic assumptions about the central driving forces in international politics, the differences between these perspectives are small. They share the same assumption of actors as rational in the sense that they seek to maximize their own interests. Politics is in other words the outcome of adverse self-interested behaviour. Furthermore, their underlying scientific position leads them to over-emphasize material structures and to neglect 'ideational' or social structures in their analyses. They operate with a conception of monological actors to whom '… other people are just external, objective facts of reality, on the line with material things, only with the distinctive quality that they carry out strategic actions too' (Eriksen and Weigård 1997: 221). According to Risse 'neo-liberal institutionalism should not be regarded as part of the liberal paradigm. This "co-operation under anarchy" perspective shares all realist core assumptions, but disagrees with structural realists on the likelihood of international co-operation among self-interested actors' (Risse-Kappen 1995). Others have suggested that the difference between the classical realists and the neo-realists/liberals is principally one of methodology (Linklater 1995). Thus, although the rational choice perspective can go a long way in modelling international co-operation, in terms of providing an alternative perspective from the classical realist position on the CFSP, with alternative micro-foundations, these recent theories are of limited use. They still define state behaviour as self-interested behaviour. Thus, they see collective institutions come about '… because they distribute goods in a way that [is] in somebody's interest' (Eriksen and Weigård 1997: 224).

Several alternative ways of studying the EU's external policies that do not rely on rational choice assumptions have however been suggested.

Alternative conceptualizations

Allen and Smith have emphasized the difficulty in studying Western Europe's international role as long as 'the notion of a "foreign policy" carries with it a conceptual framework which is inseparable from the state-centric view of world politics' (Allen and Smith 1990: 95). They identify the problem to be that we tend to get stuck in a state-centric view when analysing Europe's external policy, and therefore find it difficult to account for the growing significance of the EU's international role. They suggest that by using the concept of international 'presence', it is possible to study the impact of the EU in different policy areas of the international system, and to show that the EU 'has considerable structure, salience and legitimacy in the process of international politics' (Allen and Smith 1990: 116).

Building on the notion of the EU's 'presence' in the international system, as well as Sjøstedt's (1977) analysis of the EC's international actor-status, both Brian White (2001) and Christopher Hill (1994) have suggested that the EU is best seen as a system of external relations in which 'the Europeans represent a sub-system of the international system as a whole … a system which generates international relations – collectively, individually, economically, politically – rather than a clear-cut "European foreign policy" as such' (Hill 1994: 120). In order to understand policy-making in external relations we should thus pay attention to the following three dimensions of this European sub-system: i) the national foreign policies of the member states, ii) the CFSP and iii) the 'external relations' of the first Community pillar.

Perhaps most relevant for the argument here however is Michael Smith's (1996) suggestion that we should conceptualize the EU's external policy-making as an evolving negotiated order. He argues that within the administrative, institutional and political structures established over the life of the EU there is a constant, rule-governed process of negotiation between actors, which produces policy positions and international policy outcomes. He further connects this conceptualization to broader processes of transformation within the global arena.

These transformations are characterized by the fact that they challenge the privileged position of the state. The challenges are both domestic and international. The state can no longer control political, economic and in some cases even military movements across national borders. Neither is the nation-state able to draw on the same type of loyalty from domestic actors, as traditionally assumed. Actors' loyalties will follow other logics and be defined according to other premises in addition to loyalty to the nation-states. At the same time, the state has to relate to an increasing number of international agreements that put constraints on its behaviour. Most importantly, political, legal and normative dimensions are considered to have a direct influence on states' behaviour at the international level. In short, other types of actors than states have a foreign policy of sorts and contribute to shape the international political agenda. The EU can be considered to be one such actor. One might of course argue that after the events of 11 September 2001, the state has come back with a vengeance. However, these events also illustrate some of the new types of vulnerabilities of the state and the processes of global transformation that affect even the area of security. Often, however, these alternative conceptualizations of the EU's international actions are not explicit in identifying the driving forces in the political process or in specifying an alternative set of micro-foundations to that of the rational choice/interest-based model. In other words, they suggest alternative ways of conceptualizing the EU but do not help us that much in terms of explaining how we got to this peculiar international 'actor'. If the process that leads to change in national foreign policies, and to an increasingly important international 'presence' for the EU, is not a process of bargaining between exogenously determined national interests, what is it? How is an actor such as the EU constituted? What are the mechanisms of change?

The 'constructivist' perspective in international relations seeks to bring such issues into focus. They start from the insight that the structures of international society are not only material but also 'ideational' and explore the role of identity and norms as the social basis of global politics. Norms are intersubjective beliefs about the social and natural worlds. They define actors and constitute their preferences and worldviews. In contrast to rationalist approaches the constructivist take would be that the nature of actors' interests and goals depends on their identities and social roles. Furthermore, these preferences and worldviews are shaped and reshaped through social interaction rather than defined as exogenous to the policy-making process. Thus the 'constructivists' problematize what realists take for granted; they are interested in the content and the source of state interests and identity.

Of the many variants of 'constructivism' several rely on the institutionalist account in which actors conform to institutional roles by following a 'logic of appropriateness' (March and Olsen 1989). Actors behaving according to this logic would consider what kind of action would be appropriate given their particular role or identity. They would in other words seek to be rule-followers rather than utility-maximizers. March and Olsen argue that '… the logic of appropriateness is a fundamental logic of political action. Actions are fitted to situations by their appropriateness within a conception of identity. Second, we see action – including action in politically important and novel situations – as institutionalized through structures of rules and routines'. The fact that actors, for most of the time, follow rules rather than calculate costs and benefits of alternative courses of action does not preclude disagreement: '... although rules bring order we see rules as potentially rich in conflict, contradiction and ambiguity thus producing deviation as well as conformity' (March and Olsen 1989: 38). Central to these processes is also the element of trust that develops between actors: 'We see the network of rules and rule bound relations as sustained by trust, a confidence that appropriate behaviour can be expected most of the time. Trust, like the rules it supports, is based on a conception of appropriateness more than a calculation of reciprocity' (1989: 38).

Such perspectives are also increasingly adopted in analyses of the CFSP (Aggestam 1999; Tonra 1997; Manners 2002; Bretherton and Vogler 1999). From such perspectives the habit of co-ordination, for example, is more easily understood if we have a conception of actors as rule-followers.

'Appropriateness' as a logic of action seems to fit with the observations that co-ordination is a 'reflex' – a habit – and not an act that is based on rational calculations of utility. Furthermore the 'constructivist' take might help explain first the criticisms that Germany was faced with on the issue of the recognition of the former Yugoslav republics, and second, that those member states who were strongly against this recognition did not revert to independent national policies in the face of German pressure but worked hard to achieve a compromise. What is more, after this failure the EU continued to develop stronger institutions in order to make sure that in the future such solo-playing would become more difficult to pull off. Germany's behaviour was a breach of agreed norms of appropriate conduct. As for the gain of the other EU's members' solidarity, this is not automatically evident and must be better understood as a commitment to a particular community and a belief that they must act collectively.

Actors as communicatively rational

However, what are the mechanisms that lead to an accumulation of norms? Why are these norms accepted? In order to explain the binding character of norms we need a theory in which the actor is conceived of as capable of assessing the validity of norms. We need a conception of actors as communicative and not simply strategic (Eriksen and Weigård 1997). Without this competence collective norms will not be produced in the first place. Neither will they be adhered to and reproduced in concrete situations (Eriksen 2000). Some norms will be adhered to and others not, depending on the actor's rational assessment of their validity and legitimacy. Hence it is the commitment to norms that are considered legitimate which allows us to understand particular decisions. Such a conception of actors as communicative is missing in much of the 'constructivist' literature.

Such mechanisms can be found in a deliberative approach.[2] Here it is posited '... that co-operation comes about when the process of reason-giving generates a capacity for change of viewpoints' (Eriksen and Fossum 2000: 257). This deliberative approach builds on Jürgen Habermas' theory of 'speech acts' and communicative action. Habermas considers that our communication through linguistic expressions – 'speech acts' – 'play a central role in regulating and reproducing forms of social life and the identities of actors' (Cronin and de Greff 1998: X). This perspective is similar to rational choice analysis in the sense that both are action theoretical approaches. Social phenomena are in other words considered to be products of individual action. However, rather than focusing on monological actors with fixed preferences, the theory of communicative action focuses on dialogical actors '… who co-ordinate their plans through argumentation, aimed at reaching mutual agreement.' (Eriksen and Weigård 1997: 221).

A further difference with the rational choice perspective is that according to Habermas' theory of communicative action actors are rational when they are able to justify and explain their actions and not only when they seek to maximize their own interests (Eriksen and Weigård 1999). These reasons could be material gain, but they could also be formulated with reference to an actor's sense of identity or understanding of the 'good life'. Finally, actors could explain their actions with reference to principles that, all things considered, can be recognized as 'just' by all parties, irrespective of their particular interests, perceptions of the 'good life' or cultural identity. This is indeed a condition for the functioning of liberal democracy, where citizens are expected to be able to distinguish between different forms of justification for policy-choices and to assess which of them are acceptable and which are not (Eriksen 1999).

In such a perspective, institutions and norms are not only practical arrangements, held together through '… mutual agreement about their advantageousness or through the use of coercive power' (Eriksen and Weigård 1997: 224–225). Rather, social norms and institutions are upheld because the actors consider them valid. Contrary to rational choice perspectives, the theory of communicative action can thus show how shared respect for norms and institutions is established as the outcome of a process of deliberation in which different viewpoints are communicated and scrutinized.

As the empirical literature confirms, most of the interaction that takes place in the context of the CFSP takes the form of language, and very little interaction takes the form of monetary payments or military action. For example, an important instrument in the CFSP is the COREU network, through which the member states of the EU share information and exchange ideas, analysis and comments as well as draft common statements (Cameron 1998). With over 17,000 messages per year, this constitutes an enormous pool of information and the network is crucial to the entire functioning of the CFSP. It is on the basis of this network that the formulation of common foreign policies proceeds. Consequently it makes sense to employ a theory of action that gives weight to the importance of language as action. However, a distinction between verbal and non-verbal behaviour is not a suitable indicator for distinguishing an interest-based bargaining process from a deliberative process (Eriksen 2000). During bargaining processes parties employ speech acts strategically in order to achieve results, or even to misrepresent their preferences and deceive others. Thus in order to distinguish strategic bargaining from what takes place in a deliberative process we need other indicators. We need to show that standpoints have been moved not because actors are persuaded (through threats) but because they are convinced that an alternative course of action or objective is in the equal interest of all. Typically in such cases agreement has been reached because the actors make use of the force of a norm, a principle or a common authoritative value. Agreements are created because the participants agree to let their divergences and grievances be regulated by impartial norms or common good considerations. This would also mean that they have similar reasons for complying with an agreement. In a bargaining situation on the other hand, parties will have different reasons for complying (Eriksen and Weigård 1999).

This approach would be helpful if we sought to substantiate a description of the CFSP as a process of 'Europeanization' of foreign policy in which shared norms and rules are gradually accumulated (Hill and Wallace 1996). The binding force of norms and institutions, and thus the resilience of the CFSP, is perhaps less of a puzzle if it can be documented that at least part of the *acquis* in this policy-field is the outcome of a process of argumentation where actors' '... aim of reaching a mutual understanding is based on a reasoned consensus' (Risse 2000). Furthermore the suggestion that foreign policy-making within the EU is a dynamic process where interests and objectives are not exogenous but emerge as a result of interaction at the national, European and international level seems more plausible if this process of interaction is conceptualized as a process of exchange of arguments. Finally the possibility that the clear distinction between the 'national' and the 'European' might gradually be blurred, even in the area of 'high politics', would perhaps appear less fanciful if we consider actors to be capable of reasonable argumentation aimed at common understanding. Thus the transformative effects of the CFSP on member states might be easier to explain if we have a conception of communicative rationality.

For example the findings on the role of small states in the CFSP might be given a stronger foundation with this perspective. In his study of Ireland, Denmark and the Netherlands in the CFSP Ben Tonra (1997) has found that in these cases 'political co-operation improved the effectiveness, broadened the range and increased the capabilities of foreign policy making' (Tonra 1997: 197). He further reported that these smaller states have not only adapted to the CFSP but also that they themselves considered that their influence on the foreign policy of their European partners had increased as a result of participation in the CFSP. Given that these are small states, this influence cannot have been gained on the basis of preponderant power, as the realist perspective would expect. It must have been based on something else. In a deliberative process one would indeed consider it possible for small states to be able to influence processes in a manner disproportionate to their size. This would be due to particular knowledge or the ability to convince others through argumentation, rather than as a result of disproportionate economic or military power. Other examples of the ability of small states to influence decisions within the CFSP would be the establishment of the Northern dimension, launched by Finland, or the Baltic Sea Co-operation Council (Østersjøsamarbeidet) promoted by Denmark.

However, the understanding of the role of large states might also be improved with the help of this perspective. In a study of France, Britain and Germany's role in the CFSP Lisbeth Aggestam (1999) finds that there is also a process of 'Europeanization' of the foreign policies of the larger states in the EU. She also notes that there is a sense of solidarity in foreign policy between EU members. She argues that central features of the CFSP are transparency, consultation and compromise. To support this proposition she quotes the former British Foreign Secretary, Malcolm Rifkind (1996), and former European Correspondent and Political Director of the British Foreign and Commonwealth Office, Pauline Neville-Jones. According to Rifkind: 'consultation and co-operation are now instinctive'. And Neville-Jones underlines that:

> … the foreign policy process has become Europeanized, in the sense that on every international issue, there is an exchange of information and an attempt to arrive at a common understanding and a common approach – compared to how things were in the past, where most issues were looked at in isolation without addressing the attitudes of other member states or a European dimension [Interview January 1996].
>
> (Aggestam 1999: 6)

Likewise our understanding of the changes in Germany's foreign and security policy, which is also, at least in part, due to participation in the CFSP, can be improved with this approach. Takle (2002) argues that the change that emerged towards the end of the 1990s in Germany's security posture was possible and considered legitimate because it was justified with reference to human rights. As a state whose tradition since the end of the Second World War has been a commitment to multi-lateralism, peaceful conflict resolution and emphasis on non-military means – in particular economic means – in security policy, a fully sovereign and reunified Germany was in many ways ahead of its Western European colleagues in terms of adapting to the new security environment. However, the 'normalization' of Germany also meant facing difficult choices about the degree of political and military involvement in international affairs. This became traumatic for both public authorities and citizens at large. The argument used to justify such participation shifted the focus from concerns about German historical legacy towards a focus on Germany's responsibility also to contribute to the upholding of respect for human rights and democracy outside its own borders.

A central element in the CFSP is in Aggestam's view '…the high density of multilateral interactions and the continuous communication and adjustment' which she suggests leads to a learning process. This concept is central to the 'constructivist' perspective (Ruggie 1998). Learning here is seen as something other than a mere adaptation as the result of external constraints, or as a result of calculations of expected benefits of changing behaviour. They argue that learning is, or at least can be, a more fundamental change in beliefs '… whereby actors change not only how they deal with particular problems but also their very concept of problem solving – resulting from the recognition that they and other actors face similar conditions, have mutual interests, and share aspirations' (Ruggie 1998: 20). In order to understand how such learning is possible we must have a conception of actors as communicatively competent. In other words, we recognize that actors are able to make normative evaluations about different courses of action.

The EU's international role

Can this approach help us to understand not only the basis for internal cohesion in the CFSP and for the transformation of national foreign policies but also the EU's international role?

A growing literature highlights in various ways that the EU not only has an impact on the international system but that it has a *particular* impact due to its emphasis on international co-operation and respect for human rights (Rosencrance 1998; Menéndez 2002; Manners 2002; Aggestam 2000). In a study of the EU's international pursuit of the abolition of the death penalty Manners (2002) argues that the EU represents a normative power in world politics. He argues that the EU's work for the abolition of the death penalty cannot be understood on the basis of material incentives and instrumental bargaining because there are few rewards for promoting this issue in terms of domestic political support and because this policy creates difficulties for the EU in its relations with close allies such as the United States. He thus concludes that the EU can be conceptualized as a changer of norms in the international system. Rosencrance (1998: 22) also defines the EU attainment in international politics as 'normative rather than empirical'. Furthermore he observes that it is paradoxical that the European states, with their history as imperial powers ruling the world with the help of physical force, now set normative standards for the world.

These conceptions of the EU as representing something different from states in the international system seems to some extent to be reflected in the way member states describe the EU. In France for example there is '…an emphasis on Europe as an ethical and responsible power' (Aggestam 2000). Thus, the emphasis on the need to maximize interests seems to have been if not abandoned altogether then at least modified by an emphasis on the universal principles and the rights of individuals under a collective security regime. This is further illustrated by the following quote from Jacques Chirac: 'So a Europe which is more ethical, which places at the heart of everything it does respect for a number of principles which, in the case of France, underpins a republican code of ethics, and, as far as the whole of Europe is concerned, constitute a shared code of ethics' (Aggestam 2000: 75).

Such arguments are reinforced by the fact that there are now several legal sources that create a link between the EU and the promotion of human rights and democracy. Some sources date back a long way, such as the affirmation by the European Assembly in 1961 that respect for fundamental rights and democratic principles was a condition for membership in the EC, although the founding treaties of the EU made little reference to human rights. During the treaty revisions starting with the Single Act, and also the TEU and the Amsterdam Treaty, there was a concern with developing the EU's legal and political basis with regard to this area. The Amsterdam Treaty stipulates that 'the Union is founded on the principles of liberty, democracy, respect for human rights and fundamental freedoms, and the rule of law' (Article 6), while paragraph 2 asserts that 'The union shall respect fundamental rights, as guaranteed by the ECHR'. It also refers explicitly to the EU's foreign policy: 'The Union shall define and implement a common foreign and security policy covering all areas of foreign and security policy, the objectives of which shall be: ... to develop and consolidate democracy and the rule of law, and respect for human rights and fundamental freedoms' (Article 11, TEU). Finally, as Menéndez (2002) argues, the legal competence of the Union to promote human rights has been strengthened as a result of the proclamation of the Charter of Fundamental rights. Furthermore, the charter is likely to become a central benchmark in assessing compliance with fundamental rights by third countries. Such developments in the Treaties have led EU Foreign Affairs Commissioner, Chris Patten, to state that 'we have a legal framework for human rights in our external policy' (Patten 2000).

However, both the hypothesis that the CFSP is held together by a collective set of norms and that this implies that it will in turn, in its external action, be faithful to these norms need closer examination. It thus seems plausible that the EU is more predisposed to act in this particular way than states but we need not only more empirical data but also better theoretical tools for explaining why this might be the case. The deliberative perspective might be useful in doing so.

It is also important to note that there are clear limitations to such policies – even for a non-state actor such as the EU. Unless the principles of human rights become positive legal rights that can be enforced it is difficult to avoid noticing both that the most powerful actors only use a 'moral' foreign policy for their own interest and that when they don't they are still suspected of doing so (Eriksen 2001; Sjursen 2002). In turn this leads to arbitrariness, as human rights are not universal principles applied to all. Such arbitrariness is also visible in the EU's foreign and security policy (Smith, M. 2001). In order to overcome this problem all international relations would have to be subordinated to a common judicial order that would transform the parameters of power politics:

> Things look different when human rights not only come into play as a moral orientation for one's own political activity, but as rights which have to be implemented in a legal sense. Human rights possess the structural attributes of subjective rights which, irrespective of their purely moral content, by nature are dependent on attaining positive validity within a system of compulsory law.
>
> (Habermas 1999: 270)

With the strengthening of the United Nations, the principles of human rights have gained more force in international politics. Thus one might see a gradual change in the content of norms at the international level away from an exclusive emphasis on state-sovereignty and a strengthening of the principles of human rights. However, the international system is still one in which legal procedures for protecting human rights are weak and where their enforcement is therefore dependent on the willpower of the great powers. Hence, the deliberative perspective might be helpful in providing analytical building blocks that are necessary for understanding both the particular role of the EU in the international system, and for highlighting its limitations, as actors are seen to be led to act strategically or communicatively depending to a large extent on the specific context in which they find themselves. Hence internally in the EU the incentives to act communicatively are far stronger than in the international system.

Conclusion

It would be naïve to pretend that national foreign, security and defence policies do not remain strong and that reaching a consensus, in particular in situations of crisis which require rapid responses, remains difficult for the European Union. Identifying shared interests and reconciling different national policy traditions is a challenge. I have not suggested, in neo-functionalist fashion, that it is only a matter of time before control of security and defence policy is moved from the national to the supra-national level. I have suggested that it is possible to detect a gradual process of change even in foreign and security policy and that perhaps this will follow also in defence. Whereas analyses that conceptualize actors as strategic or instrumental have few difficulties explaining why the EU is often an ineffective and incoherent actor in world politics, they have more difficulties explaining the transformative character of the CFSP with regard to national foreign policies. The continued commitment of member states to building common institutions despite the lack of immediate material gains from such efforts is also difficult to understand on the basis of rational choice assumptions. Certain standards have been set internally in the CFSP and although they are not always upheld they are considered legitimate and set the standard for appropriate behaviour that is used against those who do not respect it.

A deliberative perspective might help by providing the analytical tools necessary in order for us to account for such changes. The underlying assumptions of this perspective stand in contrast to the view of states as 'billiard-ball' actors whose interests are defined exogenously and where the decision-making process is characterized by intergovernmental bargaining and unlimited state interests. This approach focuses on communicative processes and sees the increased co-operation as the product of the spread of supra-national norms and identities. Most importantly, its conception of actors as capable of assessing the validity of norms provides the microfoundations necessary for explaining their gradual accumulation and their binding character. The story of the CFSP as a community of information that later led to a community of views and then a community of action might become easier to appreciate from this perspective. Much more research on these issues is required, however, for any firm conclusions to be drawn.

Notes

1 'Franco-British summit – Joint declaration of European Defence' 4 December 1998.
2 The deliberative approach as outlined here is based primarily on Eriksen (1999) and Eriksen and Weigård (1997, 1999).

References

Aggestam, L. (1999) 'Role Conceptions and the Politics of Identity in Foreign Policy', ARENA Working Paper, 8.

Aggestam, L. (2000) 'Europe Puissance: French Influence and European Independence', in Helene Sjursen (ed.) *Redefining Security? The role of the European Union in European Security Structures*, ARENA Report, 7.

Allen, D. (1998) 'Who Speaks for Europe?: the Search for an Effective and Coherent External Policy', in John Peterson and Helene Sjursen (eds) *A Common Foreign Policy for Europe? Competing Visions of the CFSP*, London: Routledge: 41–58.

Allen, D. and Smith, M. (1990) 'Western Europe's Presence in the Contemporary International Arena', *Review of International Studies*, 16, 1: 19ff., reprinted in Martin Holland (1991) (ed.) *The Future of European Political Co-operation*, London: Macmillan: 95–120.

Bretherton, C. and Vogler, J. (1999) *The European Union as a Global Actor*, London: Routledge.

Cameron, F. (1998) 'Building a Common Foreign Policy: do Institutions matter?', in John Peterson and Helene Sjursen (eds) *A Common Foreign Policy for Europe? Competing Visions of the CFSP*, London: Routledge: 59–76.

Cronin, C. and De Greff, P. (eds) (1998) *The Inclusion of the Other. Studies in Political Theory. Jürgen Habermas*, Cambridge: The MIT Press.

Eriksen, E. O. (1999) 'Towards a Logic of Justification. On the Possibility of Post-national Solidarity', in M. Egeberg and P. Lægreid (eds) *Organizing Political Institutions. Essays for Johan P. Olsen*, Oslo: Scandinavian University Press.

Eriksen, E. O. (2000) 'Integration and the Quest for Theory. On the Micro-foundations of Supranationalism', Paper prepared for the ARENA/IDNET Workshop, 12–17 June, Oslo.

Eriksen, E. O. (2001) 'Why a Charter of Fundamental Rights?' in Erik Oddvar Eriksen, John Erik Fossum and Agustín Ménendez (eds) *The Chartering of Europe. The Charter of Fundamental Rights in Context*, ARENA Report, 8: 29–52.

Eriksen, E. O. and Fossum, J. E. (2000) 'Conclusion: Legitimation through Deliberation', in E.O. Eriksen and J. E. Fossum (eds) *Democracy in the European Union: Integration through Deliberation?* London: Routledge.

Eriksen, E. O. and Weigård, J. (1997) 'Conceputalizing Politics: Strategic of Communicative Action?', *Scandinavian Political Studies*, 20, 3: 219–241.

Eriksen, E. O. and Weigard, J. (1999) *Kommunikativ handling og deliberativt demokrati: Jürgen Habermas' teori om politikk og samfunni*, Oslo: Fagbokforlaget.

Habermas, Jürgen (1999) 'Bestiality and Humanity: a War on the Border between Legality and Morality', *Constellations*, 6, 3: 263–273.

Hill, C. (1994) 'The Capabilities-Expectations Gap, or Conceptualizing Europe's International Role', *Journal of Common Market Studies*, 31, 3: 305–28, reprinted in S.

Bulmer and A. Scott (eds) *Economic and Political Integration in Europe: Internal Dynamics and Global Context*, Oxford: Blackwell: 103–126.

Hill, C. (1998) 'Closing the Capabilities-Expectations Gap?', in J. Peterson and H. Sjursen (eds) *A Common Foreign Policy for Europe? Competing Visions of the CFSP*, London: Routledge: 18–38.

Hill, C. and Wallace, W. (1979) 'Diplomatic Trends in the European Community' *International Affairs*, 55: 47–66.

Hill, C. and Wallace, W. (1996) 'Introduction: Actors and Actions' in Christopher Hill (ed.) *The Actors in Europe's Foreign Policy*, London: Routledge: 1–16.

Hoffmann, S. (2000) 'Towards a Common European Foreign and Security Policy?', *Journal of Common Market Studies*, 38, 2: 189–198.

Howorth, J. (2000) *European Integration and Defence: the Ultimate Challenge? Chaillot Paper*, 43, Paris, Institute for Security Studies West European Union.

Ifestos, P. (1987) *European Political Cooperation. Towards a Framework of Supranational Diplomacy?* Aldershot: Averbury.

Kintis, Andreas (1997) 'The EU's Foreign Policy and the war in former Yugoslavia' in Martin Holland (ed.) *Common Foreign and Security Policy. The Record and Reforms*, London: Pinter: 148–173.

Linklater, A. (1995) 'Neo-realism in Theory and Practice', in Ken Booth and Steve Smith (eds) *International Relations Theory*, Cambridge: Polity Press.

Manners, I. (2002) 'Normative Power Europe: A Contradiction in Terms?', *Journal of Common Market Studies*, 40, 2: 235–258.

March, J. and Olsen J.P. (1989) *Rediscovering Institutions: The Organizational Basis of Politics*, New York: Free Press.

Menéndez, A. (2002) 'Exporting Rights: The Charter of Fundamental Rights, Membership and Foreign Policy of the European Union', ARENA Working Paper, 18.

Morgenthau, H. (1946) *Politics Among Nations: the Struggle for Power and Peace*, New York: Knopf.

Nuttall, S.J. (1992) *European Political Co-operation,* Oxford: Clarendon Press.

Patten, C. (2000) *Human Rights: Toward Greater Complementarity within and between European Regional Organisations*. Speech by the Rt Hon Chris Patten, CH, Council of Europe Conference on 'The Protection of Human Rights in the 21st Century, Dublin, March 3, 2000, available at http://europa.eu.int/comm/external_relations/news/patten/hr_dublin_03_march_2000.htm

Pijpers, A. (1991) 'European Political Cooperation and the Realist Paradigm', in Martin Holland (ed.) *The Future of European Political Co-operation*, London: Macmillan: 8–35.

Pijpers, A. (1996) 'The Netherlands: the Weakening Pull of Atlanticism', in Christopher Hill (ed.) *The Actors in Europe's Foreign Policy*, London: Routledge: 247–267.

Risse, T. (2000) '"Let's argue!": Communicative Action in World Politics', *International Organization*, 54, 1: 1–39.

Risse-Kappen, T. (1995) *Co-operation among Democracies*, Princeton: New Jersey.

Rosencrance, R. (1998) 'The European Union: A New Type of International Actor', in Jan Zielonka (ed.) *Paradoxes of European Foreign Policy*, Hague: Kluwer Law International: 15–23.

Ruggie, J. (1998) *Constructing the World Policy. Essays on International Institutionalization*, London: Routledge.

Sjøstedt, G. (1977) *The External role of the European Community*, Farnborough: Saxon House.

Sjursen, H. (2000) 'Coping – or not Coping – with Change: Norway in European security', *European Foreign Affairs Review*, 5, 4: 539–559.

Sjursen, H. (2002) *The United States, Western Europe and Poland. International Relations in the Second Cold War*, Basingstoke: Palgrave.

Smith, H. (2002) *European Union Foreign Policy: What it is and What it Does*, London: Pluto Press.

Smith, K. E. (2001) 'The EU, Human Rights and Relations with Third Countries: "Foreign Policy" with an Ethical Dimension?', in Karen E. Smith and Margot Light (eds) *Ethics and Foreign Policy*, Cambridge: Cambridge University Press: 185–203.

Smith, M. (1996) 'The EU as an International Actor', in Jeremy Richardson (ed.) *European Union: Power and Policy-making*, London: Routledge.

Smith, M. E. (2000) 'Conforming to Europe: the Domestic Impact of EU Foreign Policy Co-operation', *Journal of European Public Policy*, 7, 4: 613–631.

Smith, M. E. (2001) 'The Quest for Coherence: Institutional Dilemmas of External Action from Maastricht to Amsterdam', in Alec Stone Sweet, Wayne Sandholtz and Neil Fligstein (eds) *The Institutionalization of Europe*, Oxford: Oxford University Press: 171–193.

Takle, M. (2002) 'Towards a Normalisation of German Security and Defence Policy: German Participation in International Military Operations', ARENA Working Paper, 10.

Tonra, B. (1997) 'The Impact of Political Co-operation', in Knud Erik Jørgensen (ed.) *Reflective Approaches to European Governance*, London: Macmillan: 181–198.

Tonra, B. (2001) *The Europeanisation of National Foreign Policy: Dutch, Danish and Irish Foreign Policy in the European Union*, Aldershot: Ashgate.

Torreblanca, J. (2001) 'Ideas, Preferences and Institutions: Explaining the Europeanisation of Spanish Foreign Policy', ARENA Working Paper, 26.

Utenriksdepartementet (2001) *USA-Strategi*, Norwegian Ministry of Foreign Affairs, Oslo.

White, B. (2001) *Understanding European Foreign Policy*, London: Palgrave.

3   What game? By which rules?

Adaptation and flexibility in the EC's foreign economic policy

Alasdair R. Young

Whatever its shortcomings in foreign and security policy, the European Community is now generally accepted as an international actor in economic affairs. Despite an extensive literature, however, how this international organization functions as an international actor is still poorly understood. I argue that the failure to come to grips with the complexity and subtlety of the EC's role as an international economic actor stems from an insufficiently nuanced application of Robert Putnam's (1988) two-level game metaphor.

This lack of nuance has been sustained because most studies of EC foreign economic policy focus narrowly on trade in goods and only on specific international negotiations. By broadening the scope of investigation beyond trade in goods and by situating it in an historical context, this chapter reveals a much more dynamic process in which the EC's dual nature as an international organization and international actor plays a central role. Although it may seem like stating the obvious to point out that the EC is an international organization, many analyses, while acknowledging that fact, fail to engage fully with the implications for the EC's foreign economic policy.

By depicting the EC as a flexible framework for co-operation, this analysis helps to explain why the EC is a more effective international actor across a broader array of issues than a narrow focus on formal institutions would suggest. This chapter also raises implications for how the multi-level game metaphor might be better applied to the EC and, by extension, to other political systems.

I begin with a brief exposition of the multi-level game metaphor and its popularity in analyses of the EC's foreign economic policy. I then address two shortcomings in the literature: not adequately problematizing co-operation; and understating the impact of interdependencies between EC member states on the power relations among them. I illustrate these criticisms with a focused overview of the development of the EC's foreign economic policy. In the light of this assessment, I discuss the most recent and most significant change to the EC's formal foreign economic policy institutions – the 2001 Treaty of Nice. I conclude by reflecting on how best to understand the EC's capacity as an international economic actor and on how to better apply the multi-level game metaphor.

The multi-level game and its popularity

Analyses of international co-operation tend to focus on either structural (international) factors (e.g. neo-realism, interdependence theory) or domestic factors (society-centred, state-centred or state-society) (Gourevitch 1978; Moravcsik 1993). In the international approaches the reactions of states to particular problems are driven by their places in the international system. In the domestic approaches, state behaviour is explained by domestic politics. The two-level game metaphor provides a framework for analysing the interaction between domestic and international factors on international bargaining (Evans *et al.* 1993; Putnam 1988; Milner 1997).

In the two-level game the negotiator operates on two 'tables' at once: the domestic and the international. Diplomatic options, therefore, are constrained by what the other negotiators will accept and what domestic constituents will ratify. The range of possible outcomes that would command sufficient domestic support for ratification is referred to as the 'win-set'. The worse the alternative to international co-operation (the higher the cost of no agreement), the larger the domestic win-set is. Any international agreement must fall within the win-sets of all of the participating governments (see Figure 3.1). One implication of this is that within these constraints, the negotiator has autonomy in choosing the outcome that (s)he prefers.

Recent analyses of EC external economic relations draw, either explicitly or implicitly, on Putnam's metaphor. Most often the EC is treated as a third level between the international and national levels (Collinson 1999; Meunier 1998; Odell 1993; Patterson 1997). Some authors (Devuyst 1995) treat the EC itself as the 'domestic' level in a two-level game.

Treating the EC's participation in international negotiations as a three-level game actually means linking two two-level games at the EC level (see Figure 3.2). In one game the EC is the international level (Level I in the parlance) at which the member governments representing their domestic interests (Level II) seek to find a common position. In the second game the EC is the domestic level (Level II) and the Commission (or the Council presidency) negotiates at the international

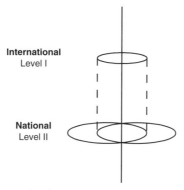

International
Level I

National
Level II

Figure 3.1 Depiction of a two-level game

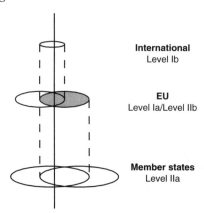

International
Level Ib

EU
Level Ia/Level IIb

Member states
Level IIa

Figure 3.2 Depiction of a three-level game

level (Level I). Level I in the first game and Level II in the second game are the same game on the same level, but looking in opposite directions.

One implication of this double two-level game is that, all else being equal, one might expect the EC's win-set to be smaller than those of other governments. This is due to the EC's win-set being the product of a pre-negotiation among (currently) 15 governments before negotiating with other partners. In some circumstances, at least, this lends the EC enhanced negotiating leverage (Meunier 1998), but contributes to it being a rather unwieldy negotiating partner.

As the subsequent discussion will illustrate, the fact that the EC is an international organization raises additional implications for the application of the metaphor: who is the negotiator? What are the mechanisms for overseeing the negotiator? What are the rules of ratification? None of these implications invalidate the metaphor's application to the EC, but they do suggest that care is needed when applying the metaphor.

Shortcomings of the prevailing approach

Although conceptualizing the EC's participation in international negotiations as a three-level game is valuable, its application has been insufficiently sophisticated (Young 2001). First, co-operation among the EC's member governments is treated as the only option; a three-level game is the only game in town. Under certain circumstances, however, the member governments have a choice about whether to co-operate in international negotiation or to participate unilaterally (a choice between three- and two-level games).

Second, the influence of the EC's institutional framework tends to be reduced to the impact of qualified majority voting and the Commission's role as negotiator on whether EC policy is protectionist or liberal (see, for example, Bilal 1998; Hayes 1993; Johnson 1998; Meunier 1998; Meunier and Nicolaïdis 1999; Wolf 1983). When the member governments do not have to co-operate, but choose to, they have to decide who will negotiate on their behalf and how they will structure their co-operation. In addition, whether co-operation is required or not, the high level of interdependence among the member governments shapes their preferences regarding international negotiations and the power relations among them (Hanson 1998; Smith, M. 2001).

The shortcomings in the prevailing analysis have been obscured by the empirical focus on trade in goods within the scope of the EC's common commercial policy. Such a focus is understandable as only since the mid-1980s have other trade issues – such as trade in services, foreign direct investment, competition policy, environmental policy – gained a heightened degree of prominence on the international agenda. When negotiating on issues within the common commercial policy, the member governments must co-operate and the procedures for co-operation and ratification are well established. Such traditional at-the-border measures affecting trade in goods, however, have never been the sole subject of international trade negotiations and have become even less so since the mid-1980s.

This narrow substantive focus has been compounded by the narrow temporal focus of most analyses. The tendency to look at only a specific negotiation, while understandable, means that the development of the EC's foreign economic policy over time is missed. In such snap shots the EC's institutional framework appears fixed. Extending the focus over time, however, reveals significant adaptation.

By broadening the empirical focus beyond trade in goods and by exploring the evolution of the EC's foreign economic policy since its inception, this chapter illuminates these shortcomings.

The dynamics of EC foreign economic policy

The picture of EC foreign economic policy depicted in this chapter is both messier and more adaptable than is usually presented. The crux of the argument is that because the EC is an international organization, the power relations between the member governments and the EC as such and among the member governments profoundly shape the EC's capacity as an international actor. These relationships are in tension and, over time, new equilibria are established until accumulated tension makes them no longer adequate. The result is an uneven and sporadic process of political and institutional adaptation.

Limited Treaty change

The EC is the world's most highly institutionalized international organization. The most fundamental impact of the EC's institutional framework, known collectively as *acquis communautaire*,[1] on foreign economic policy is in determining whether authority (competence in EC parlance) for particular issues resides with the EC, the member states or both. In other words, the *acquis* determines whether the member governments must participate in international negotiations through the EC or if they can choose to participate unilaterally. Where exclusive external competence resides with the EC (as is the case with trade in goods), the member governments cannot pursue unilateral policies. In such circumstances the *acquis* establishes clear procedures, and decision rules facilitate collective participation in international negotiations. Where competence resides with the member states, the governments can choose whether or not to co-operate at the European level in order to influence international negotiations. If they choose to co-operate, they must also agree on how to co-operate.

Disputes about the allocation of competence between the EC and its member states have been a persistent feature of EC foreign economic policy since the signing of the Treaty of Rome in 1957. The keystone of the EC's foreign economic policy, the common commercial policy, was the product of two cross-cutting tensions: liberal versus protectionist; strong Commission role versus strong member government role (Lindberg 1963; Moravcsik 1998). The ensuing compromise included an open-ended definition of the scope of the common commercial policy (see Box A). It provided only an indicative list of commercial policy instruments, leaving open the question of precisely where the boundary between EC and member state authority lies. This indicative list reflected the main preoccupations of the time – tariffs and quantitative restrictions – but meant that the policy did not include many elements that later became the subject of multi-lateral negotiations. The scope of the common commercial policy in the Treaty was not altered until the February 2001 Treaty of Nice (to which I return below).[2]

Box A The scope of the common commercial policy prior to Nice (Article 133)

… the common commercial policy shall be based on uniform principles, particularly in regard to changes in tariff rates, the conclusion of tariff and trade agreements, the achievement of uniformity in measures of liberalisation, export policy and measures to protect trade such as those to be taken in case of dumping or subsidies.

The creative tension of adaptation

The EC's member governments and the European Commission have repeatedly agreed to co-operate beyond what is strictly required by the legal allocation of competence. Such 'soft' co-operation has been facilitated by non-binding arrangements – 'soft' institutions – which clarify who will negotiate and how common positions will be agreed. Significantly, the frequent disagreements over the allocation of competence have tended to come after the internal co-operation has succeeded and the external agreement has been concluded.

The European Court of Justice (ECJ), in passing judgement on the compatibility of the resulting arrangements with the Treaty's provisions, changes the institutional backdrop against which co-operation in the next international negotiation must be decided. Yet it is up to the member governments and the Commission to interpret and apply the implications of the Court's judgements.

The following history of the EC's foreign economic policy focuses on five pivotal negotiations conducted between the creation of the customs union and the agreement of the Treaty of Nice. Each required co-operation beyond what was strictly required by exclusive EC competence. Each involved the agreement of 'soft' institutions to structure the participation of the EC and its member states. And almost all altered the context in which subsequent co-operation would be considered.

The European Road Transport Agreement

The 1970 European Road Transport Agreement was one of the first examples of 'soft' co-operation in European foreign economic policy. In 1967 the members of the United Nations' Economic Commission for Europe (ECE), including the then six EC member governments, sought to conclude a Europe-wide agreement on lorry drivers' hours. The EC as such, however, was (and is) not a member of the UN, although there were mechanisms for its participation in the ECE, and the Commission did not advance proposals for an EC negotiating position (ECJ 1971). Nonetheless, the member governments agreed to pursue a common negotiating position and to be collectively represented by the government of the country holding the six-month rotating presidency (ECJ 1971). Thus, although each member government would adopt the ensuing agreement individually, they chose to participate in a three-level game, structured by 'soft institutions' and using existing procedures.

The Commission objected to the ECJ, especially as the EC had just adopted a common policy on lorry drivers' hours. Although the Court upheld the agreement on practical grounds, it held that the EC, as such, should have negotiated the agreement. In doing so, the ECJ advanced the 'doctrine of implied powers'. According to this doctrine, in addition to the enumerated powers bestowed on the EC, the EC's power is co-extensive with its internal powers (Emiliou 1996). The Court thus established parallelism between the internal development of the EC and its exclusive external competence. In doing so, this judgement had profound implications for the balance of power between the EC and the member states in subsequent international negotiations.

The International Rubber Agreement

In May 1976 the United Nations Conference on Trade and Development, of which the EC's member states but not the EC were members, agreed to seek to achieve stable conditions in commodity trade. The Commission asserted that only the EC was competent to participate in the negotiations on the basis of the common commercial policy and proposed negotiating guidelines. Some of the member governments, however, considered that aspects of the negotiation, particularly the funding of the buffer-stock system, fell within the member states' competence. Agreeing to co-operate nonetheless, the member governments responded to the disputed allocation of competence by adopting a 'soft' institution, a so-called 'formula,' to structure their co-operation (ECJ 1979).

Under this formula the EC and its member governments were represented in the negotiations by a joint Community delegation and nine national delegations. The joint delegation was composed of the Commission and the President of the Council plus one official from each of the then nine member governments. Negotiations would be based on a 'common standpoint' agreed in advance. Where the EC was competent, the Commission would be the negotiator. On issues outside Community competence but of 'particular interest to the Community' the Commission representative would 'usually' act as the joint spokesperson for the EC, and views expressed by the member governments had to be in line with the common standpoint (quoted in ECJ 1979: 2878). This co-operation was explicitly without prejudice to the legal arguments about the allocation of competence. Again the member governments had chosen to engage in a three-level game and had agreed non-binding procedures ('soft' institutions) to structure their co-operation.

The Commission, whose opinion on how to proceed had been ignored, challenged the 'formula' before the ECJ, requesting an opinion on the extent of the EC's powers to negotiate the agreement. Although this legal challenge coincided with the start of the negotiations, the intra-EC co-operation during the negotiations proceeded essentially along the lines outlined in the 'formula'.

The Court's ruling, in Opinion 1/78 (ECJ 1979), broadened the scope of the common commercial policy, stating that it was not restricted to the use of instruments intended to affect only traditional aspects of trade. This, in turn, built upon an earlier judgement concerning an agreement within the Organization for Economic Co-operation and Development (OECD) – Opinion 1/75 (Re: OECD Local Cost Standard) (ECJ 1975) – which clarified that the EC has exclusive competence under the common commercial policy and that the content of the common commercial policy is the same as that in the national context.

The Tokyo Round

Although the scope of the common commercial policy had expanded considerably during the 1970s as the result of ECJ jurisprudence, it was still tested by the Tokyo Round of General Agreement on Tariffs and Trade (GATT) negotiations (1973–1979), which embraced issues, notably technical barriers to trade (TBTs), that fell primarily within the member states' responsibility (European Commission 1973). Nonetheless, the member governments approached the negotiations pragmatically, treating them like previous GATT negotiations. Although the EC was represented at the September 1973 Tokyo Ministerial Summit by a joint delegation and the nine national delegations that participated, the Commission conducted the negotiations on the basis of directives from the Council as if under the common commercial policy (Bourgeois 1982).

The allocation of competence, however, became an issue just as the negotiations were due to conclude (Bourgeois 1982). The sticking point was whether the EC alone should conclude the agreements on TBTs. It was at this stage the ECJ issued its Opinion 1/78 on the Natural Rubber Agreement. In the light of the ECJ's opinion that the common commercial policy could not be restricted to just those instruments intended to have an effect on only the traditional aspects of external trade, the Council's lawyers and some member governments accepted the Commission's view that the common commercial policy conferred on the EC the necessary powers to conclude all of the Tokyo Round agreements (Bourgeois 1982; Pescatore 1981).

The British and French governments, however, were not convinced. After 'arduous' discussions, and faced with a US-imposed deadline for acceptance, the member governments agreed that the Commission, on behalf of the EC as a whole, would conclude all of the agreements, except for the protocol on tariffs relating to coal and steel products,[3] and that the member governments would also conclude the codes on TBTs and civil aircraft (Bourgeois 1982: 21). Thus, the tool of a 'mixed' agreement – one concluded and ratified by the EC *and* the member states and which is not provided for in the Treaty of Rome – was employed to settle the disputed allocation of competence.

The Commission, as it made clear in its written answers to parliamentary questions (*Official Journal* C105/31 and C137/36 1980), was dissatisfied with this solution and stuck by its position that the EC was competent to conclude all of the agreements, except the protocol on coal and steel products. It did not, however, challenge the outcome before the ECJ.

The Uruguay Round

The Uruguay Round of GATT negotiations (1986–1994) addressed an even wider range of issues than the Tokyo Round. Agriculture, services, intellectual property and investment measures were all brought within the multilateral framework for the first time. All of these new issues, except for agriculture, raised competence questions for the EC.

The member governments, however, used to negotiating collectively and aware of the increased negotiating leverage that a collective position would bring, agreed to negotiate with one voice even in areas of mixed competence (Johnson 1998; Hodges and Woolcock 1996). The member governments, however, noted that the decision to authorize the Commission to open the negotiations did 'not prejudge the question of the competence' on particular issues (quoted in ECJ 1994: I-5282).

The fact that competence was mixed in some areas, however, did not seriously impede the conduct of the EC's negotiations. This was because the member governments maintained close scrutiny of the Commission during the negotiations and because of the broad support among the member governments for the positions being pursued, particularly with respect to trade-related intellectual property issues (TRIPs) (Devuyst 1995; Hodges and Woolcock 1996). Intra-EC co-operation in the services negotiations was helped by the adoption of internal measures as part of the single market programme and by the relatively unambitious aims of the General Agreement on Trade in Services (GATS) negotiations, which sought only to 'bind' existing levels of 'domestic' liberalization (Hoekman and Kostecki 1995).

The allocation of competence did become a problem when it came to signing and ratifying the agreement because the Commission asserted that only it should sign the agreement on behalf of the EC as a whole – essentially an assertion of exclusive EC competence across the full breadth of the agreement. The member governments insisted on also signing the agreement. The Commission referred the matter to the ECJ. Pending the ECJ's opinion, the Commission and the member governments signed the Uruguay Round Agreement on 15 April 1994 in Marrakech.

The Commission claimed that the common commercial policy gave the EC exclusive competence with regard to both GATS and TRIPs. It argued that if the ECJ did not agree with its interpretation of the common commercial policy, the EC still had exclusive competence by virtue of the 'doctrine of implied powers' (ECJ 1994).

Most of the member governments interpreted the common commercial policy and the extent of the EC's implied external powers much more narrowly than did the Commission. While some were willing to accept that cross-border services (but only cross-border services) fell within the common commercial policy, others restricted the common commercial policy to only those services intrinsically related to the sale of goods, such as after-sales service.

When the Court ruled in November 1994 it held that although the cross-border supply of services falls within the scope of the common commercial policy, other modes of supply do not. Further, it judged that the preservation of the single market did not justify the conclusion of the GATS by the EC alone. The Court also ruled that although the EC has competence with respect to harmonizing intellectual property rights, it had not yet exercised it internally and so could not claim exclusive external competence for TRIPs. Thus, Opinion 1/94 resulted in a very limited broadening of the scope of the common commercial policy.

The post-Uruguay Round negotiations

Although the Uruguay Round negotiations were formally concluded in December 1993, some participants felt that progress on certain key issues related to the GATS – the movement of natural persons supplying services, financial services, 'basic' telecommunications services, and maritime transport – had not been satisfactory and agreed to continue negotiations starting in May 1994. All of these issues fell within the area of disputed competence that was before the ECJ at the time. Pending the Court's opinion and without the broader sectoral coverage of the Uruguay Round, in which the weight of EC competence was greater, the issue of the division of competence was more pressing and the procedures for negotiating less clear.

Nonetheless, the member governments again agreed to engage in a 'three-level game'. The awkward issues of co-operation were addressed by a non-binding code of conduct (a 'soft' institution) drawn up between the member governments, the Council and the Commission and agreed by the General Affairs Council in May 1994 (ECJ 1994: I–5366). The code of conduct, without settling the distribution of competences, enabled the Commission to negotiate on behalf of the EC and its member states as it had done during the Uruguay Round. The code, however, did institutionalize the member governments' participation in the negotiations as observers and underline the Commission's duty to keep the member governments fully informed of developments.

Adaptation and the changing playing surface

The preceding discussion illustrates the variety of forms and formulations of co-operation that the member governments and the European Commission have adopted in order to facilitate their participation in international negotiations outside the disputed scope of the common commercial policy. These forms are summarized in Table 3.1.

The preceding discussion also illustrates how, in the absence of formal amendments to the Treaty, judicial interpretation played a crucial role in adapting the EC's institutional structure to the changing demands of the international political economy (European Commission 1995, 1996). The accumulation of the ECJ's rulings in disputes between the member governments and the Commission has amounted to a 'mutation' of competence in European foreign economic policy, shifting authority for a wide range of issues from the member states to the EC (Bermann 1993; Hendry *et al.* 1996; Weiler 1991: 2431). This mutation occurred along two dimensions: broadening of the scope of the common commercial policy itself; and establishing parallelism between the internal development of the EC and its exclusive external competence through the 'doctrine of implied powers'. In most of the cases brought before it the Court interpreted the Treaty as giving the EC more authority than at least some of the member governments wanted (Young 2000).

Expanding competence and changing preferences and power

The extension of EC competence has shaped the member governments' preferences and relative power by curtailing some unilateral policies. By foreclosing some forms of unilateral action, the *acquis* can change how member governments view co-operative solutions. This effect is clearest with regard to international trade in goods, where the member governments have ceded exclusive competence to the EC and can no longer act individually. Constraints exist on unilateral action with regard to other areas of European foreign economic policy as well. The ECJ Opinion 1/94, for example, implied that, had the member governments not already been doing so, they would have had to co-operate on some aspects of the post-Uruguay Round 'basic' telecommunications services negotiations (Young 2002).

The willingness of the member governments to co-operate with each other is also influenced by the potential effectiveness of those unilateral policies that they can still pursue. Here the EC being an international organization is critical. The *acquis*, particularly as a result of the single European market programme – which reinforced the principles of free circulation of goods, services, people and capital – has progressively reduced the member governments' capacity to insulate themselves against the policy decisions or business practices of their EC partners.

Table 3.1 Flexibility in EC external negotiations

Negotiation	Negotiator	'Soft' institution	Ratification by	Implications for future negotiations
European Road Transport Agreement	Council president	Council agreement	Member states	'doctrine of implied powers'
International Rubber Agreement	Joint Committee and 9 national delegations	Council agreement	EC and member states	broader scope of the common commercial policy
Tokyo Round	Commission	Council approval of Commission's 'overall approach'	EC and member states	mixed agreement
Uruguay Round	Commission	Council approval of the Punta del Este declaration	EC and member states	limited extension of the common commercial policy
Post-Uruguay Round	Commission	Code of conduct	EC and member states	

In areas where there is no common external policy, this intra-EC interdependence can translate into indirect extra-EC interdependence, in parallel with more conventional (external) interdependence. The impact of intra-EC interdependence is greatest on those member states with policies more protectionist than those of their partners (Hanson 1998). Thus, if a common position is pursued, the member governments that can pursue effective national policies (if only because they are liberal), will exercise greater leverage in shaping that common position (Hanson 1998; Young 2002). For example, it is the member governments whose airlines are least exposed to competition from the airlines of other member states that have blocked an EU–US 'open skies' air service agreement (Young 2002).

The EC's capacity as an international economic actor

The preceding discussion suggests that the EC is a more effective international actor in areas of mixed competence than is the common perception (see, for example, Meunier and Nicolaïdis 2000). This perception is based on two principal implications of mixed competence, which are essentially opposite sides of the same coin: that it encourages protectionism and that it impedes the EC's ability to play a leading role in negotiations.

A protectionist outcome is more likely where competence is mixed because all member governments must accept an agreement, and the least liberal government will usually set the tone for the whole EC (Woolcock 2000). This is because when a common position is pursued in negotiations that address issues including elements of both exclusive EC and mixed competence, the requirement of unanimity pervades the entire negotiation (Meunier 1998; Woolcock 2000).

One advantage of the need for unanimity is that it strengthens the EC negotiator's (whether the Commission or Council Presidency) hand with respect to the other countries in the negotiation (Meunier 1998). The need to keep all member governments on-side makes granting concessions difficult. Consequently, any concessions by the EC command a high price from the negotiating partners. While having to maintain unanimous support for a negotiating position might have benefits where the EC is on the defensive, the need for unanimity arguably undermines the EC's capacity to play a proactive role in multi-lateral negotiations (Meunier 1998).

This largely negative view of mixed competence – that it encourages protectionism and hampers activism – may be overstated. While this view may apply to wide-ranging negotiations, such as the periodic multi-lateral trade rounds, it is not obvious that it applies to all aspects of foreign economic policy, or for that matter other aspects of external relations. For a start, as discussed above, the ability of protectionist member governments to dictate a common negotiating position may be undermined by their interdependence with other member states with more liberal policies. The preceding brief overview of EC foreign economic policy, for instance, did not reveal any instances in which mixed competence unduly impeded the effectiveness of the EC's participation in international negotiations.

The absence of exclusive Community competence may actually be beneficial. The absence of the requirement to co-operate permits flexibility in how the EC and its member governments participate in multi-lateral negotiations. Where there are wide differences among the member governments' preferences, such flexibility may be necessary for the EC to participate at all. The EC's ultimately unsuccessful co-operation in the Multilateral Agreement on Investment negotiations might not even have got off the ground if the member governments, with their very different approaches to foreign direct investment, had had to agree a common negotiating position (Young 2002).

Further, mixed competence might not be such a comprehensive impediment to EC activism as some fear. Certainly where the member governments have agreed an internal regime that is more ambitious than that under negotiation at the multi-lateral level (usually the case, especially with respect to services), the obstacle of unanimity is neutralized. This was evident in the ERTA negotiations and during the Uruguay Round. In the 'basic' telecommunications services negotiations the existence of an agreed internal regime enabled the EC and its member governments to play a leading role (Young 2002). Likewise, the EC and its member governments were able to demonstrate leadership in the 1997 negotiations of the Kyoto Agreement on climate change because there was a prior internal agreement on reducing greenhouse gas emissions (Sbragia with Damro 1999). Thus there is a link between the adoption of internal EC rules and the member governments' collective ability to overcome the unanimity hurdle associated with mixed competence so as to play a leadership role in multi-lateral negotiations.

European foreign economic policy after Nice

The February 2001 Treaty of Nice[4] marks a sharp departure from the sporadic and gradual process of adaptation described so far in this chapter. By extending the scope of the common commercial policy to encompass all trade in services, with a few notable exceptions, as well as all trade-related aspects of intellectual property rights, the Treaty of Nice, when ratified, will improve the fit between the EC's procedures and the breadth of the international trade agenda (see Box B).

This chapter, however, has argued that mixed competence has not impeded the EC and its member governments as much as is often assumed. Further, to the extent that mixed competence increases the leverage of the most reluctant member government on any issue, it is a problem that Nice did not fully solve. A number of particularly sensitive service sectors – audio-visual, education, health care and social services – were explicitly identified as being of mixed competence, and foreign direct investment in non-service sectors was not incorporated in the revised common commercial policy (European Commission 2000). The round of multi-lateral trade negotiations launched in Doha in November 2001 addresses a number of such issues, including audio-visual, education and transport services, and the 'trade and ...' issues – environmental protection, competition policy and investment – may be brought on to the agenda later.[5] This

---

Box B The scope of the common commercial policy in the Treaty of Nice (Article 133)

5   Paragraphs 1 to 4 shall also apply to the negotiation and conclusion of agreements in the fields of trade in services and the commercial aspects of intellectual property, insofar as those agreements are not covered by the said paragraphs and without prejudice to paragraph 6.

      By way of derogation from paragraph 4, the Council shall act unanimously when negotiating and concluding an agreement in one of the fields referred to in the first subparagraph, where that agreement includes provisions for which unanimity is required for the adoption of internal rules or where it relates to a field in which the Community has not yet exercised the powers conferred upon it by this Treaty by adopting internal rules.

      The Council shall act unanimously with respect to the negotiation and conclusion of a horizontal agreement insofar as it also concerns the preceding subparagraph or the second subparagraph of paragraph 6.

6   An agreement may not be concluded by the Council if it includes provisions which would go beyond the Community's internal powers, in particular by leading to harmonisation of the laws or regulations of the Member States in an area for which this Treaty rules out such harmonisation.

      In this regard, by way of derogation from the first subparagraph of paragraph 5, agreements relating to trade in cultural and audiovisual services, educational services, and social and human health services, shall fall within the shared competence of the Community and its Member States.

---

means that the member governments will still have to ratify the agreement individually, which implies that aspects of the negotiations that fall within the common commercial policy can still be held hostage by protectionist member governments.

So long as issues of mixed competence are situated within the WTO framework, however, co-operation among the EC's member governments, while not necessarily easy, will not be fundamentally questioned. Where these issues are based in other international fora, such as the Organization for Economic Co-operation and Development or one of the UN's subsidiary bodies, of which the EC as such is not a member, co-operation will be more problematic. Nonetheless, intra-EC co-operation may well be accepted, particularly if the member governments' preferences are reasonably congruent.

My analysis also suggests that while the Nice reform is likely to have only limited impact on the conduct of European foreign economic policy in the short- to medium-term, it may have as yet unforeseen implications for the allocation of competence between the EC and the member states, despite the efforts of the member governments to ring fence the changes they agreed at Nice.

Implications for the two-level game metaphor

More broadly, my analysis of the dynamics of EC foreign economic policy also provokes an assessment of Robert Putnam's (1988) two-level game metaphor. The main appeal of the metaphor is that it furnishes a way of linking domestic politics and international relations. 'Domestic' institutional structures, however, are often incorporated inadequately when the metaphor is deployed. This reduces its applicability and masks some of its insights. Most treatments of EC foreign economic policy are a case in point, applying the metaphor only loosely without addressing fully how it must be adapted to accommodate the specific institutional context of the EC.

The EC context affects the two-level game metaphor in two key ways. First and foremost, a common EC negotiating position is itself the product of a two-level game. Thus, the EC's participation in international negotiations could be thought of as two two-level games that intersect at the European level. This is why having an already agreed internal regime to provide the foundation for a common external negotiating position is so important to the EC's effectiveness as an international actor.

Crucially, however, despite Nice, the member governments' participation cannot be taken for granted. The EC's institutional framework with respect to at least some 'new' trade issues, such as services and investment, is incomplete and open to interpretation. How the existing institutions are interpreted plays a pivotal role in shaping whether the member governments act unilaterally or collectively, and affects the dynamics of co-operation when they choose a collective response.

Second, the member governments, which as the Council are responsible for ratification of agreements involving EC competence, are much more closely engaged in negotiations than are traditional legislatures. One would expect this to restrict the scope for the negotiator (usually the Commission) to move the agreement towards its preferred outcome, at least without the member governments' knowledge. It should also make it more difficult for the Commission to leverage an international agreement to affect internal change, at least without the complicity of the member governments. Conversely, the close involvement of the member governments in negotiations suggests that the negotiator is more aware of the parameters of acceptable outcomes, which should reduce the risk of ratification failure (Sbragia with Damro 1999). The implications of these features for the conduct of the EC's foreign economic policy are only beginning to be explored.

The EC is in many respects an extreme case, but the challenges it poses for the two-level game metaphor should encourage us to think more carefully about how we apply it. In particular, much greater care needs to be paid to the impact of 'domestic' institutions – including parliamentary v. presidential democracy, ratification by referenda or multiple tiers of governance – on the functioning of the metaphor. In essence this is a call for building comparative politics more firmly into the metaphor.

Conclusions

This chapter has challenged the common perception that the EC's foreign economic policy is firmly supra-national (see, for example, Smith, M.E. 2001). It has
also illustrated how the institutional context in which the member governments
choose whether to co-operate has changed over time and not always in ways that
they favoured. Thus this chapter has demonstrated that the EC's status as an international actor is complicated even within economic policy. In doing so it has
revealed that there is a variety of forms of co-operation among which the EC's
member governments can choose if they decide to co-operate. This suggests that
it may be worth thinking about the different forms of co-operation in EC foreign
economic policy as forming a spectrum ranging from no co-operation through
'soft' co-operation to 'hard' co-operation, where exclusive EC competence
applies. Considered in this light, the differences between the practices in the EC's
different external policies may not be so stark as it might at first appear.

Notes

1 The EC's treaties, European Court of Justice judgements, secondary legislation and the
   norms and principles embedded in them.
2 The 1997 Treaty of Amsterdam introduced a procedure under which the scope of the
   common commercial policy could be extended without an intergovernmental
   conference, but this mechanism was not deployed.
3 Coal and steel have a special place in the EC's external trade relations because they are
   subject to the 1951 Treaty of Paris, which confers few express external trade powers on
   the European institutions and states explicitly that beyond those provisions it does not
   affect the member states' powers with respect to commercial policy.
4 The Treaty of Nice, *Official Journal*, C 80, 10 March 2001.
5 'Doha WTO Ministerial 2001: Ministerial Declaration,' WT/MIN(01)/DEC/1, 20
   November 2001, available at: http://www.wto.org/english/thewho_e/minist_e/
   min01_e/mindecl_e.htm.

References

Bermann, G. A. (1993) *Cases and Materials on European Community Law*, St Paul: West
   Publishing.
Bilal, S. (1998) 'Political Economy Considerations on the Supply of Trade Protection in
   Regional Integration Agreements', *Journal of Common Market Studies*, 36, 1: 1–25.
Bourgeois, J. (1982) 'The Tokyo Round Agreements on Technical Barriers and on
   Government Procurement in International and EEC Perspective', *Common Market Law
   Review*, 19, 1: 5–33.
Collinson, S. (1999) '"Issue-Systems," "Multi level Games" and the Analysis of the EC's
   External Commercial and Associated Policies: A Research Agenda', *Journal of
   European Public Policy*, 6, 2: 206–224.
Devuyst, Y. (1995) 'The European Community and the Conclusion of the Uruguay
   Round', in C. Rhodes and S. Mazey (eds) *The State of the European Community, III,
   Building a European Polity?*, Boulder: Lynne Rienner: 449–467.

European Commission (1973) 'Development of an Overall Approach to Trade in View of the Coming Multilateral Negotiations in GATT: Memorandum from the Commission to the Council', *Bulletin of the European Communities*, 2: Supplement.

European Commission (1995) *Commission Report for the Reflection Group*, May, Brussels.

European Commission (1996) 'IGC – External Economic Relations: Why must Article 113 be Adjusted?', April, Brussels: European Commission – DG I.

European Commission (2000) 'The Reform of Article 133 by the Nice Treaty: The Logic of Parallelism' http://europa.eu.int/comm/trade/faqs/rev133_en.htm.

ECJ (European Court of Justice) (1971) 'Commission of the European Communities v. Council of the European Communities', Case 22/70 (ERTA), *European Court Report*, 1263.

ECJ (European Court of Justice) (1975) 'Opinion 1/75,' *European Court Report*, 1355.

ECJ (European Court of Justice) (1979) 'Opinion 1/78,' *European Court Report*, 2871.

ECJ (European Court of Justice) (1994) 'Opinion 1/94,' *European Court Report*, I-5267.

Emiliou, N. (1996) 'The Allocation of Competence between the EC and its Member States in the Sphere of External Relations', in N. Emiliou and D. O'Keeffe (eds) *The European Union and World Trade Law: After the GATT Uruguay Round*, Chichester: John Wiley & Sons: 31–45.

Evans, P. B., Jacobson, H. K. and Putnam, R. D. (1993) (eds) *Double-Edged Diplomacy: International Bargaining and Domestic Politics*, Berkeley: University of California Press.

Gourevitch, P. (1978) 'The Second Image Reversed: The International Sources of Domestic Politics', *International Organization*, 32, 4: 881–912.

Hanson, B. T. (1998) 'What Happened to Fortress Europe? External Trade Policy Liberalization in the European Union', *International Organization*, 52, 1: 55–85.

Hayes, J. P. (1993) *Making Trade Policy in the European Community*, New York: St Martin's Press.

Hendry, I. D., MacLeod, I., and Hyett, S. (1996) *The External Relations of the European Communities*, Oxford: Clarendon Press.

Hodges M. and Woolcock, S. (1996) 'EC Policy in the Uruguay Round', in H. Wallace and W. Wallace (eds) *Policy-Making in the European Union*, 3rd edn, Oxford: Oxford University Press: 301–324.

Hoekman, B. and Kostecki, M. M. (1995) *The Political Economy of the World Trading System: From GATT to WTO*, Oxford: Oxford University Press.

Johnson, M. (1998) *European Community Trade Policy and the Article 113 Committee,* London: Royal Institute of International Affairs.

Lindberg, L. N. (1963) *The Political Dynamics of European Economic Integration*, Stanford: Stanford University Press.

Meunier, S. (1998) 'Divided but United: European Trade Policy Integration and EC-US Agricultural Negotiations in the Uruguay Round', in C. Rhodes (ed.) *The European Union in the World Community*, Boulder: Lynne Rienner: 193–211.

Meunier, S. and Nicolaïdis, K. (1999) 'Who Speaks for Europe? The Delegation of Trade Authority in the EC', *Journal of Common Market Studies,* 37, 3: 477–501.

Meunier, S. and Nicolaïdis, K. (2000) 'EC Trade Policy: The Exclusive versus Shared Competence Debate', in M. G. Cowles and M. Smith (eds) *Risks, Reform, Resistance and Revival: The State of the European Union*, 5, Oxford: Oxford University Press: 325–346.

Milner, H. V. (1997) *Interests, Institutions and Information: Domestic Politics and International Relations*, Princeton: Princeton University Press.

Moravcsik, A. (1993) 'Introduction: Integrating International and Domestic Theories of International Bargaining', in P. B. Evans, H. K. Jacobson and R. D. Putnam (eds) *Double-Edged Diplomacy: International Bargaining and Domestic Politics*, Berkeley: University of California Press: 3–42.

Moravcsik, A. (1998) *The Choice for Europe: Social Purpose and State Power from Messina to Maastricht*, Ithaca: Cornell University Press.

Odell, J. S. (1993) 'International Threats and Internal Politics: Brazil, the European Community and the United States, 1985–1987', in P. B. Evans, H. K. Jacobson and R. D. Putnam (eds) *Double-Edged Diplomacy: International Bargaining and Domestic Politics*, Berkeley: University of California Press: 233–264.

Patterson, L. A. (1997) 'Agricultural Reform in the European Community: A Three-Level Game Analysis', *International Organization*, 51, 1: 135–165.

Pescatore, P. (1981) 'Contribution to the Discussion', in C.W.A. Timmermans and E. L. M. Völker (eds) *Division of Powers Between the European Communities and their Member States in the Field of External Relations*, Deventer: Kluwer: 69–75.

Putnam, R. (1988) 'Diplomacy and the Logic of Two-Level Games', *International Organization,* 42, 2: 427–460.

Sbragia, A. M. with Damro, C. (1999) 'The Changing Role of the European Union in International Environmental Politics: Institution Building and the Politics of Climate Change', *Environment and Planning C: Government and Policy*, 17, 1: 53–68.

Smith, M. (2001) 'The European Union's Commercial Policy: Between Coherence and Fragmentation', *Journal of European Public Policy*, 8, 5: 787–802.

Smith, M. E. (2001) 'The Quest for Coherence: Institutional Dilemmas of External Action from Maastricht to Amsterdam', in N. Fligstein, W. Sandholtz and A. Stone Sweet (eds) *The Institutionalisation of Europe*, Oxford: Oxford University Press.

Weiler, J. H. H. (1991) 'The Transformation of Europe', *The Yale Law Journal,* 100, 8: 2403–2483.

Wolf, M. (1983) 'The European Community's Trade Policy', in R. Jenkins (ed.) *Britain and the EEC*, Basingstoke: Macmillan: 151–177.

Woolcock, S. (2000) 'European Trade Policy: Global Pressures and Domestic Constraints', in H. Wallace and W. Wallace (eds) *Policy-Making in the European Union*, 4th edn, Oxford: Oxford University Press: 373–399.

Young, A. R. (2000) 'The Adaptation of European Foreign Economic Policy: From Rome to Seattle', *Journal of Common Market Studies,* 38, 1: 93–116.

Young, A. R. (2001) 'Adapting Two-Level Games to Explain European Foreign Economic Policy', *ECPR News*, 12, 2: 15–16.

Young, A. R. (2002) *Extending European Co-operation: The European Union and the 'New' International Trade Agenda*, Manchester University Press.

Part II

Internal decision-making on external policies

The challenges of multiple levels and multiple pillars

4   Framing an American threat

The European Commission and the technology gap[1]

Ulrika Mörth

This chapter discusses how the activity of framing legitimizes certain interests and actors in the EU's political process. It argues that frames play a vital part in constructing a European actorness and identity. Framing is important in many political systems but it is especially salient in the EU, where policy processes are both fluid and open. Indeed, policy-making in the EU is an exercise in the mobilization of ideas and common policy conceptualizations. The emphasis in this chapter is on how the issue of defence equipment has been framed by the European Commission in the 1990s as part of the classic European discourse on the European 'malaise' towards the US. It is argued that even though the political breakthrough for the issue of defence equipment is evident in the ongoing formation of a defence policy and a defence capacity in the EU, it has also for a long time been considered to be a question of Europe's (civilian) economic and technological capacity towards the US. This was especially true in the 1990s, when the need for the EU to address the issue of European economic competitiveness and technological development was articulated more than it had been during any earlier period of EU's history.

The empirical section of the chapter is divided into two parts. In the first it is argued that the perceived need to strengthen Europe's economic and technological competitiveness towards the US is a regular feature in EU politics. Three waves of technology gap threats can be identified. The first occurred in the mid-1960s, the second in the early 1980s and the third during the 1990s. The second section analyses how defence equipment has been part of this technology gap threat in the 1990s, and how a market frame on the issue of defence equipment has enhanced a sense of a European actorness and identity.

Frames and institutional settings

Frames are referents for action and give direction to the political process (Schön and Rein 1994; Jachtenfuchs 1996; Mörth 2000). They legitimize certain decisions and activate different actors. Actors also use frames in order to gain influence in the political process. This means that frames can be seen as instruments for pursuing various interests. Actors can use 'globalization' and other catchwords in order to promote a specific set of policy solutions to various external threats (Rosamond 1999). An issue can be framed as a threat to certain values and will therefore be the focus of political attention. Indeed, actors are not merely 'finding' circumstances but are also very much in the making of circumstances (Ruggie 1998a, 1998b). However, conflicts over how to define and conceptualize a policy or an issue are not only explained by different interests. They are also about constitutive rules, in other words how the rules of the game are shaped (Ruggie 1998b: 871). It is argued that:

> The environment in which actors operate is given meaning through ongoing processes of social construction. This means that there is an inherent connection between the social construction of the 'external' environment and the interests that actors acquire.
>
> (Rosamond 1999: 658)

I argue that both the power and the identity dimensions are important in frame analysis.[2] The power dimension of the analysis focuses on conflicts between actors pursuing different frames. The identity dimension of the analysis is essential in order to study how an issue is interpreted and how actors organize collectively. In other words, I am not only interested in why actors compete over how to categorize and define an issue but also how definitions and conceptualizations direct the political process and determine the rules of the game.

Why does one particular frame appear rather than another?[3] Why are certain issues framed as threats whereas others take on more positive connotations? Major political and economic events seem to function as important triggers for a certain policy process and make it possible to pursue policy activities that previously were considered to be political 'dead-ends' (Sandholtz 1992a). The general political development is thus an important factor behind the process of political attention. The end of the Cold War or the war in Kosovo cannot, however, in themselves explain why certain issues are on the European political agenda or why they are framed in a certain way.

I argue in this chapter that how an issue is framed partly depends on the institutional and organizational setting (DiMaggio and Powell 1991; Bourdieu 1996). Frames do not come out of the blue. They consist of certain ideas that travel both in space and in time (Merton 1965). An institutional and organizational approach takes into account that actors strive for influence, but this approach emphasizes that they are also part of institutions which consist 'of cognitive, normative and regulative structures and activities that provide stability and meaning to social behaviour' (Scott 1995; Peters 1999: 106). Indeed, European political integration can be viewed as a continuous process of institutionalization – the process by which social processes take on rule-like status in social thought and action (Meyer and Rowan 1991).

Europe's competitiveness: three waves of technology gap 'fever'

The First Wave

Since the early and mid-1950s research and technological development (RTD) and industrial issues have been at the heart of the European Communities. The first RTD programmes that were launched were not based on any article in the treaties but rather on the general Article 235 in the Treaty of Rome[4] (Sharp and Shearman 1987).

In the mid-1960s technology policy and industrial policy became increasingly linked to each other, both in national politics and at the EC level. Sandholtz (1992a: 70) argues, 'At the same time, a panicky debate erupted in Europe over technology gaps that left European industries dangerously behind the American competitors'. Both national actors, such as governments, and European and international organizations, especially the OECD, recognized the technology gap (Sandholtz 1992a; Mörth 1996). The well-known book by Jean-Jacques Servan-Schreiber, *The American Challenge* (1968), illustrates the general sense of a European 'malaise' towards the US that existed in the late 1960s. National programmes were launched at the national level and the aim was to create national high-tech champions (Ibid.; Mörth 1996, 1998).

Another policy response toward this perceived American threat was the decision to create a more coherent RTD policy and industrial policy at the European level. An important component in this endeavour was to create the framework programme on RTD in 1983. This process started in the late 1960s when the Council adopted RTD plans that were elaborated by the Commission.[5] The Commission advocated supra-national RTD and industrial policies, especially by the Commissioner Altiero Spinelli (1970–1976). In contrast, the national governments pursued a more intergovernmental policy-making style (Nau 1975; Hodges 1983). The Commission and the national governments both shared, however, the view that the EC should take a greater responsibility for RTD and for industrial issues that were regarded as strategic for the future of Europe. Under the leadership of Pierre Aigrain, French Delegate-General for Scientific and Technical Research 'over forty projects for European-owned companies (to avoid encouraging further U.S. penetration) were put forward under the sectoral headings already identified' (Peterson and Sharp 1998: 31). In 1971 an outline plan was decided for a European programme of Cooperation in Science and Technology (COST).

The Second Wave

The second wave of technology gap 'fever' came in the early 1980s and was even more visible in the period after the Single European Act (SEA) in 1986–1987. The policy responses this time were more focused on the European level than during earlier periods. One reason for this was the perceived threat from Japan.

Three major European RTD programmes were launched between 1982 and 1985. Two programmes were sponsored by the EU: ESPRIT (the European Strategic Programme for R&D in IT) and RACE (R&D in Advanced Communications

Technologies for Europe). The then Commissioner for research questions, Etienne Davignon, initiated the programmes for industry, and maintained close dialogue with the directors of the 12 largest European IT companies (Sandholtz 1992a; Peterson 1992). They were, together with other high-tech programmes, part of EU's framework programme for research and technological development that was decided by the Council in 1983. The third programme, EUREKA (European Research Co-ordination Agency) was initiated by the then French President Mitterrand in 1985 as a first response to the American Strategic Defence Initiative programme (SDI) (Mörth 1996). EUREKA was formally organized and financed outside the framework programme but it 'responded to the same fears about the status of high technology that motivated ESPRIT and RACE' (Sandholtz 1992a: 5). The framework programme and EUREKA comprised a European Technological Community and provided an umbrella for the promotion of a technological fortress Europe (Wyatt-Walter 1995).

The Third Wave

The EU's RTD policy was characterized in the 1990s and in the early 2000s by the continuous build up of Europe's structural base of civilian power – so-called 'soft power' (Nye 1990; Nye and Owens 1996). The image of a declining Europe is still vivid, but the focus has changed somewhat. The framing of Europe's competitiveness is less focused on the technology gap and more on unemployment 'and the EU's failure to match either the fast growth-rates of South-East Asia or the faster employment creation of the U.S.' (Peterson and Sharp 1998: 12). Thus, the inability in Europe to create jobs is considered to be an important symptom of its 'declining competitiveness' (Ibid.).

The most comprehensive EU approach towards a common industrial policy emerged out of the White Paper on 'Growth, Competitiveness and Employment,' which was published in December 1993 (European Commission 1993). The report identified a number of issues concerning EU competitiveness and aimed to 'lay the foundations for sustainable development of the European economies, thereby enabling them to withstand international competition while creating the millions of jobs that are needed' (Ibid.: preamble). The Commission had already, in 1990, presented the so-called Bangemann Report (European Commission 1990), which outlined major problems that European industry was facing in an increasingly open and competitive environment. It was argued that Europe's competitive position in relation to Japan and the US had worsened with regard to employment, shares of export markets, R&D, etc (Ibid.).

In the 1993 White Paper it was suggested that a solution to the problem of European competitiveness lay in a strong knowledge-based economy. This was, according to the communication, most evident within the fields of telecommunications, information technology, consumer electronics and so on, in which strategic alliances between firms were increasing. The former Commissioner for Industry, Martin Bangemann, recurrently emphasized the need for the European nation-states to act as one entity in response to the global competition.

The world is now becoming a global economy, thanks to Information and Communications Technology. In the global economy, wealth will only come from our ability to compete. We are in a race for competitiveness [...] competitiveness is not everything. But without competitiveness, everything is nothing.

(Bangemann 1996a)

The problems of co-ordination between various political levels and policy activities were also at the centre of various communications during the 1990s. According to the Commission this was especially a problem in the RTD sector, where national policies were still developed largely without reference to one another (European Commission 1992; European Commission 1993). The Commission argued that the lack of co-ordination between various RTD activities and other policy areas was an important factor behind Europe's limited capacity to convert scientific breakthroughs and technological achievements into industrial and commercial successes. This European weakness was explicitly in contrast to the US, which, according to the Commission, had succeeded in transforming research accomplishments into the commercial market (Ibid.). The diagnosis of Europe's problem vis-à-vis the US is also well elaborated in the Commission's Green Paper on Innovation in 1995. In the paper the European paradox is presented – Europe is good at research but not at transforming these skills into a competitive advantage. The reason for this paradox is that the European effort is fragmented. In an interview, the former commissioner for research, Edith Cresson argued:

I am afraid that we are wasting resources by spreading them too thinly over too many fields. This is why, together with my colleagues Commissioners Bangemann and Kinnock, I introduced the Task Forces. Their aim is to strengthen co-operation and co-ordination between research and industry, and to target our research efforts more precisely.

(Cresson 1996)

What was needed was a 'genuine European strategy for the promotion of innovation' (European Commission 1995: 5).

Clearly, technology policy has thus been closely linked to other policy areas, such as trade, competition and economic policy (Cini and McGowan 1998). Indeed, by the late 1990s, the EU's technology policy had a far clearer and more widely accepted rationale than ever before (Peterson and Sharp 1998: 114). The changed technology policy was evident in the framework programme during the 1990s. The redistributive component of the programme changed, and became more targeted at strengthening Europe's competitiveness. In April 1997 the Commission presented a proposal for the fifth framework programme (F5P) for research and technological development (European Commission 1997a). The overall theme of the proposal was how to cope with globalization on a European level by making European research more effective, thereby giving Europe added value. The programme covered a very broad area, including issues such as the knowledge-based society, employment, economic globalization, European competitiveness and foreign policy.

The importance of the information society and Europe's technological and economic competitiveness has been a concurrent theme in the Presidency Conclusions of the European Council during the 1990s and in the early 2000s.[6] There has thus been no disagreement between the Commission and the European Council on how to diagnose Europe's problem. One difference, however, between the Commission's communications and the Presidency Conclusions of the European Council, is that the Commission has underlined the problematic relationship between Europe and the US, while the European Council hardly ever explicitly mentions the European malaise towards the US. This could be explained by the fact that the Commission is more focused on thinking about Europe as an entity and how to transform a 'fragmented' European into a more coherent actor in a globalized economy.

To sum up, the three waves of technology gap 'fevers' in the EU all share the general notion of a technologically declining Europe. The responses to this perceived threat to Europe's prosperity have consisted of various RTD programmes at the European level. The Commission and the European Council have recurrently stressed the importance of co-ordinated EU activities and that Europe must be seen as an entity. We now turn from this general discourse on Europe's technological and economic competitiveness to the issue of defence equipment and how the future of Europe's defence industry has contributed to the notion that Europe is 'lagging-behind'.

The Commission and the marketframe

In January 1996 the Commission took the unusual step of explicitly discussing the difficulty of separating civilian and defence-related technology and argued that this overlap had to be considered in various ways in EU policy-making (European Commission 1996a). An important argument for the perceived need to increase linkages between the civilian and defence-related spheres was the changed dynamics in the technological and industrial sector. Traditionally it was the military sphere that gave the civilian sphere technology – the so-called spin-off effect. However, the spin-off effect has more or less been replaced by the so-called spin-in effect (Ibid.). This means that the defence industry has become more dependent on civilian industry and civilian RTD programmes. The interlinkages between the two spheres were especially evident in the space and aerospace sectors, which were greatly in need of a co-ordinated approach (European Commission 1996b).

The 1996 communication showed the Commission's ambition to pursue a more comprehensive industrial policy – an action plan – that drew not only on the civilian industry in Europe but also the defence-related industry. Although the future of the defence industry had been discussed earlier, the communication was the first comprehensive document from the Commission that addressed the problems of the

European defence industry. This was a rather bold initiative due to the fact that this sector has been regarded as an area of exclusive national prerogative. Article 223 in the Treaty of Rome (now Article 296) may be evoked by member states in their defence industry deals, which means that rules on mergers, competition and procurement are not applicable. The deals are normally considered by the Commission within the market rules for possible overlaps that might raise antitrust concerns. However, to date the Commission has never opposed a defence industrial merger. The Court has also never investigated a country for breaking the rules requiring merger notification within the defence industry.[7]

It is clear that the Directorate General on Industrial Affairs, formerly DG III, tried to introduce more industrial policy into the defence industry. This policy meant that the rules of the internal market could, after necessary adaptations, be used for this industry as well. DG III already had close relations with this industry, both bilaterally and with EDIG and AECMA.[8] There have been several meetings between DG III and EDIG on the issue of defence equipment in order to create a European defence industrial strategy.[9] The Commission and EDIG agree that a collective effort is needed, 'to tackle the various sensitive issues leading to the establishment of a European Defence Equipment Market where Defence Industry will survive to remain competitive and capable of catering for the European Armaments needs' (EDIG 1995: 2).

According to DG III the incorporation of the defence industry into the first pillar must be implemented systematically. Although DG III recognizes that the defence industry is a very special market, with its close relationship to the state, it is also obvious that it can be approached from a cost-effectiveness perspective. This is also DG III's task within the Commission. In the autumn of 1997, DG III presented a 'Draft Action Plan for the Defence-Related Industry' outlining measures for the short as well as the long term. A first step is to begin a process of standardization of European defence equipment, intended to rationalize the different sets of standards currently being used by the defence ministries in the member states. This process of standardization also entails common rules of public procurement. In a longer perspective, this standardization process must also extend to differing national export policies with regard to conventional arms (see below). The next step would be to incorporate the defence industry sector into the EU's competition policy and state-aid regulations. During this stage there would also be a need for a European Armament Agency in charge of conducting armament co-operative and R&D programmes.

Clearly, the profile of DG III and its then Commissioner Martin Bangemann was very high on defence industry issues. They organized seminars, informal meetings with representatives of the industries, national administrators and other European bodies (Mörth 1998, 2000). At a conference in June 1996 – titled 'The Future of Europe's Defence Industry' – Bangemann urged the national administrators to take part in the 'decision-finding process', initiated by the Commission. It was argued that national administrators needed to identify ' the main problems and priorities' (Bangemann 1996b). The Commissioner emphasized the problems that the European defence industry faced with the US:

First, if European defence industry will not overcome its structural problems we may lose the capacity either to compete efficiently or to co-operate on equal terms with the USA. Secondly, we will be challenged with technology gaps and a disappearance of technological skills. As nowadays, dual-use technologies are widespread, this may also have impacts in the commercial sphere. Given the long period of time for developing new technologies and new systems, these gaps could not be filled in a few years. This would have substantial economic and political consequences.

(Ibid.)

We can thus conclude that the activity of the Commission, especially DG III and EDIG, was intense during the early to mid-1990s on the future of the European defence industry. In November 1997 the Commission presented another communication on the defence industry in which the market frame is less salient than outlined in 1996. In fact, in the communication the Commission argues that the issue of defence equipment must be conceptualized from both a market and a defence frame (European Commission 1997c).

To reiterate, the Commission has been very active in framing the issue of defence equipment as a market issue. We now turn our attention to the defence industry, especially the aerospace industry in Europe, and its activities during the 1990s and early 2000s.

The European defence industry and the fear of US competition

There have been major changes in the European industrial landscape during the 1990s and in the early 2000s. National companies – or national 'champions' – have been transformed into European and transatlantic companies.[10] The transnational linkages between the companies are multiple and complex (Schmitt 2000b). Major industrial changes took place in 1999, which could be explained by the general development in the European defence policy process (Heisbourg 2000). It is difficult to imagine that complex cross-mergers between defence industries would have taken place if there were no credible political development in the European defence policy. That said, it is also quite clear that the industry itself created pressure for political initiatives and that the process towards a strong European defence industry is driven by market factors and not only by the defence policy process.

The aim in this section is to discuss the industrial and the political idea of creating a European aerospace company: the European Aerospace and Defence Company (EADC). As noted above, the general rationale behind creating a strong European defence industry rests with the fact that the borders between technologies are considered to be blurred and that the national protection of the defence industry is an obstacle to a common European effort to strengthen its industrial and RTD base.

This diagnosis of the aerospace industry is presented in several communications from the Commission during the 1990s (see, for example, European

Commission 1996b). In contrast to the situation in the US, national boundaries and separate research and defence policies create the perception that the European industry is fragmented (Ibid.).

The US is the market leader in both civilian and military aerospace, and the recent history of US industry has been one of consolidation. In 1993 the then US defence minister Les Aspin invited the defence industry for a 'last supper' in which he made it clear that the industrial defence companies had to restructure (James 1998). This was not only a rhetorical change by the American government. It was followed by a merger wave in the American defence industry (Ibid.). The European defence industry, and the European Commission, closely monitored the American defence industrial consolidation. One major turning point from the European defence and civil aerospace industry was the Boeing and McDonnell-Douglas merger in 1997. Until then the civil European aircraft project, Airbus, had challenged Boeing but after the American merger the power balance between the American and European companies changed profoundly.[11]

The comparison with the US is striking in various reports from the Commission (European Commission 1997b). Indeed, it was argued that the European consolidation of the European defence industry needed to include measures to create mechanisms that would prevent American companies from buying European companies.[12] In a report from the Brussels-based think-tank CEPS (Centre for European Policy Studies), which is made up of representatives from the industry and from the EU, WEU and NATO, it is stated that the 'European defence industry suffers from a widely fragmented "home market base", overcapacity and duplication of official procedures and processes. Its ability to compete in the global defence equipment market is threatened by these impediments' (CEPS 1999: 22; AECMA 1996: 55). Thus, what is needed is both 'rationalization' and 'consolidation' of the sector and the creation of European companies (Ibid.).

The framing of a technology and capability gap between the US and Europe is also presented by several journals specializing in defence industry matters (see *Aviation Week & Space Technology*, *Defence News* and *Jane's Defence Weekly* (JDW)). Comparisons between the US and Europe for instance concerning defence budgets or RTD budgets always show that the US spends more (see, for example, JDW 29 March 2000). Implicitly, sometimes even explicitly, these journals present a model for Europe – that of the US. The journals also underline the image of a 'war' between the US and Europe on defence equipment matters (see for instance the case of Meteor, *Aviation Week & Space Technology*, 22 May 2000: 25).

Hence, the general image of the European defence and aerospace industries is that of fragmentation. The synopsis is that the industry needs to be consolidated in order to compete with American companies. In December 1997 the French, German and British governments issued a statement in which they stressed the vital political and economic interest of restructuring the European defence industry. The political initiative has been interpreted as a reaction to the industry and its demand for political activities to enhance the creation of transnational defence companies.[13] Until then the European governments had been rather silent on the question of the future of the European defence industry and the most active actor at the European level was the Commission (Mörth 2001).

In the summer of 1998 the three governments plus the governments of Sweden, Spain and Italy presented the Letter of Intent initiative (LoI), which aimed to enhance the creation of Transnational Defence Companies. In July 2000 a general agreement was signed by the six governments to bring the national defence industry policies closer to each other (Ibid.). The statement in November 1997 was thus the pre-phase to this political initiative and agreement. In that statement the three governments made it clear that they wanted to launch various measures to enhance transnational industrial collaboration, and in it they urged the national champions to present a plan and timetable for industrial restructuring and integration (Schmitt 2000c).

Paradoxically, the political vision at the time was focused on the creation of *one* company, a European Defence and Aerospace Company.[14] Rather soon the industrial development turned away from the creation of one company. In January 1999, British Aerospace confirmed that it would buy General Electric Company's Marconi Electronics, which created the third largest defence and aerospace group in the world. Germany's DASA warned that the creation of a pan-European aerospace and defence company might be postponed indefinitely (*Financial Times*, 25 January 1999). Prior to the take-over the specialized press reported that the best way to push forward plans for a consolidated European Aerospace and Defence Company (EADC) was through a link-up between BAE and DASA.

In October 1999, a merger between Aérospatiale Matra and DASA was announced. The new company, which would form a military aviation joint venture, was named EADS (European Aeronautic Defence and Space Company), not to be confused with EADC. What is interesting with the new company (EADS) is the fact that

> ... for the first time, 'national champions' are merging all their assets (with the exception of DASA's aero-engine subsidiary MTU, which will be retained in the DaimlerChrysler group). With the recent inclusion of CASA, what began last October as a Franco-German rapprochement is turning into a truly European grouping.
>
> (Schmitt 2000a: 4)

The new European grouping will enjoy a dominant position in the European aerospace industry. In May 2000 the European Commission cleared the creation of the new company (*Financial Times*, 14 May 2000).

Thus, the political vision of one big European company, EADC, is dead. The idea has been questioned from an industrial competitiveness perspective and as a symbol for fortress Europe. An interviewee in the Commission argued in September 1999 that very few believed in the creation of *one* company. Rather, the notion of EADC was an effective way to provoke and thus generate action to get rid of various trade and market barriers.

From a European political perspective the crucial question of what kind of linkages the European companies will have with American companies remains. In August 1999 John Weston stated, 'We never conceived EADC as something that represented Fortress Europe, with everything in it. We actually saw it as a mechanism for how to get some of these deals together across the national boundaries of Europe' (John Weston, *Defense Daily*, 10 August 1999). In fact, it appears that the companies are already mixed up with each other.[15] Interestingly, in February 2000 the French co-president executive of EADS, Philippe Camus, stated that EADS would not constitute a fortress Europe (*Le Monde*, 25 February 2000).[16]

In December 1999 it was stated that BAE Systems of the UK and Boeing, the US aircraft and defence manufacturer, were engaged in exploratory talks which could result in a merger of their defence businesses (*Financial Times*, 13 December 1999). BAE and Boeing are already involved in a number of collaborative defence-related projects and the two governments have stressed the potential benefits of defence co-operation between the UK and the US (Ibid.). Indeed, one scenario is that BAE's linkages with Boeing will intensify in roughly five years time and that Lockheed Martin 'could become the American friend of EADS' (the *Economist*, 23 December 2000 – 5 January 2001: 112). BAE also has a long-standing partnership with Lockheed Martin. In November 2000 BAE bought components of Lockheed Martin, making it one of world's largest defence groups (Ibid.).

The logic that makes the Atlantic option attractive is of course compelling. The military hardware budgets have been decreasing on both sides of the Atlantic. The production of high technology, which is so important for the military, is dependent on global and commercial business. Hence, a market-driven consolidation tends to manifest closer transatlantic relations. Politically, however, governments seem to be rather reluctant to accept both a more market-driven policy and a transatlantic consolidation. One political problem is the uncertainty regarding the future role of the US and NATO in European security affairs. From an industrial and business community perspective it could be argued that the political polarization of the US and Europe will be (or is perhaps already) less relevant among the defence companies. It could therefore be argued that in the long run there will be US firms 'that become European and European firms that become American, within and across product lines, enhancing companies and efficiency in a broader transatlantic market' (Gordon Adams, *Financial Times*, 3 February 1999).

Euro-American competition: the case of the Eurofighter

From the European Commission's perspective it is, however, very important to create a strong Europe to counter the US. Indeed, the European consolidation of the European defence industry must include measures to create mechanisms that will prevent American companies from buying European companies.

An illustration of the competition between Europe and the US is the arming of the Eurofighter, a fighter project involving the United Kingdom, Germany, Spain and Italy. Whether the European countries chose the missile manufactured by

Raytheon or one produced by the European Meteor consortium was seen as an indication of whether US fears of a 'fortress Europe' may be realized or not. Indeed, the decision by the governments in the UK, Germany, Spain and Italy was crucial in the ongoing consolidation of the aerospace industry (*Financial Times*, 18 February 2000). From a European industrial as well as political perspective Meteor is primarily about breaking a US monopoly in the missile sector. The European consortium consists of a joint venture by Aérospatiale Matra and BAE Systems and the American company Boeing. In February of 2000 the deputy chief director of Matra BAE, Alan Garwood, declared that this co-operation provided 'a very clear signal to the U.S. government that strong relationships with American industry are very important to us' (*Financial Times*, 18 February 2000). In May 2000 the British government decided it would buy Meteor air-to-air missiles and not the American Amraam missile (*Financial Times*, 17 May 2000). 'For the first time Europe will equip its fighter aircraft with a European air-to-air missile, creating interoperability and independence to export' (Fabrice Bregier, CEO of Matra BAE Dynamics, *Aviation Week & Space Technology*, 22 May 2000: 25).

In sum, the European defence industry is traversing a period of dramatic change. The earlier vision of one European aerospace company is dead. Instead, Europe is doing what the US did earlier. It is creating a small number of large companies who have the capacity to compete with the US giants.

Conclusion

By using the concept of framing which emanates from general theories in political science this case has shown that the EU struggles with how to conceptualize multi-pillar issues and furthermore, that this struggle is linked to the European effort to become an equal player with the US. In the wake of the end of the Cold War and the creation of the internal market the Commission has revitalized the classic lagging-behind theme between Europe and the US. Like a Trojan horse the Commission has pursued a market frame in order to gain influence over an issue that has traditionally been framed as a defence and security issue. The Commission has, together with industry, special journals and policy centres such as CEPS, created a political crisis awareness pointing to various economic, industrial and technological threats from the US.

An image of a Europe in disarray is presented which legitimizes a stricter interpretation of Article 296 and the protection of national security interests. Important values are at stake, which make it necessary to think both in European and global terms. In the 1980s the economic threat that SDI (the Strategic Defence Initiative) posed to the Europeans was one of the driving forces behind the creation of the internal market (Sandholtz 1992b: 82).

The nation-state as the important territory for technological innovations was replaced by the notion of a European territory. In the 1990s the turn has come to the defence industry. Thus, the ongoing liberalization of the national defence industries is part of the liberalization trend in the European Union that started with the creation of the internal market. This market integration entails the gradual harmonization of standards, or at least the creation of a framework within which a standardization process could take place.

The US is clearly perceived as the model for Europe and has become an important component in EU policy-making and European identity building. The technological and economic threat of the US is not simply a matter of objective and exogenous changes. It is a social construction. Ideas must be conceptualized and put on the political agenda. By interpreting the issue of defence equipment within a market frame the Commission and industry have assigned a clear meaning to the issue and guided future political actions – to deregulate the national defence industry. Through the market framing activity – by contrasting Europe against the US – a sense of European unity and identity is created. Thus, framing is not only about strategic interests, it also constitutes the identity of actors. A sense of European actorness is created.

Scholars who study the linkage between security and international political economy suggest that the end of the Cold War has led to a power struggle between states on economic and technological terms. States' struggle for economic growth, knowledge and competitiveness has partly replaced the more military and territorially-oriented security policy (Crawford 1995; Strange 1992). Nye and Owens (1996: 22) argue that '[i]n assessing power in the information age, the importance of technology, education, and institutional flexibility has risen, whereas that of geography, population and raw materials has fallen.'

The popular notion of competitiveness 'has been widely used to create a sense that the U.S. and Europe are "losing" to each other in some kind of knock-out competition' (Cable 1995: 310; Hart 1992). The increasing competitiveness is thus often described in realist terms – as economic warfare between leading countries in the world. There is a struggle between independent actors striving to maximize their own utility – the classic logic of anarchy in the international system. The US, the EU, Japan (and increasingly China):

> ... are essentially adversaries though the weapons in countering threats to national security are economic policy measures rather than Cruise missiles and Stealth bombers. By combining a 'realist', Machiavellian, approach to international relations with the language of security and the economic insights of 'strategic trade theory', advocates of a more mercantilist approach have achieved some intellectual respectability and made some impact, in the U.S. especially.
>
> (Cable 1995: 307)

The empirical analysis in this chapter shows that the European Commission has now transferred this reasoning on the importance of knowledge-based power and the view of the adversary to the European defence industry context. The emerging alliances between European and American defence companies are, however, driven by market frames. In markets there are no enemies, only competitors. In a world of economic globalism, in which production becomes de-coupled from individual states, 'it becomes more and more difficult to constitute an Other that might be transformed into a threatening enemy' (Lipschutz 1995: 220).

Notes

1 This chapter has previously been published in slightly different form in *Threat Politics*, ed. Johan Eriksson, Aldershot: Ashgate, 2001.
2 This means that 'actors both calculate consequences and follow rules' (Laegreid and Roness 1999: 308; March and Olsen 1998; Marcussen *et al.* 1999; Green-Cowles *et al.* 2001).
3 See for example Foucault (1972).
4 The new number after the Treaty of Amsterdam is 308.
5 See for instance the Marchécal report in 1967 (Nau 1975; Peterson and Sharp 1998).
6 See for instance Presidency Conclusions from Copenhagen in 1990, Dublin and Florence in 1996, Luxemburg in 1997, Cardiff and Vienna in 1998 and the so-called Vienna Strategy for Europe, Helsinki in 1999 and Lisbon in 2000.
7 Interview with senior official in DG IV.
8 EDIG stands for the European Defence Industrial Group and AECMA stands for the European Association of Aerospace Manufacturers.
9 Interviews with officials at DG III and the General Secretary of EDIG.
10 For an overview of European Aerospace Consolidation see, for instance, *Aviation Week & Space Technology*, 24 July 2000.
11 Lars Gissler, Vice President, Saab Aerospace Strategy, Saab AB, Conference at SIPRI, 13 October 2000.
12 Interview with senior official, DG III, September 1999.
13 Interviews with officials with the Commission, EDIG and Saab.
14 The company would include the Airbus partners (France-Aérospatiale, Germany-DASA, United Kingdom-British Aerospace, Spain-CASA) and Italy's Finmeccania-Alenia and Sweden's Saab. Initially, however, the companies involved were Aérospatiale, BAE and DASA.
15 Interview with former Secretary-General of EDIG, Woodcock, September 1999.
16 The transatlantic linkages already exist, for instance, in October 1999 it was announced that Marconi Electronic Systems (owned by BAE), Aérospatiale Matra and DaimlerChrysler Aérospace agreed to merge their space activities into a new company, Astrium (*Aviation Week & Space Technology*, 25 October 1999, and 5 June 2000). Furthermore, the same month it was also announced that Aérospatiale Matra, British Aerospace and Italy's Finmeccanica were about to merge their missile businesses (Ibid.). If Finmeccanica enters into Airbus a transatlantic problem is created. This is because Finmeccanica already has a close relationship with Boeing – the arch-rival of Airbus (*Financial Times*, 14 April 2000).

References

AECMA (1996) *Towards a European Aerospace Policy – Perspectives and Strategies for the Aerospace Industry,* AECMA: Brussels.
Bangemann, M. (1996a) Opening speech at the Tenth World Congress, 'Technology and Services in the Information Society', Bilbao, 3 June.
Bangemann, M. (1996b) 'The Future of Europe's Defence Industry', Opening Speech at 'The Future of Europe's Defence Industry Conference', Brussels, 18 June.
Bourdieu, P. (1996) *The Rules of Art – Genesis and Structure of the Literature Field,* Cambridge: Polity Press.
Cable, V. (1995) 'What is International Security?', *International Affairs*, 2: 305–324.
CEPS (1999) 'Future Cooperation among European Defence Industries in the light of European Multinational Forces', Report of a CEPS Working Party.

Cini, M. and McGowan, L. (1998) *Competition Policy in the European Union*, London: Macmillan.

Crawford, B. (1995) 'Hawks, Doves, but no Owls: International Economic Interdependence and Construction of the New Security Dilemma', in R. Lipschutz (ed.) *On Security,* New York: Columbia University Press.

Cresson, E. (1996) 'Industry and Technology', *Innovation and Technology Transfer*, no. 2.

DiMaggio, P. J. and Powell, W. W. (1991) 'The Iron Cage Revisited: Institutional Isomorphism and Collective Rationality in Organizational Fields', in W. W. Powell and P.J. DiMaggio (eds) *The New Institutionalism in Organizational Analysis*, London: University of Chicago Press.

EDIG (European Defence Industries Group) Position papers 1995–1999.

European Commission (1990) 'Industrial Policy in an Open and Competitive Environment: Guidelines for a Community Approach', COM (90) 556 final, Brussels.

European Commission (1992) 'Research After Maastricht: an Assessment, a Strategy', SEC (92) 317 final, Brussels.

European Commission (1993) 'Growth, Competitiveness, Employment', COM (93) 700 final, Brussels.

European Commission (1995) 'Green Paper on Innovation', Brussels.

European Commission (1996a) 'The Challenges Facing the European Defence-related Industry, a Contribution for Action at European Level', COM (96) 10 final, Brussels.

European Commission (1996b) 'The European Union and Space', COM (96) 617 final, Brussels.

European Commission (1997a) 'Concerning the 5th Framework of the European Community for Research, Technological Development and Demonstration Activities', COM (97) 142 final, Brussels.

European Commission (1997b) 'The European Aerospace Industry is in Urgent Need of Restructuring – Meeting the Global Challenge', COM (97) 466 final, Brussels.

European Commission (1997c) 'Implementing European Union Strategy on Defence-Related Industries', COM (97) 583 final, Brussels.

Eriksson, J. (ed.) (2001) *Threat Politics*, Aldershot: Ashgate.

Foucault, M. (1972) *The Archeology of Knowledge*, London: Routledge.

Green-Cowles, M., Caporaso, J. and Risse, T. (eds) (2001) *Transforming Europe: Europeanization and Domestic Change,* Ithaca: Cornell University Press.

Hart, J. (1992) *Rival Capitalist – International Competitiveness in the United States, Japan and Western Europe*, Ithaca: Cornell University Press.

Heisbourg, F. (2000) 'European Defence: Making It Work', *Chaillot Papers,* 42, Institute for Security Studies, WEU, Paris.

Hodges, M. (1983) 'Industrial Policy: Hard Times or Great Expectations?', in H. Wallace, W. Wallace and C. Webb (eds) *PolicyMaking in the European Community,* London: John Wiley & Sons.

Jachtenfuchs, M. (1996) *International Policy-Making as a Learning Process?,* Aldershot: Ashgate.

James, A. (1998) *Post-merger Strategies of the Leading US Defence Aerospace Companies,* Research Report, Stockholm: Swedish Defence Research Establishment.

Laegreid, P. and Roness, P. (1999) 'Administrative Reform as Organized Attention', in M. Egeberg and P. Laegreid (eds) *Organizing Political Institutions,* Bergen: Scandinavian University Press.

Lipschutz, R. (1995) 'Negotiating the Boundaries of Difference and Security at Millennium's End', in R. Lipschutz (ed.) *On Security*, New York: Columbia University Press.

March, J. and Olsen, J. (1998) 'The Institutional Dynamics of International Political Orders', *International Organization*, 52: 943–969.

Marcussen, M *et al.* (1999) 'Constructing Europe? The Evolution of French, British and German Nation State Identities', *Journal of European Public Policy*, 6: 614–633.

Merton, R. K (1965) *On the Shoulders of Giants*, New York: The Free Press.

Meyer, J. and Rowan B. (1991) 'Institutionalized Organizations: Formal Structure as Myth and Ceremony', in W. Powell and P. DiMaggio (eds) *The New Institutionalism in Organizational Analysis*, Chicago: Chicago University Press.

Mörth, U. (1996) *Vardagsintegration – La vie quotidienne – i Europa*, PhD Dissertation, Department of Political Science, Stockholm University.

Mörth, U. (1998) 'Policy Diffusion in Research and Technological Development – No Government is an Island', *Cooperation and Conflict,* 33: 35–58.

Mörth, U. (2000) 'Competing Frames in the European Commission – the Case of the Defence Industry and Equipment Issue', *Journal of European Public Policy*, 7: 173–189.

Mörth, U. (2001) *The Building of Europe – the Organising of European Armaments Co-operation*, unpublished manuscript.

Nau, H. (1975) 'Global Responses to R&D problems in Western Europe: 1955–1958 and 1968–1973,' *International Organization*, 29: 616–654.

Nye, J. (1990) *Bound to Lead – The Changing Nature of American Power*, New York: Basic Books.

Nye, J. and Owens, W. (1996) 'America's Information Edge', *Foreign Affairs*, 75: 20–36.

Peters, G. (1999) *Institutional Theory in Political Science,* London: Pinter.

Peterson, J. (1992) *The Politics of European Technological Collaboration. An Analysis of the Eureka Initiative*, PhD Dissertation, London School of Economics and York University.

Peterson, J. and Sharp, M. (1998) *Technology Policy in the European Union*, London: Macmillan.

Rosamond, B. (1999) 'Discourses of Globalisation and the Social Construction of European Identities', *Journal of European Public Policy*, 6: 652–668.

Ruggie, J.G. (1998a) *Constructing the World Polity*, London: Routledge.

Ruggie, J.G. (1998b) 'What Makes the World Hang Together? Neo-utilitarianism and the Social Constructivist Challenge', *International Organization*, 52: 855–886.

Sandholtz, W. (1992a) *High-Tech Europe – The Politics of International Cooperation,* Berkeley: University of California Press.

Sandholtz, W. (1992b) *The Highest Stakes – The Economic Foundations of the Next Security System*, London: Oxford University Press.

Schmitt, B. (2000a) 'EADC is Dead – Long Live EADS!', *Newsletter*, 28, Institute for Security Studies, WEU, Paris.

Schmitt, B. (2000b) 'Task Force: "European Armaments Sector" Fourth Session, "Towards a Common European Demand for Defence Goods"', *Institute for Security Studies, WEU*, Paris.

Schmitt, B (2000c) 'From Cooperation to Integration: Defence and Aerospace Industries in Europe', *Chaillot Papers*, 40, Institute for Security Studies, WEU, Paris.

Schön, D. and Rein, M. (1994) *Frame Reflection*, New York: Basic Books.

Scott, R. (1995) *Institutions and Organizations*, London: SAGE.

Servan-Schreiber, J. J. (1968) *The American Challenge*, London: Hamilton.

Sharp, M. and Shearman, C. (1987) 'European Technological Collaboration', *Chatham House Paper*, 36.

Strange, S. (1992) 'States, Firms and Diplomacy', *International Affairs*, 68: 1–16.

Wyatt-Walter, A. (1995) 'Globalization, Corporate Identity and European Technology Policy', *Journal of European Public Policy,* 2: 427–446.

Interviews with senior officials from the European Commission (especially concerning external relations, industrial affairs and RTD), Swedish MEPs, Swedish and French officials at the Ministry of Defence dealing with the Letter of Intent Initiative, the former chairman of EDIG and other representatives from the European defence industry.

5 European external relations fields

The multi-pillar issue of economic sanctions against Serbia

Yves Buchet de Neuilly

Observing the uses of economic sanctions is one way to analyse the links between external economic relations and foreign policy.[1] Actors and commentators have for some time deplored the gap between the European economic strength and its political weakness. The series of sanctions imposed against Serbia from 1998 to 1999 is one attempt of the EU to fill this gap and to transform its economic size and weight into a real and effective foreign policy. It was not the first example of EU sanctions (De Wilde d'Estmael 1998; Nuttall 1992), but it was the first time that EU sanctions were taken autonomously. In other words, these sanctions were unique because they were not simply adopted out of UN Security Council resolutions.

European governments were heavily criticized for their impotence and divisions during the Yugoslav wars. As a result they were prompt to respond rapidly to the troubles in the Serbian province of Kosovo. In addition to diplomatic contacts and mediations, they decided to strengthen their action by using sanctions as a tool. However, the aims of the EU in the beginning of the Kosovo crisis were not as clear as expected. There was minimal consensus that sanctions should in principle be taken, but there were strong dissensions about their effectiveness and scope. The European strategy was not always clear. For example, while EU foreign ministers announced tough sanctions, they later signed regulations that did not have any economic impact.

The aim of this chapter is to provide a satisfactory explanation of this apparent contradiction in the EU sanction policy. It argues that the realist analysis is of little help, despite the fact that EU common and foreign security policy (CFSP) is generally considered to be an intergovernmental area. In this case, divergences came not from different states but from representatives of the same states. The defence of diverging interests was not the result of individual or bureaucratic disagreements, but rather a consequence of the existence of several autonomous external European bureaucratic spaces or sub-fields[2] where interests of member states are expressed.[3]

The principle judgement to sanction was always decided in the institutional framework of the CFSP pillar of the EU Treaty. Contrary to common interpretations it was easy to reach a fast agreement under this pillar. On the other hand the decision to implement sanctions under the first EC pillar, was characterized by endless meetings in the Council and a series of tight discussions. The shift of sanctions decisions from pillar two to pillar one led to deep changes in the conditions of negotiation, not only in terms of constitutional structure but also, and more decisively, in terms of actor configuration and structural distribution of power both at the member state and at the European level.

This chapter is structured as follows. First, I will briefly summarize the EU diplomatic reaction to the escalating situation in Kosovo (in the spring of 1998) and the use of a sanction strategy generally. I will then highlight the apparent contradictions between the tough political declarations of the European governments and the empty shell of the economic sanctions. Third, to understand this discrepancy, I will show the necessity to identify the relevant space structuration of the EU external relations field. This will lead me, finally, to explain the decision to impose EU economic sanctions as the result of negotiations in relatively autonomous European sub-fields.

Sanctions as a European response to the Kosovo crisis

Troubles in the Serbian province of Kosovo intensified in early March 1998. A Kosovar Albanian demonstration was barely repressed by the Serbian police, and at least 80 civilians were killed. For the first time the events in Kosovo raised a unanimous indignation in the international community. The Foreign Ministers of six major diplomatic countries met on 9 March in the framework of the *ad hoc* Contact Group for the former Yugoslavia. The Contact Group had been set up in 1994 to co-ordinate the positions of the United States, the Federation of Russia, the United Kingdom, France, Germany and the incumbent president of the European Union during the war in Bosnia-Herzegovina (Boidevaix 1997: 64). After the Dayton Agreement, the Contact Group's activities resumed, focusing on the tensions in Kosovo.

On 9 March 1998, the Contact Group condemned the large-scale police action of Serbia and decided to take new measures to increase pressure on the authorities in Belgrade. Ministers called for:

1   UN Security consideration of a comprehensive arms embargo against the Federal Republic of Yugoslavia (FRY);
2   refusal to supply equipment to the FRY which might be used for internal repression or for terrorism;
3   denial of visas for senior FRY and Serbian representatives responsible for repressive action by FRY security forces in Kosovo;
4   a moratorium on government financed export credit support for trade and investment, including government financing for privatizations in Serbia.[4]

The Foreign Ministers used a stick-and-carrot strategy. They gave the FRY President Slobodan Milosevic ten days to withdraw its special police units and to cease security force action. They threatened to impose further international sanctions and, specifically, to pursue a freeze on the funds held abroad by the FRY and Serbian government. This tough statement was not easily finalized and had to be translated into binding norms before it could have a concrete effect. This was the case in part because the Contact Group had no legal statute and depended on other international or national arenas.

The attention immediately turned to the UN Security Council where substantive discussions on sanctions began. Drezner (2000) argues that countries often look for broad multi-lateral support in such diplomatic processes. In New York, however, the divisions expressed during the preparation of the Contact Group statement were more acute. The Russian Federation's hesitation slowed the decision-making process, making the probability of adopting measures within the Contact Group deadline highly unlikely.

In the end, the European governments decided not to wait for the UN Security Council Resolution and instead took autonomous sanctions for the first time (Karagiannis 1999). A draft common position was drawn up by the CFSP Counsellors' working group of the Council and finalized by the Committee of Permanent Representatives (COREPER) in Brussels. Thus, the Contact Group's deadline was met when the Council adopted a common position on restrictive measures against the FRY on 19 March.[5] In line with the Contact Group's recommendations, sanctions consisted of an interdiction to supply equipment for internal repression, a moratorium on government financed export credit support for trade and investment and a visa ban for senior FRY and Serbian representatives.

The next week, on 25 March, the Contact Group noticed some movement in Belgrade's position.[6] Talks were beginning on the autonomy of Kosovo, and an agreement seemed to be reached on the implementation of an education accord. In the meantime, however, it was feared that nationalist radicalism would rise again following the appointment of Vojislav Seselj, the leader of the ultranationalist Serbian Radical Party, as deputy prime minister. Foreign ministers decided in the Contact Group to maintain the first restrictive measures. Milosevic was given a new four-week deadline to avoid further sanctions, and the UN Security Council Resolution 1160, imposing an arms embargo on the FRY, was finally adopted on 31 March.[7]

Tensions continued to be high. There was FRY army activity at the Kosovo border and its police repression intensified. The Contact Group met in Rome on 29 April, 'to decide on next steps regarding the increasingly dangerous situation in Kosovo'.[8] Foreign ministers (excluding Russian) recognized Belgrade's non-compliance to the requirements that they had set out. They decided to freeze the funds of the FRY and Serbian government and threatened to stop new investment in Serbia by 9 May if dialogue was still blocked. The EU rapidly approved the freezing of funds in the common position adopted on 7 May.[9]

In a preparation meeting for the G8 Birmingham Summit (London 8–9 May) foreign ministers insisted on 'Belgrade's primary responsibility' in the failure to start a dialogue. They also decided (again without Russia) to stop new investment in Serbia.[10] Meanwhile, Kosovo Albanian leader Ibrahim Rugova and his delegation agreed to meet Slobodan Milosevic in Belgrade on 15 May. The dialogue was supposed to begin with no preconditions, and this new move toward dialogue was welcomed by the withdrawal of the EU's new common position from the agenda.

It was a short-lived calm. A new level of violence was reached by widespread Serbian security forces inflicting arson and artillery attacks on villages in Kosovo. The conflict prompted a growing stream of refugees into northern Albania and threatened regional security and stability. In response, the EU foreign ministers adopted a third common position on sanctions on 8 June.[11]

European governments were increasingly preoccupied by the deteriorating situation on the ground in Kosovo. During the Cardiff European Council (15–16 June) they agreed to adopt further sanctions by imposing a ban on Yugoslav carrier flights between the FRY and the EU. The Council adopted this fourth restrictive measure on 29 June.[12]

There were further sanctions imposed on the FRY during the diplomatic phase of the Kosovo crisis including: refused entry in the member states to persons in the FRY acting against the independent media;[13] an oil embargo;[14] an extension of visa bans; a freeze of FRY funds; a prohibition of export finance; an extension of the investment ban;[15] and a comprehensive flight ban. None of these restrictive measures had any legal effect on EU economic relations with the FRY, as long as they were not implemented by EC regulations. After fast consultations and reactions from the foreign ministers and the CFSP bureaucratic machinery, the decision-making process slowed down when it entered the EC arenas.

Apparent contradictions of the EU sanction policy

A short week was enough to adopt the first EU common position. No more than one meeting was necessary to reach an agreement on the second common position, and the third was also finalized in one meeting after the Council Conclusions. Contrary to common anticipation about diplomatic negotiations, the process was particularly smooth and fast. More difficult talks took place in other arenas, especially in the Contact Group and in the UN. Some EU member states showed a little reluctance to follow decisions devised by a 'directory' of the 'big', but there was never a break from the common decision.

Things were completely different at the second stage of the sanction's decision-making process. To have a legal impact on economic relations with Serbia, sanctions had to be implemented by the adoption of Community legislation in all areas that fell within European Community competencies. An EC regulation was necessary for each common position, and the second negotiation was far more difficult than the first stage. This is surprising given that there was already unanimity of votes for the common positions and that the EC regulations needed only majority consent. Realistically, however, it took weeks and even months of tireless internal negotiations. As a result the sanctions were deprived of any substance.

As a Dutch diplomat noted:

> … in Maastricht, we made the provision that if the Union wants to use its economic instruments for sanction measures, then there should be a political

common position first. But there are two decisions. One is the political decision, which comes first, then we have a decision on the sanctions regulation.
And if you look at the sanction regulation negotiation then you see that member states that do agree to the political decision first, very often have very
different points of view of the actual need for the sanction if they start discussion on the economic measures. There is a huge difference of views. We have
to negotiate several weeks and very intensely on a piece of paper with very
mixed arguments, technical arguments, institutional arguments, legal arguments and economic interest arguments. So it's a very complicated field.[16]

The Council adopted the first EC regulation on 11 May 1998, more than two
months after the Contact Group statement and the Community's common position
and two weeks after the new Contact Group statement for further restrictive measures. The fourth regulation on the ban of flights that came into force on 7
September 1998 was even more difficult. It took 83 days from the initial political
decision to agree.

The member states who pushed first for fast and tough sanctions were the
same states first to strongly oppose the adoption of real economic sanctions. The
explanation for this rests in part on fears that the sanctions would have adverse
consequences for domestic industries. There were complaints from companies
'such as Telecom Italia and Siemens, German textile-makers and governments,
including Greece, which was funding construction of a motorway in Serbia.'[17]
Greek and Italian Telecom firms had bought 49 per cent of the Serb Telecom
organism (Srbija), and a Greek consortium had signed two significant co-operation
contracts with the Mines of Treptka and Bor in Kosovo.[18] However, this does not
explain why the member states waited until the implementation regulation stage
of the sanction decision-making process to raise those objections. Before turning
to this question, I will show how they managed to reduce the restrictive measures
to empty shells.

Table 5.1 Adoption timing of the first economic sanctions against Serbia

Political decision	Nature of economic sanctions	CFSP Common Position	**Interval**	EC Regulation	Interval with Common Position	**Interval with political decision**
9 March	Embargo on equipment for repression	19 March	**10 days**	27 April	39 days	**49 days**
29 April	Freezing of funds	7 May	**8 days**	22 June	46 days	**54 days**
8 June	Prohibition of new investment	8 June	–	24 July	46 days	**46 days**
16 June	Ban of flights	29 June	**13 days**	7 September	70 days	**83 days**

The main strategy of the member states was to use a legal strike. 'Technical limits'[19] were the recurrent issue. First, they contested the community competencies, putting forward restrictive definitions of the Community Treaty – mainly Article 133 (former 113). Second, the binding effect of some parts of the regulation was contested.

A third strategy was to accept only a restricted definition of the scope of sanctions. The wording of the common positions was always very vague and could be clarified in the EC regulation in two opposite ways. For instance, financial sanctions could be limited to a freezing of funds or extended to a suspension of capital flows. The narrow definition adopted in the regulation threw doubt on the effectiveness of sanctions. The Serbian government had, of course, taken precautions to transfer its funds outside the EU before the regulation came into force.

Similar problems of interpretation were raised by the notion of 'investments'. An extensive definition could lead to a comprehensive economic embargo and a restrictive definition would result in a lack of economic effects. The Commission proposed that EU companies be forbidden to 'obtain ownership or control, directly or indirectly, of any kind of asset in the Republic of Serbia, including companies, shares, bonds, loans, and intellectual property rights. This provoked a strong hostility among the member states that had tried to water down tough European Commission proposals'.[20] In the end, they only agreed on an interpretation of investment that prohibits the transfer of funds or financial assets to Serbia. The policy was ineffective, given that there was no such type of investment in Serbia.

Finally, they also contested the applicability of the regulation due to international commitments. The most visible example was the UK failure to enforce the European ban on Yugoslav commercial flights. British officials explained that existing air services agreements made between the UK and Yugoslavia in 1959 took precedence over EU law. Therefore the sanction measures could not apply before a one-year notice period.[21]

The economic sanctions against Serbia adopted in 1998 had no visible economic impact. They were considerably watered-down during the negotiations of the EC regulation implementation. What explanations account for this seeming U-turn? Did the member states simply change their minds? On the contrary, the explanation lies in the domestic political arena. Scientific literature on bureaucratic politics has shown for 30 years (Allison 1971) that states are not unitary actors. Foreign policy is the result of compromise, conflict, and confusion between officials with diverse interests and unequal influence. Allison's model is certainly helpful, but like its competitors it presents the difficulty of developing reasoning based on a separation between national and international (or European) level games.

Relevant sub-fields of the EU external relations field

We could find useful theories offering insights into the preference formation and decision-making process in the growing literature on EU public policies and international relations. One of the main contributions to the understanding of EU and international negotiations was the introduction of different levels of analysis. The logic is that policies are not formulated in a single arena but are the consequences of multiple games bargaining. Multi-level game theory and the multi-level governance approach certainly diverge on many points. Nonetheless, they both share a common interest in the complexity of the EU or international decisional architecture. Negotiations and outcomes are the result of complex linkages between the games, and one must take into account what is going on in one game to understand the actions of the main protagonist in the other.

In his well-known article published in 1988, Robert Putnam proposed a convincing articulation of the link between the domestic level and the international level, which he used to explain the outcomes of multi-lateral bargaining. He focused on the size of the 'win-set' each state is assumed to have, or in other words the set of potential international agreement acceptable at domestic level (Putnam 1988; Evans *et al.* 1993). This model was expanded to encompass the European level for the explanation of the agriculture policy reform in 1992 (Patterson 1997). The EU is presumed to be a third intermediate level between the national and the international arena. It is argued that change in public policy is the result of simultaneous changes in those interlocking levels. The multi-level game theory has been integrated into neo-realist and intergovernementalist approaches of the European construction. The intergovernmentalist theory could not be entirely reduced to a state-centric approach, as it takes into account the domestic conflict and 'national interests'. Nonetheless, states representatives are considered to be the decisive actors connecting domestic interest and European affairs.[22]

The multi-level governance analysis contests state-centric approaches which emphasize 'European level policy-making as the aggregation of domestic interests' (Marks *et al.* 1996: 346; see also Kohler-Koch 1996). Rather, it is argued that decision-making competencies are shared by state and non state actors – such as supra-national institutions and in our case more specifically the European Commission – at different levels as well as subnational actors. Transnational interests could act independently in the European scene, shattering the traditional separation between domestic and international politics. While contesting the prominent and exclusive role of the state, the governance approach of course does not call into question the multi-level analysis. The articulation between multiple arenas is at the heart of this model. Sutcliffe (2000: 291) argues that 'Policy-making responsibility is now shared among a variety of actors at European, national and subnational levels', and attention has been focused on the strategies of alliance between actors of those levels (Ansell *et al.* 1997).

When distinguishing between the levels of European games, researchers very often focus exclusively on the separation between a European level and a national or domestic level (Moravcsik 1998; Evans *et al.* 1993). They explore the relation between domestic politics and EU foreign policy (Hill and William 1996) and the changes in national foreign policy structure caused by the development of the CFSP (Smith 2000). Although there are fundamental differences between multi-level game and multi-level governance theories, both encompass a similar pattern of level division: a vertical territorial level distinction. On the other hand, the theories offer divergent explanations for the articulation between the levels and on the actors involved in both different arenas.

But in the sanction case, such levels of division are of little help. The apparent contradiction of the EU sanction policy could not be attributed to the complex relations between member states, EU and international level negotiations, as far as those contradictions appeared between decisions drawn up at the same territorial level. A territorial division of the games could be relevant for the explanation of each decision process (the CFSP common position and the EC Regulation) but not to understand the links and differences between those decisions.

In one recent article, Sarah Collinson (1999) combined the vertical game division of Putnam's theory with the horizontal division of James Rosenau's 'issue-systems' model. This concept allows her to 'steer the analysis to focus on the interaction of overlapping systems and subsystems of political action that form around specific issues or combinations of issues' (Collinson 1999: 207). Therefore, attention could be turned to the analysis of 'overlapping and interacting policy arenas within the EU governance system' and the effects on the policy process and the outcomes of this interaction. This distinction of overlapping policy arenas and the analysis of their relations to each other are particularly appropriate in the external relations field. The next step is to identify the distinctive systems. Collinson suggests two different and tying ways to locate them: one is to focus on the legal and institutional framework; the second is to focus on the issue.

The constitutional structure is certainly the most visible sign of distinction between the external EU policy areas. The Maastricht Treaty is divided into three pillars with important legal distinctions. Commercial and development policy fall under Article 133 (former 113) and Article 310 (former 238), while foreign and security policy is defined by pillar two provisions. In the first pillar, the European Commission has a monopoly of initiative and leads the implementation of decisions often taken under the rule of majority. In the second pillar, member states keep their faculty to initiate the negotiations and to block the decisions in a so-called intergovernmental system. Of course, the decision-making process cannot be reduced to a legalistic view and we should always be aware of the variation of power in each area. But it seems quite obvious that the first and second pillars are dealing with different issues and therefore are constitutive of two separate issue-systems, including several narrowly defined issue-systems or issue-'subsystems' – such as external commercial policy or development policy (Collinson 1999: 213).

The two systems or subsystems may have the same issue on their agenda (Rosenau 1990) and the way an issue is handled in one system may have repercussions on its handling in the other system. The political use of an economic instrument, as is the case for economic sanctions, is particularly interesting as far as it spreads some light on the autonomy and interdependency of two important EU external sub-fields. The sanctions were at stake at both first and second pillar levels. One similarity between the two pillars was the effect that CFSP decisions (the sanctions common positions) had on EC agenda setting (the necessity to adopt implementing EC regulations). At the same time this sanction process shows the autonomy of the two sub-fields allowing strong differences in the policy outcomes (i.e. tough sanctions in the first pillar and very weak sanctions in the second pillar).

Such divergent policy outcomes are generally attributed to differences of constitutional structures. A widely accepted hypothesis about the effect of institutional rules in the Council is that, under the rule of unanimity voting, the common position eventually reached is the lowest common denominator. By contrast, the majority rule has the effect of mitigating the extreme position (Garrett and Tsebelis 1996; Meunier 2000). In the sanction case, the institutional hypothesis does not work. Tough economic sanctions were easily adopted under the rule of unanimity in the CFSP pillar and weak economic sanctions were more difficult to adopt under the majority rule of the EC pillar. Common positions were not the voice of the more conservative EU member states. Greece, for example, was very reluctant but did not threaten to use its veto right in the CFSP pillar. Furthermore EC regulations under qualified majority voting in the first pillar were radically different from the proposal originally made by the Commission, and were limited to the lowest common denominator.

These facts either undermine the link between institutional rule and the outcome of Council decisions, or mean that institutional rules are less decisive than other variables to explain the variation of degree in EU decisions. The second is the more plausible explanation, because voting rules do not fully help us understand the EU's decision to reduce the scope of economic sanctions against Serbia. One of the tacit assumptions of an institutional explanation would have been that the national interest of a state would be the same in all areas. But in our case, the representatives of the *same* states pushed for a fast adoption of tough sanctions when they took part in the negotiation of the CFSP common position. However, they were strongly opposed to any substantial sanction when it came to the adoption of EC regulations. The problem came not precisely from the multiplicity of national interests but from the diversity of sub-fields, where national interest had to be expressed. This distinction is fundamental. The diverging interests of the member states over time can be attributed to the existence of two different sub-fields, one generally referred to as traditional foreign policy and the other as external economic policy. The differentiation is not caused by the institutional structure of the Maastricht Treaty. If both were under the rule of EC pillar they would remain autonomous, just as the common agricultural policy is autonomous from education and culture policy. In this case, the institutional properties of the pillar do not explain the distinction between the spaces of external relations. They are only signs. The pillar structure of the Treaty is, above all, an institutional translation at one time of a pre-existing structural differentiation.

I do not deny that institutional structures have consequences for the negotiation process and partially explain the outcomes. The argument, however, is that we can not attribute policy system differentiation only to the institutional differences. Otherwise, we need to explain the diverging positions of the member states in the two sub-fields by institutional arguments.

One other significant sign of structural change between the CFSP diplomatic sub-field and EC economic relations sub-field was the mobilization capacity of interests. This change enables us to explain why private or public industrial interests are linked to domestic or transnational constraints during the EC regulation negotiations and not during the CFSP common position negotiations. Within a sub-field, an issue (for example economic sanctions) may or may not be an activator for domestic or transnational interests. Strategies of private or public industrial interests, which seek to gain access to the decision-makers, highlight the line of differentiation between the relevant sub-fields of the EU external relations field. Multiple channels of contact were used simultaneously at the national and the European level. These channels were used mainly when negotiating the EC implementation regulation, because this is where they had the greatest opportunity to exert influence.

EU economic sanction decisions are issues that are simultaneously localized in two EU external spaces: foreign policy and external economic relations. It is essential to identify this horizontal field division in order to explain how it is possible at the same time to adopt both strong and weak measures.

Explaining the EU sanction decisions

Why has the European Union not consistently been able to transform its economic size and weight into a real and effective foreign policy? The question is on everyone's lips and it surfaces on the agenda of many intergovernmental conferences for the revision of the European Treaties. The failure of the European foreign policy is generally put down to the institutional framework of its decision-making process. Unlike external economic action, the Common Foreign and Security Policy (CFSP) remains in the hands of the member states in the intergovernmental second pillar of the Maastricht Treaty. It is certainly true for European security policy, as it exists in the European Security and Defence Policy (ESDP). However, European foreign policy is less clear. As noted above, the watering-down of sanctions does not originate in the constitutional pillar structures.

The change of sanctions was first and foremost a change in the sub-field. It was not necessarily a change of players,[23] or a change of institutions. Rather, differences between the foreign policy sub-field and the external economic relations sub-field are structural. The positions and power of the actors are different, as are effective means of action, expectations and concerns. In the first space, they negotiate the economic sanctions as a political issue, bearing in mind their impact on the diplomatic arena. In the second space, sanctions are negotiated mainly as an economic issue, considering their impact on trade and financial relations between the EU and the FRY. Political consequences are the priority in the CFSP sub-field, whereas economic consequences are the principal concern in the external economic relations sub-field.

According to Robert Pape (1997: 95), what policy-makers 'most want to know [is] when the strategy of economic sanction can change another state's behaviour without resorting to military force'. The change of state behaviour is a political change, which is to be expected in the diplomatic sub-field. It is not an economic change. The political and economic impact of sanctions is not necessarily connected. An economic sanction could have diplomatic effects without any economic effect. Talks between Milosevic and Rugova began just after the announcement of new economic sanctions and before the adoption of the implementation measure of the previous sanctions. These economic sanctions were a success, but they were not implemented and therefore could not have any economic impact. The success of the policy was purely political, which is acceptable as long as the real economic impact was not directly connected to the political impact. Economic sanctions may have political costs for the target with or without economic costs. However, neither the Contact Group nor the UN Security Council's aims can be discussed exclusively in economic terms. 'Resonant norms' (Drezner 2000: 81), defined as a legitimate vision of action shared by the diplomatic community, also factor into the analysis.

A priority in the foreign relations sub-field is not necessarily a priority in the external economic sub-field. In the classical diplomatic space, the timing is very important. One should react quickly to any event in the international scene. Deadlines are fixed and respecting them gives credibility. To exert presssure on Milosevic, diplomats and foreign ministers fixed very short deadlines (nine days to withdraw security forces, etc.). Considering the strong reservations of the Russian Federation, it was too short a deadline for a UN security resolution. In the absence of consensus the European and American governments decided, each one for their part, to adopt the sanctions. The first EU common position on restrictive measures against the FRY met the deadline. This was in itself a success. According to the former US Foreign Secretary of State Madeline Albright, it enabled the Western security community to 'maintain credible pressure on Belgrade to end repression and restore autonomy [in Kosovo]'.[24] Setting a deadline and upholding it signalled diplomatic determination, the effects of which were noticeable during the diplomatic negotiations. The situation in the economic implementation sub-field was different. The interval between the political decision and the economic implementation was far more important. There was pressure to accelerate the negotiation process, but the expectation for fast action could not overcome the defence of economic interests. The hierarchy of priorities was not the same in this sub-field.

The identification of the two autonomous sub-fields is not sufficient to explain why the EC regulation was hard to negotiate when it was easy to adopt the CFSP common position. Given that the preferences of the principal member states were aligned in both sub-fields, why was it so difficult to adopt the EC regulations? Here we should introduce the constitutional variable in the analysis. The move from the second pillar to the first pillar comes with a change of the relative power position in the space. This change lies partly on the redistribution of institutional resources. For the European Commission, the most sensible evolution occurred. Weak and often marginalized in the CFSP sub-field, the Commission has a strong position in the EC sub-field. Its formal monopoly of initiative gives it the means to formulate strong proposals, allowing the

Commission to play a major role in the sanction policy. Tough economic sanctions were not acceptable for the representatives of the principal member states, but they had to wait for the official adoption of the Commission proposal. In addition, they needed to find unanimity on all points to overcome the Commission's text.

Conclusion

External economic relations are a well established EU competence, while foreign policy is still considered an intergovernmental matter. The use of economic pressure for political goals is one of the most visible overlaps between these areas. Many authors have shown the complexity of the 'hydra of European Foreign Policy' (Hill and Wallace 1996: 2; Holland 1997), but they tend to focus almost exclusively on the states, trying to understand their strategies and interests and whether they act under CFSP or community arenas (adding the European Commission in the second case). In order to understand the role of the EU in international relations and its capacity to lean on its economic power to increase its political weight, it is useful to identify the relevant spaces of the external relations field. We could move our attention from the interaction between the national and European levels to the relations between political and economic bureaucratic sub-fields.

During 1998, while foreign ministers and EU diplomats were engaged on a test of strength with the Yugoslav government, ministries and bureaucrats interested in the EU's economic interest were trying to minimize the economic cost of the retaliation against Milosevic. What appears as a contradiction of the EU foreign policy was only the effect of the differentiation of the sub-fields of the EU external relations field. Diplomatic and external economic policies could peacefully co-exist and develop in different directions. It is only in situations where calls for more consistency are made that the divergent outcomes of the structurally differentiated EU external relations field become a problem. Expectation for consistency is one way of thinking about the competence struggles (between COREPER and Political Committee) that often characterize interpillar relations (Ginsberg 1997). However, this was not the case during the first diplomatic stage of the Kosovo crises. Economic sanctions were an issue that crossed over into the two sub-fields, but the horizontal repercussion was essentially limited to the impulse of the negotiation in the EC external economic space after the adoption of the CFSP common positions. Thus, there was every chance that the actors involved in the two distinctive and relatively autonomous sub-fields of the EU external relations would produce dissonant strategies.

The purpose of this chapter was not to explain why tough sanctions were adopted in the second pillar and empty sanctions in the first pillar (although this could have raised questions about the costs of sanctions in the first pillar where they were probably more specific than in the second pillar) but to explain why the same states could adopt both tough and empty sanctions at the same time. These 'contradictory' outcomes are puzzling as long as we confront activities from the two pillars using a single framework. In other words, we are puzzled if we look at what is happening in the economic external relations field using political diplomatic lenses or when there are crossed field feedbacks – for example, if a diplomat contests the EU political sanction strategy arguing that economic measures have no economic impact. In practice, it is generally not necessary for states to have consistent economic and political interests. Governments can, without difficulty, manage the diversity of their interest as far as they do not cross over into a single issue area. A theoretical approach based on the structural notion of 'fields' offers us the possibility to identify different areas where states (or the EU) are acting out their specific social properties. In our case, the two sub-fields correspond to an institutional particularity of the European Union: the pillar structure. Thus, in order to understand the multi-pillar process, it is important to take into account the differences of logics of actions that lead to specific interest framing.

Notes

1 This chapter is based on the empirical material gathered for my PhD thesis (Yves Buchet de Neuilly 2001: 338) including 31 recorded and transcribed interviews and dozens of informal discussions with actors in Brussels (in the European Commission, the General Secretariat of the Council and Permanent representations of Member States), in Paris (in the Ministry of Foreign Affairs and the General Secretariat for Interdepartmental Coordination) – as well as participant observation as a *stagiaire* to the CFSP Counselor of the Commission, from March to July 1998, which afforded me the opportunity to attend many Council group meetings where sanctions were negotiated.

2 A field or a sub-field is a configuration 'of objective relations between positions. These positions are objectively defined, in their existence and in the determinations they impose upon their occupants, agent or institutions, by their present and potential situation (*situs*) in the structure of the distribution of species of power (or capital) whose possession commands access to the specific profits that are at stake in the field, as well as by their objective relation to other positions (domination, subordination, homology, etc.)' (Bourdieu and Wacquant 1992: 97).

3 In the sanction case these are the diplomatic sub-field and the external economic relations sub-field.

4 Contact Group Meeting, *Statement on Kosovo,* London, 9 March 1998, http://www.ohr.int/docu/d980309a.htm

5 2075th Council meeting – Justice and Home Affairs, Brussels, 19 March 1998, C/98/73. Common position of 19 March 1998 on restrictive measures against the Federal Republic of Yugoslavia, OJEC, L 95, 27/03/98: 1–2.

6 Contact Group Meeting, *Statement on Kosovo*, Bonn, 25 March 1998, http://www.ohr.int/docu/d980325b.htm

7 Resolution 1160, adopted by the Security Council at its 3868th meeting, on 31 March 1998, S/RES/1160 (1998).

8 Contact Group Meeting, *Statement on Kosovo,* Rome, 29 April 1998, http://www.ohr.int/docu/d980429a.htm

9 2091st Council meeting – Industry, Brussels, 7 May 1998, PRES/98/129. Common position of 7 May 1998 concerning the freezing of funds held abroad by the FRY and Serbian Government, 98/326/CFSP.

10 http://birmingham.g8summit.gov.uk/forfin/foreign.shtml

11 2104th Council meeting – General Affairs – Luxembourg, 8/9 June 1998, PRES/98/190. Common position of 8 June 1998 concerning the prohibition of new investment in Serbia, 98/374/CFSP.

12 2111th Council meeting – General Affairs – Luxembourg, 29 June 1998, PRES/98/227. Common position of 29 June 1998 concerning a ban on flights by Yugoslav carriers between the Federal Republic of Yugoslavia and the European Community, 98/426/CFSP.
13 Common position of 14 December on restrictive measures to be taken against persons in the Federal Republic of Yugoslavia acting against the independent media, 98/725/CFSP.
14 Common position of 23 April 1999 concerning a ban on the supply and sale of petroleum and petroleum products to the Federal Republic of Yugoslavia, 1999/273/CFSP.
15 Common position of 10 May 1999 concerning additional restrictive measures against the Federal Republic of Yugoslavia, 1999/318/CFSP.
16 Interview, Brussels, April 2000.
17 'Discord erodes force of Serbia sanctions', *European Voice*, 16–22 July 1998.
18 AFP, Athena, 11/06/98.
19 Interview with a French high civil servant, General Secretariat for Interdepartmental Coordination (SGCI), Paris, April 2000.
20 'Discord erodes force of Serbia sanctions', *European Voice,* 16–22 July 1998.
21 Reuters, Brussels, 10 September.
22 'The prospects for international agreement will depend almost entirely on the configuration of societal preferences; in negotiations, governments have little flexibility in making concessions, proposing linkages, managing adjustment or otherwise settling on the "lowest common denominator". International agreement requires that the interests of dominant domestic groups in different countries converge; where they diverge, co-ordination is precluded.' (Moravscik 1993: 487)
23 Foreign Ministers and CFSP Counsellors participate in the two games, but in the individual capitals there were quite different actors involved.
24 Inter Press Service, Bonn, 25 March 1998, http://www.oneworld.org/ips2/mar98/20_58_081.html

References

Allison, G. T. (1971) *Essence of Decision: Explaining the Cuban Missile Crisis*, New York: Harper Collins.
Ansell, C. K., Parsons, C. A. and Darden, K. A. (1997) 'Dual Networks in European Regional Development Policy', *Journal of Common Market Studies,* 35, 3: 347–372.
Boidevaix, F. (1997) *Une Diplomatie pour l'Europe. Le Groupe de Contact Bosnie*, Fondation pour les Études de Défense, Paris.
Bourdieu, P. and Wacquant, Loïc J. D. (1992) *An Invitation to Reflexive Sociology*, Chicago: University of Chicago Press.
Buchet de Neuilly, Y. (2001) *The Chaotic Path of European Foreign Policy: Interdependences, Competitions, Crossed Exchanges and Institutionalisation Process in a World of Differentiated Fields,* PhD dissertation, University of Paris 1 – Panthéon-Sorbonne.
Collinson, S. (1999) '"Issue-systems", "Multi-level Games" and the Analysis of the EU's External Commercial and Associated Policies: a Research Agenda', *Journal of European Public Policy*, 6, 2: 206–224.
De Wilde d'Estmael T. (1998) *La Dimension Politique des Relations Économiques Extérieures de la Communauté Européenne. Sanctions et Incitants Économiques comme Moyens de Politique Étrangère*, Brussels : Etablissements Emile Bruylant.

Drezner, D. W. (2000) 'Bargaining, Enforcement, and Multilateral Sanctions: When is Cooperation Counterproductive?', *International Organization*, 54, 1: 73–102.

Evans, P. B., Jacobson, H. K. and Putnam, R. D. (eds) (1993) *Double-Edged Diplomacy*, Berkeley: University of California Press.

Garett, G. and Tsebelis, G. (1996) 'An Institutional Critique of Intergovernmentalism', *International Organization*, 50, 2: 269–299.

Ginsberg, R. (1997) 'The EU's CFSP: the Politics of Procedure', in M. Holland (ed.) *Common Foreign and Security Policy. The Records and Reforms*, London: Pinter: 12–33.

Hill, C. and William W. (1996) 'Introduction. Actors and actions', in C. Hill (ed.) *The Actors in Europe's Foreign Policy*, London: Routledge: 1–16.

Holland, M. (ed.) (1997) *Common Foreign and Security Policy. The Records and Reforms,* London: Pinter.

Karagiannis, S. (1999) 'Sanctions Internationales et Droit Communautaire. A propos du Règlement 1901/98 sur l'Interdiction de Vol des Transporteurs Yougoslaves', *Revue Trimestrielle de Droit Européen*, 35, 3: 363–394.

Kohler-Koch, B. (1996) 'Catching up with Change: the Transformation of Governance in the European Union', *Journal of European Public Policy*, 3, 3: 359–380.

Marks, G., Hooghe, L. and Blank, K. (1996) 'European Integration from the 1980s: State-Centric v. Multi-level Governance', *Journal of Common Market Studies*, 34, 3: 341–378.

Meunier, S. (2000) 'What Single Voice? European Institutions and EU-US Trade Negotiations', *International Organization*, 54, 1: 103–135.

Moravcsik, A. (1993) 'Preference and Power in the European Community: A Liberal Intergovernmental Approach', *Journal of Common Market Studies*, 31, 4: 473–524.

Moravcsik, A. (1998) *The Choice for Europe: Social Purpose & State Power from Messina to Maastricht*, Ithaca: Cornell University Press.

Nuttall, S. (1992) *European Political Co-operation*, Oxford: Clarendon Press.

Pape, R. (1997) 'Why Economic Sanctions Do Not Work', *International Security*, 22, 2: 90–136.

Patterson, L. A. (1997) 'Agriculture Policy Reform in the European Community: a Three-level Game Analysis, *International Organization*, 51, 1: 135–165.

Putnam, R. D. (1988) 'Diplomacy and Domestic Politics: The Logic of Two-Level Games', *International Organization*, 42, 3: 428–460.

Rosenau, J. (1990) *Turbulence in World Politics: A Theory of Change and Continuity*, Princeton: Princeton University Press.

Smith, M. E. (2000) 'Conforming to Europe: the Domestic Impact of EU Foreign Policy Co-operation', *Journal of European Public Policy*, 7, 4: 613–631.

Sutcliffe, J. B. (2000) 'The 1999 Reform of the Structural Fund Regulations: Multi-level Governance or Renationalization?', *Journal of European Public Policy*, 7, 2: 290–309.

6 Negotiating when others are watching

Explaining the outcome of the association negotiations between the European Community and the countries of Central and Eastern Europe, 1990–1991

Dimitris Papadimitriou

More than a decade has passed since the conclusion of the first association agreements between the (then) European Community (EC) and the Central and Eastern European countries (CEECs). Indeed the new agreements marked an important turning point in the EC's relations with post-communist Eastern Europe remaining rich in both symbolism and ambition. Their name – Europe Agreements (EAs) – was meant to emphasize the end of the continent's division and the beginning of the new era of co-operation and interdependence. By the time of its launch in January 1990, the association process was the clearest manifestation yet of the EC's determination to assist the CEECs' 'return to Europe'. In terms of substance the association agreements provided for the comprehensive regulation of trade relations between the EC and the CEECs (eventually leading to the creation of a Free Trade Area) as well as for co-operation on a wide range of issues including finance, transport, culture and environmental protection. These provisions, in both their depth and width, went well beyond the pre-existing frameworks of co-operation between the EC and the CEECs such as the First Generation Agreements or the Phare programme. In addition, the Europe Agreements were equipped with institutions and procedures designed to facilitate political dialogue and the regular exchange of information between the EC and its associated partners.

Poland, Hungary and Czechoslovakia were the first group of countries to begin association negotiations with the EC in February 1991, followed by Bulgaria and Romania in May 1992. Subsequently, the EC negotiated association agreements with the successor republics of the former Czechoslovakia in 1993, the Baltic states in 1994 and Slovenia in 1995. Despite the initial optimism surrounding the launch of the association process, however, the EA negotiations soon evolved into a rather turbulent process, tarnished by delays, quarrels and disillusionment, particularly as the EC often failed to match the expectations that the East European applicants had attached to the association agreements. The EC's cautious offers to the association applicants has been one of the most striking features of the association negotiations as they not only contradicted the earlier EC pledges for economic assistance for the new democracies in Eastern Europe, but were also disproportionate to the relatively small economic threat posed by the association applicants whose combined share of the EC's total external trade in 1990 was just 2.37 per cent (European Commission 1994: 545).

In the decade that followed the conclusion of the first wave of association agreements, an extensive literature has developed on the subject (Bonvicini 1991; Pinder 1991; Reinicke 1992; Baldwin *et al.* 1992; CEPR 1992; Rollo and Smith 1993; Van Ham 1993; Baldwin 1994; Inotai 1994; Sedelmeier 1994; Guggenbuhl 1995; Sedelmeier and Wallace 1996; Maresceau 1997; Mayhew 1998; Sapir 2000; Papadimitriou 2001, 2002). Yet, despite the substantial body of literature available on the wider theme of association agreements, our knowledge of this important turning point in post-Cold War Europe remains somehow incomplete. Perhaps the greatest difficulty in this respect is our inability to account fully for the EC's bargaining position during the association negotiations. There is little disagreement amongst scholars in the field that the EC's refusal to agree upon a generous package of trade concessions in favour of its Eastern neighbours was in stark contrast to the rhetoric used by EC leaders prior to the opening of the association negotiations. Moreover, there is widespread consensus that the EC's protectionism in the negotiations was, if not completely unjustified, at least disproportionate to the economic threat posed to the EC by the association applicants (Baldwin *et al.* 1992; Rollo and Smith 1993). The same can also be argued in relation to the EC's caution to agree upon a more generous 'political' package for the CEECs – most notably the EC's repeated refusal to incorporate a specific membership clause into the agreements (Bonvicini 1991; Inotai 1994). Yet, despite making well informed arguments against the EC's economic and political strategy in Eastern Europe, the existing literature sheds little light upon the fundamental question of *why* such policy came about, with the EC's caution frequently explained with general references to its 'instinctive tendency towards protectionism'; 'bold pursuit of self-interest'; or 'lack of imagination and strategic planning'.

On a different level, despite the rich empirical evidence available, the conceptualization of the association negotiations has attracted, with few exceptions (Reinicke 1992; Van Ham 1993; Guggenbuhl 1995; Friis 1997, 1998), rather limited attention. That is certainly the case when it comes to the examination of the association negotiations through the lens of the 'wider' rational choice tradition. The term 'wider' is used here to refer to the body of literature that acknowledges the limitations caused by real-life situations on the notion of optimization (which is central to full-blown game theory), but at the same time maintains an overall rationalist framework of analysis where puzzles are explained on the assumption that the actors that participate in them are purposive and driven by cost-benefit considerations (Opt 1999; Fierke and Nicklson 1999). In recent years, tools borrowed from the 'wider' rational choice literature such as game theoretic representations and multi-level bargaining models have provided useful insights into the study of a wide range of issues relating to the EU's integration process (Tsebelis 1994; Schneider and Seybold 1997; Radaelli 1999). Nevertheless, similar theoretical tools have only been used sporadically in the study of the EC's relations with Eastern Europe (Shaffer 1995; Friis 1998).

This chapter attempts to fill some of the gaps in the existing literature by offering an analysis of the association negotiations between the EC and the Visegrad three (Poland, Hungary and Czechoslovakia) that is both historically and theoretically informed. For this purpose, the next section will seek to contextualize the association negotiations by looking at a number of issues that dominated the EC's domestic and international agenda during the early 1990s. It will also borrow from the existing 'wider' rational choice literature in an attempt to place the narrative of the association negotiations into an explanatory framework that could help us better understand the factors that shaped the EC's strategy vis-à-vis the association applicants. Following that, the attention of this chapter will shift onto the main points of contention during the association negotiations where an attempt will be made to account for the differing degrees of caution with which the EC responded to the association applicants' demands for faster trade liberalization and fast-track integration into the structures of the European Community.

Putting the association agreements into historical and theoretical perspective

The elaboration of the EC's association strategy in Eastern Europe was a long and turbulent process. The idea that the best performing countries in Eastern Europe could be granted 'a form of Association' with the EC was first put forward by the Strasbourg European Council (8–9 December 1989). In legal terms the new agreements were based on Article 238 (EEC) and their precise structure was finalized by a series of Commission Communications to the Council during the first nine months of 1990 (European Commission 1990a, 1990b, 1990c). The scope of the Europe Agreements was indeed wide covering the regulation of trade liberalization, movement of workers, financial and cultural co-operation as well as providing a framework for the development of a political dialogue between the two parties. For trade liberalization, in particular, the Commission's proposals envisaged the creation of a Free Trade Area at the end of a 10-year transitional period (divided into two broad phases) during which the Community would move more rapidly towards free trade than its association partners. The proposed Free Trade Area, however, did not include agricultural products for which special arrangements would be negotiated 'taking fully into account their particular character and the functioning of the common agricultural and fisheries policies' (European Commission 1990c). Moreover, the speed with which the EC would liberalize trade in the so-called sensitive products (i.e. textiles, coal and steel) was also left open for the negotiations with the association applicants. The Commission's proposals also provided for the creation of new institutions to oversee the functioning of the Europe Agreements. These included an Association Council (responsible for political consultation at the highest level), an Association Committee (responsible for the management of the most technical aspects of the agreements) and a Parliamentary Association Committee (responsible for promoting dialogue between members of the European Parliament and the parliaments of the association partners). Following the Commission's proposals in August 1990 (European Commission 1990c) and the Council's endorsement in September 1990 (*Bull*-EC 9-1990), Poland, Hungary and Czechoslovakia were selected as the first wave of CEECs to begin association negotiations with the EC in early 1991.

The elaboration of the EC's association strategy in 1990 as well as the negotiation of the Europe Agreements with the Visegrad countries in 1991 ran in parallel with an unusually busy domestic and international agenda for the EC. Domestically, the EC's agenda was dominated by the decision of the Strasbourg European Council (December 1989) to open an Inter-governmental Conference (IGC) on Economic and Monetary Union (EMU), a project in which the Commission's President Jacques Delors had invested much of his political credibility and prestige during the late 1980s (Dyson and Featherstone 1999). Six months later, under immense pressure from the rapidly unfolding events in Eastern Europe, the Dublin European Council (June 1990) decided the opening of another IGC on Political Union that would run parallel to that on EMU. The IGC on Political Union aimed at deepening political integration between the EC's member states and strengthening the Community's international presence by equipping it with foreign and defence policy instruments.

The diplomatic activity for the construction of a 'deeper' European Community, however, came amidst an unfavourable economic climate at home, dominated by sluggish economic growth and controversial plans to boost the EC's international competitiveness by opening up 'traditional' sectors (i.e. textiles, coal and steel) of the European economy to international competition. By the end of the 1980s calls for the restructuring of the EC's textile, coal and steel industries had intensified considerably both as a result of the imminent completion of the Single Market and the EC's participation in the negotiations for the conclusion of the General Agreement for Trade and Tariffs (GATT). The climax of the GATT negotiations in 1991 also unleashed tremendous pressure for the reform of the EC's Common Agricultural Policy (CAP), the protectionist character of which was seen by many of the EC's international trade partners as the main obstacle for the successful conclusion of the Uruguay Round. Against this background, the Agriculture Commissioner Ray MacSharry in July 1991 announced plans for the comprehensive reform of CAP, prompting a lengthy and acrimonious debate with the farming lobby over the nature of CAP and the level of protection it offered to the EC's farming communities (*Agence Europe* 12 July 1991: 15; Rieger 1996).

The lengthy and laborious GATT negotiations formed only part of the EC's busy international agenda during the early 1990s. In Europe, the euphoria following the collapse of the Iron Curtain was soon overshadowed by the urgent need to address the growing security vacuum in Eastern Europe, as highlighted by the massive influx of East European immigrants into the EC as well as by the deepening crises in the USSR and Yugoslavia (Ullman 1991). The negotiation regarding the future relationship between the EC and the European Free Trade Area (EFTA) was another feature of the emerging new European architecture in the late 1980s. In January 1989 (*Agence Europe* 26 January 1989) the Commission's President Jacques Delors put forward his idea for the creation of a European Economic Area (EEA), a new framework of co-operation aiming to extend the four freedoms and flanking policies of the EC's Single Market to the

EFTA members (Austria, Finland, Iceland, Norway, Sweden and Switzerland), without offering them full EC membership. Despite early hopes that an EEA agreement could be clinched before the end of 1990, the negotiations proved both difficult and lengthy, leaving the EC exposed to accusations that the EEA project was nothing more than a device by the Delors-led 'deepeners' to halt the drive towards the EC's 'widening' until the two IGCs on EMU and Political Union were successfully completed. Mitterrand's calls for the creation of a European Confederation in the early 1990s, as well as Andriessen's idea on affiliated EC membership in April 1991, also received a similarly sceptical reaction from the EFTAns and East Europeans alike (Papadimitriou 2002: 45–46).

An analysis of the association negotiations without reference to the contextual factors that shape the EC's strategy in them would be misleading. The EC's bargain with the association applicants did not take place in a vacuum, but was instead conducted in parallel with important developments in the EC's domestic and international agenda.

Conceptually, the association bargain can, therefore, be understood as being nested (Tsebelis 1988, 1990) within a wider network of games, or what can be described as a 'grand game'. For purposes of analytical clarity the grand game

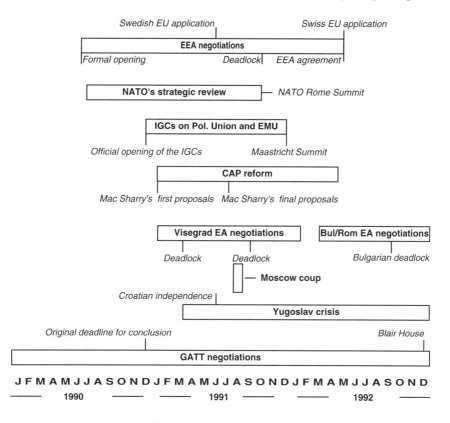

Figure 6.1 Timetable of the EC's Multiple Games, 1990–1992

can be assumed to involve a series of games played in three inter-connected arenas: the domestic arena (involving games such as the two IGCs on EMU and Political Union, the CAP reform and the restructuring of the EC's traditional industries); the association arena (involving bargains on the different items of the EAs negotiating agenda) and the international arena (involving games such as the GATT and the EEA negotiations as well as the new security environment created in Europe following the collapse of the Berlin Wall).

Because of the EC's simultaneous involvement in all three inter-connected arenas, the distribution of pay-offs within the grand game remained variable. In other words, the EC's strategy in a particular game (or arena) and the pay-offs it managed to secure from it, were inextricably linked with the EC's performance (and pay-offs) in other games and vice versa. In practical terms, the variability of pay-offs within the grand game meant that the EC's strategy during the association negotiations could not have been developed in isolation from the EC's strategies in other international and domestic games. Based on Tsebelis' (1988: 9) observation that 'an optimal alternative in one arena (or game) will not necessarily be optimal in respect to the entire network of arenas in which the actor is involved', the next section of this chapter will examine the main points of contention during the association negotiations and attempt to account for the differing degrees of caution involved in the EC's offers to the association applicants.

Why so sensitive? Towards an explanation of the EC's association strategy in Eastern Europe

The association negotiations between the Commission (on behalf of the EC) and the Visegrad countries began in February 1991 (*Agence Europe* 8 February 1991) and concluded after ten rounds on 22 November 1991 (*Bull-*EC 11-1991). Over the course of the negotiations the EC came under immense pressure from the Visegrad applicants to improve its offers on both the political and economic aspects of the agreements. The EC's refusal to match these expectations often caused dismay amongst East European officials and on two occasions (in March and September 1991) brought the talks to the verge of collapse. Much of the controversy during the negotiations revolved around three main issues: the EC's trade offers in regards to products belonging to the so-called sensitive sectors such as agriculture, textiles, coal and steel; the inclusion or not of an explicit reference to future EC membership for the association applicants; and the provisions regulating the movement of East European workers into the European Community. A game-theoretic representation of the association negotiations along the lines of Tsebelis' nested games could help us understand the different degrees of caution with which the EC responded to the demands of the association applicants with reference to five prevailing constellations.

Constellation 1: The larger the CEECs' pay-offs from the association arena the smaller the EC's pay-offs in both the international and the domestic arenas

This constellation best describes the EC's position in regards to agricultural products and the EAs' membership clause. As far as agriculture was concerned, ever since the early design of the association agreements in 1990, the East European applicants had insisted on agricultural products being included in the proposed Free Trade Area. However, their demands were largely ignored by the Commission, which in the August 1990 communication had inserted a vague and non-committing reference to the promotion of trade in the agricultural and fisheries sectors between the two parties (European Commission 1990c). When the association negotiations opened in February 1991, the Polish, Czech and Hungarian negotiators reiterated their earlier demands for the liberalization of agricultural trade within the envisaged 10-year transitional period for the creation of the FTA. Despite the profound importance of the agricultural sector for the reforming economies in Eastern Europe and against a wave of international criticism, the EC refused to give in to the association applicants' demands. As a result agriculture was excluded altogether from the proposed FTA and instead the EC's trade concessions for agriculture were to be negotiated on a product-by-product basis and annexed as a separate protocol to the association agreements.

The EC's extreme caution to proceed with more generous agricultural concessions during the negotiations can only be partially explained by the direct threat that CEECs posed to the EC's agricultural markets. Whilst it was true that agricultural prices in Eastern Europe remained only a fraction of those in the EC, the CEECs' export potential was severely compromised by the process of land reform and the disintegration of the old communist structures of agricultural production. In addition, during the early 1990s less than 3 per cent of the EC's total agricultural imports originated from the CEECs, hardly a big enough share to justify the protectionism displayed by the EC during the association negotiations (European Commission 1994: 545). However, such protectionism can be better understood by reference to international and domestic developments affecting the EC's agricultural sector.

The EC's bargain with the association applicants over agricultural concessions coincided with a turbulent period for European agriculture which was characterized by domestic quarrels over the Community's strategy in the Uruguay Round and the proposed CAP reform. In the international arena, the EC's protectionist agenda had already caused the Uruguay Round to miss the completion target of December 1990 (envisaged by the Punta del Este declaration) and left the EC isolated (Woolcock and Hodges 1996). In the domestic arena, the situation of the EC's agricultural sector was close to boiling point. Commissioner MacSharry's proposed CAP reform (itself a by-product of the EC's isolation in the GATT negotiations) in July 1991 provided for big cuts in price subsidies for cereals, beef and milk and called for a whole new strategy for the protection of the EC's farming industry (*Agence Europe* 12 July 1991: 15). This initiative, however, received a hostile reaction from the EC's agricultural lobby, which saw the proposed price cuts and the prospect of reduced protection as a 'capitulation' to the US demands in GATT (*Agence Europe* 12 July 1991 and 19 July 1991).

This state of affairs was most unfortunate for the CEECs' demands for the fast track liberalization of agricultural trade. A generous offer to the CEECs was bound to undermine the EC's negotiating position within GATT and leave it exposed to the US accusations of protectionist and discriminatory practices. On the other hand, a liberal agricultural settlement with the association applicants was also certain to further infuriate the EC's militant agricultural lobby and, therefore, reduce the chances of it accepting the proposed CAP reform which was vital for the successful completion of GATT and the reduction of CAP's burden on the EC's budget. Evidently, the EC's anticipated pay-offs from both the completion of the GATT negotiations and the CAP reform were much bigger than those anticipated from a generous agricultural offer to the association applicants. Moreover, the EC's opponents within the GATT and the CAP reform bargains were much stronger than the East European applicants for which the cost of walking out of the association negotiations remained prohibitively high. Against such an unfavourable international and domestic environment and unable either to seduce (through higher pay-offs) or bully (through credible threats) the EC into more generous offers, the association applicants faced 'maximum EC protectionism' with regards to agriculture. This was reflected in the final text of the Europe Agreements, which, as argued above, provided for only incremental changes to the trade regime on agricultural products.

A similar case of 'maximum EC protectionism' can also be observed in the case of the association agreements' membership clause. During the early stages of the association negotiations the Visegrad delegations had demanded the inclusion of a clear EC commitment to eastwards enlargement in the preamble of the agreements. It was argued that since association agreements in the past, such as the Greek (1961) one, had included specific references to accession being a 'mutual' objective, a similar clause should also be available in the Europe Agreements. The East European applicants' hopes, however, were disappointed since the EC made it clear that the EAs should be separated from the question of accession and be treated as arrangements with value of their own. The EC's refusal to give in to the Visegrads' calls for a more generous membership clause deadlocked the association negotiations in March 1991 (*Bull*-EC 3-1991). The member states' position remained unchanged on the question of membership even in the revised negotiating mandate to the Commission in April 1991 (in which certain concessions in trade-related issues were made) (*Bull*-EC 4-1991). As a result, the preamble of the Europe Agreements made no reference to the automatic passage from association to accession, or to enlargement being a mutual objective. Instead, the agreements simply recognized that they would contribute to the realization of the candidates' 'ultimate objective' of EC membership.

In a similar case to the arguments in relation to agriculture, the likelihood of a generous offer to the association applicants with regards to the membership clause was severely compromised by other bargains dominating the EC's domestic and international agenda. By the time the association negotiations with the Visegrads began in January 1991, both IGCs on EMU and Political Union were already under way. From the outset the ambitious targets set by the two IGCs gave their proceedings an aura of 'history in the making' (Dyson and Featherstone 1999). With so much effort invested in establishing the two IGCs, and with the reputation of key European politicians (including Mitterrand, Kohl and Delors) inextricably linked to the success of the new treaty on European Union, the size of the EC's pay-offs at stake in this process was indeed enormous. On a different level, the opening of the two IGCs has been the product of a long and bitter battle between those supporting the deepening of co-operation between the EC's member states (i.e. Germany, France, Italy) as a means of responding to the new post-Cold War setting and those opposing such a process in favour of a 'wider' and less integrated EC (i.e. Britain). Whilst by late 1990 the 'deepeners' had been successful in putting their integrationist plans at the top of the EC's agenda, the successful conclusion of the two IGCs was by no means certain, particularly when considering that the new treaty required the unanimous agreement of all EC member states.

Against this background the association applicants' demands for a strong membership clause to be inserted in the Europe Agreements found a rather unsympathetic audience in the majority of the EC's member states. Such a move would almost certainly deflect the EC's resources and attention away from the two IGCs whilst it would have also given precious ammunition to those wishing to sabotage the negotiations for the new treaty. A generous membership offer to the association applicants would also undermine the EC's position in the international arena, particularly with regards to the EEA negotiations with the EFTAns. As argued before, despite the high degree of economic and political development of the EFTA countries, the EC repeatedly refused to be drawn into a fast-track Scandinavian enlargement, arguing instead that, for the medium-term, its relations with the EFTA members would be best served within the framework of the European Economic Area (Wallace 1991).

With the European Community desperate not to undermine its cautious strategy vis-à-vis the EFTAns and with negotiations for the conclusion of a major new EC treaty in full swing, the association applicants' demands for a clear EC commitment on accession were doomed. As developments in both the EC's domestic and international arenas conspired against a generous Visegrad pay-off in the association arena, the association applicants were left facing 'maximum EC protectionism' with regards to the EAs' membership clause. This was reflected in the final wording of the agreements' preamble which referred to accession into the EC as the applicants' 'ultimate objective', not as an EC objective or the natural progression of the Europe Agreements.

Constellation 2: The larger the CEECs' pay-offs from the association arena, the smaller the EC's pay-offs from the association arena

This constellation refers to the EC's offers to the association applicants regarding the free movement of workers. The Visegrads' early demands on this issue called for the abolition of all restrictions in the movement of workers by the end of a 10-year transitional period. These demands, however, were rejected outright by the

Commission which also refused to accept the applicants' proposals for the legal-ization of all illegal East European immigrants in the EC (Pinder 1991: 67–68). Against this background, negotiations soon focused on the clause of non-discrimination, in other words, whether those CEE nationals (and their families) already legally employed within the EC's territory would enjoy the same working rights as EC nationals. The Visegrads' demands for the application of the non-discrimination clause for both contributory and non-contributory benefits were once again rejected by the Commission whose final offer provided for the appli-cation of the non-discrimination clause only to contributory benefits. The final agreement on freedom of movement was, therefore, an extremely cautious one. The Visegrads' only consolation was the EC's promise that the Association Council would examine further improvements in relation to movement of workers in the second phase of the transitional period (subject to the economic situation in the associated partners and the employment situation in the Community).

A look at economic developments within the EC's member states as well as at the changing security environment in post-Cold War Europe can help us put the EC's caution vis-à-vis the association applicants into a clearer perspective. By the time the association negotiations got under way in early 1991, the EC was already feeling the full impact of the seismic changes brought about by the collapse of the Berlin Wall. In the absence of a clear military threat from the former communist camp, the new post-Cold War setting elevated soft-security issues to the top of the EC's agenda. Immigration soon emerged as the single most important area of con-cern as during the period 1991–1992 more than two million legal (and an unknown number of illegal) East European immigrants entered the European Community (*Financial Times* 23 March 1993). The problem of dealing with immigration received a new sense of urgency by plans for the abolition of the EC's internal borders following the completion of the Single Market project and the ongoing negotiations for the widening of co-operation in the field of Justice and Home Affairs (JHA).

The large increase in immigration figures from Eastern Europe coincided with an unfavourable economic climate within the EC. By the early 1990s the EC's economy stood on the brink of recession. As growth stalled, unemployment began to rise putting further pressure on the member states' social security bills (Eurostat 1993, 1994). On a different front, the ECJ's ruling (ECJ 1991) on the eligibility of the spouses of nationals originating from associated countries who were legally employed in the EC to non-contributory benefits further aggravated the member states' concerns over the long-term financial implications of an increased number of East European workers residing and working in their terri-tory. Against this background the association applicants' requests for a more lax regime for movement of workers received a hostile audience in the EC. Indeed the conjunction prevailing on this issue was, alongside the one described in constella-tion 1, the most harmful for the East European applicants' pay-offs from the association arena, leading to what can be described as 'maximum EC protection-ism' during the association negotiations. In both constellations, developments in the EC's international and domestic arenas conspired against generous EC offers to the association applicants. Unlike constellation 1, however, where the East European applicants' pay-offs were sacrificed as a result of the EC's bargain with third parties, in constellation 2 the association applicants themselves were perceived as the main threat to the EC's interests. Indeed the extremely cautious provisions included in the Europe Agreements with regards to movement of workers mirrored this unfortunate conjunction for the association applicants' interests.

Constellation 3: However large the CEECs' pay-offs from the association arena, the EC's pay-offs in both the international and the domestic arena remain mixed

This constellation best describes the association bargain over textiles. At the beginning of the negotiations, the East European applicants insisted on the full liberalization of textile trade within the first phase of the transitional period (lasting no more than five years). This suggestion, however, met with strong opposition from some EC member states, which argued that the sensitive nature of the EC's textile industry merited a much slower pace of liberalization. The stalemate over textiles lasted until the late stages of the association negotiations and was broken after the second revised negotiating mandate given to the Commission by the Council in September 1991 (*Agence Europe* 9–10 September 1991: 10). On the basis of the new mandate, a compromise was finally reached between the Commission and the association applicants. According to this, the Visegrad three were forced to accept a specific safeguard clause for textiles which could be triggered in case of severe disruption of the EC's textile markets by imports originating from Eastern Europe. In exchange, the EC promised to eliminate its tariffs on East European textile imports within six years whilst all EC non-tariff barriers would be abolished within a period of not less than five years (half the period agreed by the ongoing GATT negotiations regarding the abolition of the Multi-Fibre Agreement).

The prospect of greater trade liberalization with the CEECs (and for that matter with other international competitors within GATT) found the EC's domestic audience divided. Sectoral groups representing commerce, which had lobbied the Commission hard to pursue a liberal strategy in GATT negotiations (Woolcock and Hodges 1996: 312), were also supportive of the prospect of fast-track liberalization of textile trade with the association applicants (*Agence Europe* 20 June 1991: 14 and 3 September 1991: 16). In both cases, commerce groups (which suffered a substantial decrease of their market share in the late 1980s) saw the relaxation of international trade protection as an essential element of the industry's restructuring based on the re-localization of production to low-labour-cost countries through the development of Outward Processing Trade (OPT). Yet, such a liberal agenda was opposed by trade unions and textile producer associations, particularly those representing small and medium-size businesses which lacked the resources needed for relocating production abroad (*Agence Europe* 13 July 1991: 10; 6 December 1991: 15 and 29 January 1992: 15). Moreover, the relocation of production outside the EC was also opposed by many of the EC's regions which since the late 1970s had suffered the devastating effects of the decline of the textile industry and which remained largely unconvinced by the Commission's promises (Rapid Database speech IP/91/309, 15 April 1991; speech IP/90/20 16 March 1991) that the Structural Funds would compensate those regions affected by the industry's restructuring.

The EC's association strategy with regards to textile and clothing products had, therefore, to compromise two conflicting interests. One argued for the pursuit of a liberal agenda as a means of boosting the competitiveness of the EC's troubled textile and clothing industries. The other argued for the pursuit of a protectionist agenda as a means of protecting the EC's workforce and some of the EC's poorest regions still dependent on the two industries. Indeed, the 'increased EC protectionism' displayed during the course of the association negotiations regarding trade in textile products reflected the need to compromise these conflicting objectives. Hence, in the Visegrad Europe Agreements the textile sector (unlike agriculture) was to be included in the proposed FTA, but unlike the fast track liberalization envisaged for industrial products, full liberalization of trade in textiles would not be completed until the second phase of the transitional period.

Constellation 4: The larger the CEECs' pay-offs from the association arena, the smaller the EC's pay-offs from the domestic arena

This constellation refers to the association bargain over coal and steel. Both product categories had been an important source of foreign currency earnings for all three Visegrads applicants, which from the outset of their negotiations with the Commission insisted on the full liberalization of trade in ECSC products within the first couple of years of the first phase of the transitional period. As in the case of textiles, however, the association applicants' liberal agenda met with strong opposition within the EC and was eventually rejected by the Commission (Guggenbuhl 1995). The final compromise reached for both product categories left the Visegrad applicants disappointed. For coal products the EC agreed to abolish all quantitative restrictions within one year whilst tariffs would be phased out within a period of four years (with some special derogations for Spain and Germany). Agreement over steel products proved more elusive with Spain (and to a lesser extent Germany) threatening, until the eleventh hour, to veto the conclusion of the association negotiations unless higher levels of protection were agreed for EC steel producers (*Agence Europe* 21 November 1991: 9). Hence, the Visegrad association agreements provided for the immediate abolition of quantitative restrictions and the gradual phasing out of tariffs within five years. In addition, special surveillance mechanisms were established to monitor the growth of steel imports from Eastern Europe and any possible disruption these may have caused to the EC's steel market.

This form of 'moderated EC protectionism' during the association negotiations can be best understood by reference to developments in the EC's domestic arena. The beginning of the 1990s found both the EC's coal and steel industries in deep crisis. Coal had long lost its privileged position as the EC's main energy source. Steel too was rapidly losing its pre-eminence amongst manufacturing industries. Economic recession at home had depressed demand and led to large over-capacities. In addition, exports were severely hit by increased international competition (mainly from South-east Asia and South America) and by the decision of the US government to impose severe anti-dumping measures against EC steel producers (Sedelmeier 1995: 5). In an effort to bring the situation under control, the Commission introduced painful restructuring programmes for both industries. In exchange, increased regional funding (*Agence Europe* 18-19 November 1991: 8) and the introduction of an Aid Code (authorizing public aid only for the financing of social programmes, research development and investments for environmental protection) were aimed at alleviating some of the immense social consequences of the restructuring process (Barnes and Barnes 1995).

Against this background, the powerful coal and steel sectoral groups in the EC (e.g. Eurofer) were becoming increasingly apprehensive over the prospect of a significantly improved coal and steel trade regime with Eastern Europe (*Agence Europe* 8 March 1991: 13; 10–11 June 1991: 13; 20 September 1991: 11). Such apprehension was further aggravated by accusations that, during the period between 1991 and 1993, heavily subsidized steel imports from Eastern Europe had depressed prices by up to 30 per cent, leaving the EC's steel industries unable to compete (Barnes and Barnes 1995: 237). The turmoil amongst the EC's domestic audience combined with the high cost of combating the social consequences of restructuring the coal and steel industries were evidently taken into consideration when the EC formulated its offers to the association candidates. As a result the final provisions of the Visegrad Europe Agreements regarding trade in coal and steel reflected what can be described as a form of 'moderated EC protectionism'. Coal and steel products were to be included in the proposed FTA, but full trade liberalization in both product categories would be completed in no less than four and five years respectively.

Constellation 5: The larger the CEECs' pay-offs from the association arena, the larger the EC's pay-offs from the association arena

This constellation does not describe any particular aspect of the association negotiations, but instead refers to the overall strategic importance attached to the Europe Agreements. Since their early conception in August 1990 the EAs were meant to be far more than just an instrument for the regulation of trade between the EC and its East European partners. Both EC and East European leaders recognized the value of the agreements as a stabilizing force in the fragile post-communist Eastern Europe. For the EC, the EAs were a confirmation of its willingness to assume a greater political role in the post-Cold War setting and assist the process of reform in the fragile democracies in Eastern Europe. For the association applicants, the EAs presented a platform for (and proof of) their rapid 'return to Europe' with the ultimate objective of full participation in the European structures (CEPR 1992). As the progress of the association negotiations continued to be slow and frustrating, the fragile security environment in Europe throughout 1991 was arguably the East European applicants' greatest ally in their efforts to maximize their pay-offs from their association bargain with the EC.

The EC's willingness to consider changes to its negotiating position in order to respond to wider security concerns in Europe was demonstrated twice during the course of the association negotiations. The first was in March 1991 when the Visegrad applicants refused to accept the EC's offers on a series of issues – including trade in sensitive products, movement of workers and the EAs' membership clause – leaving the association negotiations deadlocked. Amidst a barrage of criticism from the press accusing the EC of 'dashing' the Visegrads' hopes of 'returning to Europe' (*Financial Times* 26 March 1991) and a rapidly spreading instability in the former Yugoslavia, the Commission requested and finally received a new, more flexible, negotiating mandate by the Council which did just enough to persuade the Visegrads to resume their negotiation with the Commission (*Agence Europe* 10 April 1991: 11 and 13 April 1991: 8).

In mid-July 1991 the association negotiations were stalled once again, with the Visegrad applicants demanding more EC trade concessions (particularly for textiles and agricultural products) and a clear commitment of the EC's financial assistance in the region (*Agence Europe* 31 July 1991: 7). The break up of negotiations between the EC and the Visegrads during the summer of 1991 coincided with a substantial deterioration of the security outlook in Europe with the instability in the former Yugoslavia escalating into an all-out war and the Soviet leader Mikhail Gorbachev being overthrown by a military coup in Moscow. Against this background, the Commissioner for External Relations, Frans Andriessen, urged the Council for a new negotiating mandate, which would assist the rapid conclusion of the association negotiations and create '…a sense of belonging' for the Visegrad applicants (*Agence Europe* 7 September 1991: 7). Once again, the Council's new negotiating mandate did just enough to break the deadlock, paving the way for the conclusion of the Visegrad Europe agreements in late 1991.

Whilst the deteriorating security environment in Europe evidently increased the EC's cost of non-agreement (Putnam 1988) in the association negotiations, the effects of these developments for the association applicants' pay-offs should not be overestimated. In both negotiating mandates given to the Commission following the April and July 1991 deadlocks, the Council's new position only incrementally increased the Visegrads' pay-offs from the association bargain. After all, the three main demands by the Visegrad applicants – the insertion of a strong membership clause into the EAs, the inclusion of agriculture into the proposed FTA and the substantial improvement of the regime regulating the movement of workers – were all rejected by the EC. On one level the inability of the association applicants to secure a more generous deal from the EC was a reflection of the fact that the EC's pay-offs from the association bargain remained considerably smaller than those anticipated by other domestic or international bargains such as the conclusion of GATT or the process of CAP reform. This was certainly the case for all trade-related aspects of the agreements. The political significance of the EAs for the EC was much greater, but here too a generous membership clause for the Visegrads was compromised by the EC's determination to proceed uninterrupted with the conclusion of the two IGCs on EMU and Political Union.

The power asymmetry between the participants in the association negotiations was also an important determinant of the final outlook of the Europe Agreements. The EC's ability to dictate the terms of the association bargain was only temporarily threatened by the East European applicants (in most cases utilizing the 'European security' argument) whose cost of non-agreement remained immeasurably higher than that of the EC throughout the course of the association negotiations. Hence, an understanding of the association process as a joint exercise between equals would be misleading. As the dominant player in this process the EC was in a position to adjust its offers to the association applicants so that it would not undermine its strategy in other domestic or international bargains. Evidently, the scope for similar manoeuvring on behalf of the association applicants was substantially narrower.

Conclusion

This chapter looked at the first wave of association negotiations between the EC and Poland, Hungary and Czechoslovakia in 1991. It explored some of the reasons behind the EC's inability to match its strong rhetorical commitment to the reform process in Eastern Europe with generous economic and political concessions to the Visegrad Association applicants. This mismatch has been one of the most paradoxical aspects of the EC's strategy in Eastern Europe since 1989. How such a mismatch manifested itself in the Europe Agreements has been well covered by the existing literature (Guggenbuhl 1995; Sedelmeier and Wallace 1996; Maresceau 1997; Mayhew 1998), which has also provided powerful arguments as to why the EC's caution during the association negotiations was both bad economics (Rollo and Smith 1993) and bad politics (Inotai 1994).

I have sought to explain why such a strategy came to be, with reference to Tsebelis' (1988, 1990) concepts of nested games and of games in multiple arenas with variable pay-offs. Both concepts have been used in this work outside the methodological and theoretical rigidity of their parenting game theory. Instead, a game-theoretic representation of the association negotiations has been put forward in an attempt to provide an explanatory framework, which illuminates the contextual factors that shape the EC's strategy vis-à-vis the Visegrad applicants. In doing so this work builds upon an increasing number of scholars (Schneider and Seybold 1997; Friis 1998; Radaelli 1999) who have utilized tools from the 'wider' rational choice tradition to study the European Union and fully subscribes to Scharpf's observation that '...a game-theoretic representation can often provide useful and precise abstractions of extremely complicated real life constellations' (1997: 45).

The main line of argument pursued in this chapter has been that the EC's cautious offers to the Visegrad applicants cannot be fully understood if the association negotiations are studied as a one-shot game played in a vacuum. Instead the association bargain can be best characterized as being nested within a wider network of domestic and international games (named the grand game) in which the EC was engaged during the early 1990s. The interdependence between these different games and the variable distribution of pay-offs within the grand game offers some additional resources for our understanding of the EC's protectionism in the association negotiations. It was argued that such a protectionism had, in most cases, little to do with the actual 'threat' posed by the applicants themselves, but was instead dictated by the EC's need to pursue a consistent strategy in a number of domestic and international bargains and thus maximize its pay-offs from the entire grand game. Against this background five different constellations were described, each linking the EC's offers to the association applicants with a different interplay of games in the EC's domestic and/or international agenda. These constellations were subsequently used to account for the differing degrees of caution with which the EC responded to the association applicants' demands for fast-track trade liberalization in all product categories, a substantial improvement to the regime regulating movement of workers as well as for the inclusion of a strong membership clause into the Europe Agreements.

Finally, this chapter has set out to offer an analysis of the association negotiations that is both theoretically and historically informed. Conceptually the study of the association negotiations through the lens of the wider rational choice tradition is hoped to contribute to the wider literature on the EC/EU's relations with Central and Eastern Europe, which, despite its considerable wealth of empirical evidence, has remained rather atheoretical. It is also hoped that an analysis of the EC's association strategy that is sensitive to the contextual factors which affected its early development will contribute towards a better understanding of the paradoxes that surrounded it. On a more general level such a context-sensitive analysis can help us unpack rather vague references to the notion of the EC's 'self interest' and thus lead to a clearer understanding of the EC's international presence.

References

Baldwin, R. (1994) *Towards an Integrated Europe*, Centre for Economic Policy Research, London.

Baldwin, R. *et al.* (1992) *Monitoring European Integration, iii: Is Bigger Better? The Economics of EC Enlargement*, CEPR, London.

Barnes, I. and Barnes, P. (1995) *The Enlarged European Union*, New York: Longmann.

Bonvicini, G. (ed.) (1991) *The Community and the Emerging European Democracies*, Royal Institute of International Affairs, London.

CEPR (1992) *The Association Process: Making Work*, Occasional Paper, 11, Centre for Economic Policy Research, London.

Dyson, K. and Featherstone, K. (1999) *The Road to Maastricht*, Oxford: Oxford University Press.

ECJ (1991) *Office National de l'Emploi v Bahia Kziber,* Case 18/90, Report 1991, I.

European Commission (1990a) *Implications of Recent Changes in Central and Eastern Europe for the Community's Relations with the Countries Concerned*, SEC (90) 111/2, Brussels.

European Commission (1990b) *Commission's Proposals for the Visegrad EAs*, SEC (90) 717, Brussels.

European Commission (1990c) *Commission's Proposals for the General Outline of the Association Agreements,* COM (90) 398, Brussels.

European Commission (1994) 'The Economic Inter-Penetration between the European Union and Eastern Europe', *European Economy: Reports and Studies*, 6, Directorate General for Economic and Financial Affairs, Brussels.

Eurostat (1993) *Basic Statistics of the Community*, 30th edn, Luxembourg.

Eurostat (1994) *Basic Statistics of the Community*, 31st edn, Luxembourg.

Fierke, K. and Nicklson, M. (1999) 'Divided by a Common Language: Formal and Constructivist Approaches to Games', Paper delivered at the conference of the International Studies Association (ISA).

Friis, L. (1997) *When Europe Negotiates: From Europe Agreements to Eastern Enlargement?*, Institute of Political Science, University of Copenhagen, Copenhagen.

Friis, L. (1998) 'Approaching the "Third Half" of the EU Grand Bargaining – The Post-Negotiation Phase of the "Europe Agreement Game"', *Journal of European Public Policy,* 5, 2.

Guggenbuhl, A. (1995) 'The Political Economy of Association with Eastern Europe', in F. Laursen (ed.) *The Political Economy of European Integration*, The European Institute of Public Administration, Netherlands.

Inotai, A. (1994) 'Transforming the East: Western Illusions and Strategies', *The New Hungarian Quarterly*, 35, 1.

Maresceau, M. (ed.) (1997) *Enlarging the European Union*, London: Longman.

Mayhew, A. (1998) *Recreating Europe: The European Union's Policy towards Central and Eastern Europe*, Cambridge: Cambridge University Press.

Opt, K.D. (1999) 'Contending Conceptions of the Theory of Rational Action', *Journal of Theoretical Studies*, 11, 2.

Papadimitriou D. (2001) 'The European Union's Strategy in the Post-Communist Balkans', *Journal of South East European and Black Sea Studies*, 1, 3: 69–94.

Papadimitriou, D. (2002) *Negotiating the New Europe: the European Union and Eastern Europe*, Ashgate, Aldershot.

Pinder, J. (1991) *The European Community and Eastern Europe*, London: RIIA.

Putnam, R. (1988) 'Diplomacy and Domestic Politics. The Logic of Two-Level Games', *International Organization*, 42, 3: 427–460.

Radaelli, C. (1999) 'Game Theory and Institutional Entrepreneurship: Transfer Pricing and the Search for Co-ordination in International Tax Policy', *Policy Studies Journal*, 26, 4.

Reinicke, H. W. (1992) *Building a New Europe: The Challenge of System Transformation and Systemic Reform,* Brookings Occasional Papers, The Brokings Institutions, Washington, D.C.

Rieger, E. (1996) 'The Common Agricultural Policy: External and Internal Dimensions', in H. Wallace and W. Wallace (eds) *Policy Making in the European Union,* 3rd edn, Oxford: Oxford University Press.

Rollo, J. and Smith, A. (1993) 'The Political Economy of Eastern European Trade with the European Community: Why So Sensitive?', *Economic Policy,* 16.

Sapir, A. (2000) 'Trade Regionalism in Europe: Towards an Integrated Approach', *Journal of Common Market Studies*, 38, 1: 151–162.

Scharpf, F.W. (1997) *Games Real Actors Can Play,* Boulder: Westview.

Schneider, G. and Seybold, C. (1997) 'Twelve Tongues, One Voice: An Evaluation of European Political Co-operation', *European Journal of Political Research,* 31, 3.

Sedelmeier, U. (1994) 'The European Union's Association Policy towards Central and Eastern Europe: Political and Economic Rationales of Conflict', SEI Working Paper, 7, Sussex European Institute, Falmer.

Sedelmeier, U. (1995) 'Competing Policy Recommendations for Europe Association and the Limits of a Trade Liberalisation Approach to Integration: Some Illustrations from the Case of Steel', Paper presented at the UACES Research Conference: Integration within Wider Europe, Birmingham.

Sedelmeier, U. and Wallace, H. (1996) 'Policies towards Central and Eastern Europe', in H. Wallace and W. Wallace (eds) *Policy-Making in the European Union*, 3rd edn, Oxford: Oxford University Press.

Shaffer, M. (1995) 'The Applicability of Three-Game Analysis to the EC-Visegrad Negotiations for the Europe Agreements', Paper presented at the UACES Research Conference: Integration in a Wider Europe, Birmingham.

Tsebelis, G. (1988) 'Nested Games: The Cohesion of French Politics', *British Journal of Political Science*, 18.

Tsebelis, G. (1990) *Nested Games: Rational Choice in Comparative Politics*, Berkeley: University of California Press.

Tsebelis, G. (1994) 'The Power of the European Power as a Conditional Agenda Setter', *American Political Science Review*, 88.

Ullman, R.H. (1991) *Securiting Europe*, Princeton: Princeton University Press.

Van Ham, P. (1993) *The EC, Eastern Europe and European Unity. Discord, Collaboration and Integration Since 1947,* London: Pinter Publishers.

Wallace, H. (ed) (1991) *The Wider Western Europe: Reshaping the EC/EFTA Relationship*, Royal Institute of International Affairs, London.

Woolcock, S. and Hodges, M. (1996) 'EC Policy in the Uruguay Round', in H. Wallace and W. Wallace, *Policy-Making in the European Union*, 3rd edn, Oxford: Oxford University Press.

Part III

Promoting European norms, values and ideas

The EU as an exporter of models

7 Exporting 'values'?

EU external co-operation as a 'soft diplomacy'

Franck Petiteville

A great deal of literature addressing the EU's international capacity reflects a realist approach. This relative hegemony of realism is based on analyses of what *state* foreign policies are traditionally made of: diplomatic formal relations, geo-political constraints, security stakes and so on. This approach towards the EU's international capacity is biased by a 'high politics' preconception, which logically focuses on the CFSP and leads – not less logically – to highly critical conclusions about the 'failures' of EU diplomacy (Durand and Vasconcelos 1998). These include Europe's *'uncommon* foreign policy' [present author's italics] (Gordon 1997), the absence of European potential in the field of defence and security (Duke 1999), the weakness of the EU's international influence in a world of 'power politics' (Gnesotto 1999), the 'European anarchy' and its 'hard road into high politics' (Holm 2001), 'Euro-paralysis' (Zielonka 1998) and so on. After the terrorist attacks against the United States in September 2001, it would be absurd to ignore the fact that foreign policy still has a lot to do with the management of international crises and security issues, straight diplomatic influence and coalition-building capacity. In this respect, it is undeniable that the EU has not played the peace-building role that it should have in the violent conflicts since the Balkan tragedies in the 1990s. Dealing with these conflicts, the CFSP has not proved to be a practical and effective tool in its current state.

However, European foreign policy analysis must clearly go beyond the study of traditional diplomatic and military tools (White 1999). In particular, as liberal theorists of international relations advocate, the globalization era gives an increasing influence to economic actors and policies. As regards the EU's international capacity, the 'external relations' of the EU go far beyond the poor resources of the CFSP machinery (Hendry *et al.* 1996; Rhodes 1998). Analysing the EU's 'external economic dimension' (Van Dijck and Faber 2000) leads to another vision of the EU as a 'global actor' (Bretherton and Vogler 1999). This is especially true in terms of foreign economic policy, most notably EU trade policy (Young 2000; Smith and Woolcock 1999) and is demonstrated by the EU's established 'global links' in, for example, inter-regional economic co-operation (Edwards and Regelsberger 1990). The realist visions of the EU's international political hollowness can also be challenged, particularly if one underlines the political dimension of EU economic external relations which stems from a process of 'politicization' (Smith, M. 1998; De Wilde d'Estmael 1998).

This chapter aims to demonstrate that EU economic co-operation can be seen as an attempt to export 'values' worldwide through the emergence of a 'soft diplomacy' combining economic resources with political ambitions. It does so precisely by focusing on EU led economic co-operation with the rest of the world (Cox and Chapman 1999).

The chapter is divided in four parts. The first section shows that EU external economic co-operation can no longer be restricted to some historically and/or geographically privileged regions but now covers the entire world and is managed on a global scale through an institutional network set up by the European Commission with state/international/regional bureaucracies as well as with local authorities and NGOs. The second part of the chapter questions whether there are some specific 'values' which may be distinctive of a 'European identity' and exported through EU external co-operation. Specific attention is given to human rights and democratic values, which are now commonly enshrined in EU co-operation policies. It is argued that this politicization process has given birth to 'soft diplomacy'. Section three tackles the question of whether the European Commission has appropriate institutional and financial resources to manage a global policy of external co-operation. Finally, section four argues that the EU's soft diplomacy is limited by geo-political constraints and that a more effective CFSP could strengthen its international capacity.

The global scale of EU external economic co-operation

The traditional tools that the EU uses to co-operate with external partners are preferential trade agreements, financial aid and institutional dialogue. Until the late 1980s, this EC co-operation policy was commonly referred to in the Lomé agreements signed between the EC and the African, Caribbean and Pacific Group.[1] Rooted in the colonial history of the member states (mainly France, Belgium and the UK), the Lomé system was based on specific financial instruments (the European Development Fund financed by voluntary contributions of EU member states, completed by the 'Stabex' and the 'Sysmin' to compensate ACP loss in exports of primary goods). Trade relations were also very favourable for the ACP countries since they could export almost 99 per cent of their products custom free within the EC while keeping their own import duties.

After 25 years, this privileged co-operation came to an end for economic as well as for geo-political reasons. The trade preferential provisions were neither sufficient enough to trigger real economic development in the ACP countries nor to stabilize their share of EC external trade, which dropped from 6.7 per cent in 1976 to 3.4 per cent in 1997. Within that same time period, emerging Asian countries substantially increased their share of EC trade, despite having less favourable treatment from the EC. Moreover, the Lomé trade arrangements were ruled to be incompatible with WTO rules, as particularly illustrated by the banana dispute. Therefore, by the end of the Lomé IV agreement, the EU member states decided not to renew it as they had done before. The European Commission was asked to open a public debate with the ACP countries, the NGOs and experts on how to rebuild a new relationship between the EU and the ACP group. After two years of negotiation between the EU and the ACP within the Lomé institutions, the result was the Cotonou Agreement, which was signed in June 2000. The Cotonou Agreement clearly puts an end to the Lomé era. In particular, the ACP's trade advantages, which are based on non-reciprocal preferences, are set to be totally removed by a progressive evolution (between 2008 and 2020) towards free trade inter-regional agreements between the EU and ACP regional sub-groups. Therefore, after Cotonou, the ACP countries can no longer be considered as privileged countries in the EU's external trade relations. The same evolution may be observed in the allocation of EC financial aid. ACP countries are still at the top of EC financial aid, but their share in the total amount of EC aid has dropped from 67 per cent in 1986–1990 to 29 per cent in 1996–1998. Only two countries out of the 15 first beneficiaries of EC aid now belong to the ACP group, compared to 13 in 1970–1974. As a consequence of this evolution, the EDF now provides only 18 per cent of EC aid, since three quarters of the EC's aid is financed through EC budget lines.

The European external co-operation system is now developed on a global scale following a deep reorientation of EU trade co-operation and financial aid in the 1990s (Petiteville 2001). Indeed as regards trade co-operation, the EU has signed more than 35 regional trade agreements out of 120 declared at the WTO in 2000. This trade co-operation targets Eastern and Central Europe and the Mediterranean countries, but also Russia, Asia and Latin America. This trade co-operation policy establishes global links throughout the world which in turn help the EU secure its relations with its periphery, but also with emerging countries and big powers (Winters 2000).

Clearly, the Central and Eastern European Countries, which are now engaged in the enlargement process, have replaced the ACP countries as top priorities for EC co-operation. The association agreements, called 'Europe Agreements', have been accompanied by a high amount of financial aid within the framework of the PHARE program (23 per cent of EC aid in 1996–1998). With regard to the Commonwealth of Independent States (CIS), the EU has signed 'Partnership and Co-operation Agreements' with those countries that also already received 11 per cent of EC external aid in 1996–1998 (Hillion 1998).

The South Mediterranean countries have also significantly upgraded their position within the EC's external relations in the 1990s. They received a 20 per cent share of the EC's external aid in 1996–1998, up from 12 per cent in 1986–1990. As a symbol of this evolution, Egypt has become the first recipient of EC financial aid world wide. This rise in EC aid allocated to Mediterranean countries is linked to the so-called 'Barcelona Process' which re-launched the EU/Mediterranean co-operation on a multi-sectoral basis including political aspects (regional security, democracy, immigration) and a new framework for financial aid through the MEDA programme (Edwards and Philippart 1997; Gomez 1998). At the trade level, the objective is to build up an EU-Mediterranean free trade area by 2010 through association agreements. This ambitious co-operation initiative has given birth to a complex network of institutional relations in all three pillars at the ministerial level (including 15 ministerial meetings between 1995 and 2000) and the administrative level (characterized by regular meetings of the ministerial 'Euro-Med' Committee and of specialized working groups). Despite the fact that the Meda programme has been highly criticized (especially for the very low rate of financial disbursement, that is 26 per cent of the credits engaged between 1995 and 1999), a 'Meda II' programme was officially launched in December 2000.[2]

EC co-operation policy is also more clearly oriented towards the emerging countries of Asia and Latin America. The amount of EC aid allocated to Asia and Latin America (15 per cent of EC aid for both regions, mainly channelled through the 'ALA' programme[3]) is less important than the diversity of initiatives aimed at projecting European economic interests in those regions. These projects include Community support to the creation of joint-ventures, negotiations on trade, investment, intellectual property rights and so on. The institutional framework of this multi-sectoral co-operation is also impressive, especially in the case of Asia (Kirkpatrick and Richards 1999). It includes regular Asia-Europe meetings at the level of heads of states and governments, specific relations with ASEAN countries (MacMahon 1998), and a multiplication of Commission delegations in Asia (compared to one in Tokyo in the 1970s). This development of the relations between the EU and Asia is clearly the result of a new strategy pursued by the EU in the mid-1990s and formulated by the Commission in an official document in 1994 (European Commission 1994).The same kind of strategy emerged for EC co-operation with Latin America (European Commission 1999a) and has been especially geared towards MERCOSUR (Durand *et al.* 2001) with a clear political dimension rooted in former institutional co-operation (in a 'political dialogue' with the Rio Group and the 'San José dialogue' with Central America).

At the international level, the impact of EC economic co-operation as a global projection of the EU must not be underestimated. The increasing number of institutional 'customers' of EC aid throughout the world – governmental bureaucracies, international organizations, NGOs and local authorities – has led to the creation of a wide international network of institutions which recognize the EU as an international actor. Roughly 130 Commission delegations located throughout the world play an important role in this process. An interesting case study by Michael Bruter on local press coverage of the Commission delegation's activity in Mexico has shown that those delegations are often seen as fully-fledged embassies of 'Europe' (Bruter 1999).

Exporting 'values' through 'soft diplomacy': the example of human rights

According to the European Commission, EU external co-operation carries out not only trade and financial flows but also 'values':

> The global projection of European values of democracy, social justice and sustainable development calls for an EU policy of solidarity. [...]

Community development policy conveys a certain image of Europe in the world. The culture and values of co-operation and collective action carries a strong and positive message to partners in developing countries... European social values, the diversity of existing social systems and importance attached to environmental considerations give EU policy a distinct profile as regards the quality of sustainable development.

(European Commission 2000)

This official rhetoric about EU development policy raises an important question: are there specific values that would characterize a 'European identity' in the world? This is too wide a debate to be extensively tackled in this chapter, but some of the answers are laid out below. The main argument is that if EU diplomacy is inspired by common values rooted in the political culture of its member states, than there is in Europe a potential for expressing specific values which may be quite different from those carried out by the US in particular. In response to globalization, for instance, most European governments are more in favour of strong regulation than the US, whose stance is basically free-market led. As argued by Fritz Scharpf, most European states accept globalization as a new historical mutation of capitalism, but they are still seeking strategies to rescue their welfare system in one way or another (Scharpf 2000). Moreover, most member states believe that strong regulatory protection is needed in some fundamental economic sectors to escape the harsh effects of globalization. These include agriculture, which is linked to the 'CAP model' (with France trying to persuade its partners that agriculture has 'societal' functions as well as economic objectives). The audio-visual sector is another case where European governments have successfully resisted US pressure to liberalize regulation though the WTO. In this case the EU claims that audio-visual policy is a 'cultural exception' (Devuyst 1995). Such EU–US divergent views feed permanent transatlantic misunderstandings and even 'transatlantic trade wars' about hormones, genetically modified food and so on which heighten visible 'cultural gaps' (Krenzler and MacGregor 2000). With regards to the environment, the divergent positions of the EU and the US on climate policy reflect another clash of values, with the EU leading up an international coalition in favour of the Kyoto Protocol while the US Administration rejected it for economic reasons (Gupta and Ringius 2001).

Even considering the geo-political dimension of international relations, Europe's perception of 'non western cultures' is often different from the US perception. The Arabs, in particular, are considered 'Mediterranean neighbours' in many European states (and often as immigrant communities). This relationship is illustrated by Euro-Mediterranean co-operation agreements. On the other hand, Arab countries constitute a 'far' and less well-known civilization for the US, whose links to the region are often reduced to military inter-state agreements and/or oil companies' settlements. This difference of perception explains why, for example, the European position on the Israeli-Palestinian conflict is much more balanced in favour of the Palestinians (Charillon 1998).

Last but not least, one might find different values between the EU and the US on human rights, democracy and the rule of law. The conception of human rights is clearly not the same when all European states are fundamentally opposed to the death penalty, which is extensively used by the US. The perception of the role of the state towards civil society also differs. American political culture traditionally praises the primacy of civil society whereas 'European conceptions' see no individual rights without extensive social rights guaranteed by the Welfare State.

Values of democracy, rule of law and human rights are certainly among the most visible and explicit political values now promoted by EU external co-operation (Ward 1998; Smith, K. 1998). In a recent communication, the European Commission has stressed the major role played by the EU in the international promotion of human rights and democratic principles (European Commission 2001). The ACP countries have been the first EU partners to face this 'incremental politicization' of EU co-operation in the 1990s. After two decades of non-involvement from the EU in ACP domestic affairs, the Lomé IV agreement signed in 1989 included new provisions addressing human rights, democracy and the rule of law. After the revision of Lomé IV in 1995, a special procedure was included to suspend co-operation with the states violating those principles. The revised Lomé IV agreement also forecasted the establishment of a 'reinforced political dialogue' between the EU and ACP states including foreign affairs and security problems. The new Cotonou Agreement signed in June 2000 not only includes the traditional principles on democracy and so on, but also gives the co-operation new functions such as peace-building and conflict prevention. Last but not least, the Cotonou Agreement multiplies new conditionalities such as the fight against corruption and against illegal immigration, transparency and efficiency in the use of EC aid. In ten years' time, the rise of the political dimension in EU-ACP relations clearly appears as a strict multidimensional political conditionality imposed by the EU to its ACP partners. Suspension of EC co-operation has affected several ACP countries in the 1990s such as Nigeria, Rwanda, Burundi, Niger, Congo and Sierra Leone. In other countries such as Somalia and Angola, the EU combined political pressure – through CFSP measures – while keeping a minimum level of financial aid for humanitarian purposes (Visman 1998; Sanches 1999).

Political conditionality has been extended to EC co-operation agreements with many regions of the world in the 1990s including Eastern and Central Europe, the Commonwealth of Independent States, Latin America, and Mediterranean and Middle-Eastern countries. Very few partners of the EU – mainly China and ASEAN countries – have successfully resisted the EU's attempts to include provisions about democracy and human rights in EU co-operation agreements.[4] Even a big power like Russia encountered EU sanctions in 2000. The freezing of TACIS credits by the EU Council of Ministers for a few months as was an EU protest against the violation of human rights in Chechnya following the military destruction of Grozny in 1999.[5]

As 'essential elements' of the co-operation agreements, the provisions about democracy and human rights may be used as a legal basis for the suspension of co-operation. As far as possible, the philosophy of the EU is to prevent the violation of democratic principles within partner countries through an institutional support to democratic transitions (material and technical support to the organization of elections and to the reform of the judicial systems, financial support to NGOs working in the field of human rights, etc.). In cases of crises, the EU may then resort to a broad range of measures to exert pressures on the state: confidential dialogue with the authorities, downsizing of EC aid, freezing of new projects and so on. If the violation of democratic principles is very serious and if moderate pressures prove to have no effect, the EU may envisage a suspension of co-operation as a measure of last resort. It is worthwhile mentioning that the suspension of co-operation may be completed by more severe EU sanctions under the second pillar (such as an embargo, suspension of diplomatic relations or even military measures). In that case, the process of politicization of EC co-operation blurs the boundary between pillars 1 and 2.

It must also be added that the EU's goals for the international promotion of human rights have been pursued in the 1990s by a new type of EU external action in the field of humanitarian aid. In 1987, only 3 per cent of EC external aid was devoted to humanitarian aid. In 1995, this percentage reached the level of 15 per cent. Indeed in 1992, the EC created a humanitarian office (ECHO) within the Commission (under authority of the Commissioner for development policy) which now employs roughly one hundred people in Brussels plus 80 local representatives, most of them working in Commission delegations. The scope of EC humanitarian aid (covering both natural disasters and military conflicts) and the rules of co-operation between ECHO and humanitarian organizations have been settled by a 1996 regulation.[6] From 1996 to 1998, ECHO has financed humanitarian operations in more than 60 countries. Given the fact that ECHO often subsidizes several simultaneous operations in one country, the total number of operations supported by ECHO within one year is very impressive (1366 in 1998; see European Commission 1999b).

In the end, it is clear that the EU has hitherto found more resources of international influence in a politicization process of economic co-operation than in the CFSP machinery. Many reasons may explain this apparent paradox. First, economic co-operation can be seen as a simple 'externalization' of the economic powers that the Community has gained in the regulation of the internal market (Cremona 1998) whereas intergovernmental diplomatic and security co-operation has always proved to be difficult, limited and uncertain since the origins of the Community. Second, the post-Cold War/globalization era has considerably changed the conditions of international relations, giving more weight to economic actors and policies, but also to institutional regulation carried out by supranational bodies, both processes which benefited the EU. Third, the EU's international actorness has also been enhanced by the revival of regionalism which has characterized the 1990s. This revival has given legitimacy to the oldest regional integration process and opened up new opportunities for 'inter-regional networking' such as EU-Mercosur, EU-ASEAN and so on. Last but not least, the collapse of socialist regimes and the end of Cold War ideologies have spurred democratic principles throughout the world giving a second birth to human rights diplomacies. In particular the effect has been to transform the EU's traditional rhetoric on democracy and human rights into acts.

All in all, the politicization of EU co-operation is a very important evolution for the emergence of the EU as a political actor on the international scene. EU co-operation must no longer be regarded as purely economic. It is clear that it conveys political values shared by EU member states. This process has given birth to what may be called a 'soft diplomacy' which relates to the concept of 'soft power' (Nye 1990) as well as to the commonly used concept of 'civilian power' (Duchêne 1973; Whitman 1998; Smith 2000). Both concepts underline the primacy of economic and institutional co-operation over military means, and of long-term cultural influence on short-term diplomatic pressures, to achieve international political influence.

Soft diplomacy may then be defined as a diplomacy resorting to economic, financial, legal and institutional means to export values, norms and rules and achieve long-term cultural influence. This kind of diplomacy is not totally new and has, for instance, characterized the diplomacy of states like Canada and Scandinavian countries. It is mainly based on the promotion of democracy, human rights, the rule of law, peaceful resolution of conflicts, sustainable development and so on. This kind of state diplomacy is usually seen as deprived of power interests and as a useful contribution to the work of the United Nations' efforts to promote global governance. The EU's soft diplomacy is not new in itself, but the EU brings an added value because its weight in the world is comparable to the US. In this sense, the EU may pretend to compete with the US for global leadership in promoting its own conceptions of democracy (for example banning the death penalty and defending strong welfare states), promoting sustainable development (through support for the Kyoto protocol which was rejected by the US) and by regulating globalization (especially on social protection, culture, agriculture, development aid, etc.). The EU's soft diplomacy as a way of proposing values, norms and rules is all the more important given that the globalization era is characterized by a collective need for meanings other than strictly economic norms. Soft diplomacy is not a 'soft imperialism' in the sense that it does not mean imposing values on countries which would then be tied into a sort of 'learning process'. It is much more a deliberative contribution to a worldwide debate over which values, norms and rules are necessary to bind the international community together in the post-Cold War/globalization era. Of course this international debate remains open. However, the EU's soft diplomacy is also attached to some fundamental universal values. This is particularly the case where the EU may exert some real (although so far mainly economic and institutional) pressures on states which do not respect human rights and democratic principles. Last but not least, it is quite difficult to assess the global effectiveness of the EU's soft diplomacy. It is of course possible to observe a success here or there (as, for instance, when the EU successfully led the coalition for rescuing the Kyoto protocol in Bonn, July 2001). But assessing a soft diplomacy which in general terms has been defined as a long-term cultural influence will undoubtedly take time.

Now the politicization of EU co-operation into a soft diplomacy raises other fundamental questions, which are successively dealt with in the next two parts of this chapter. First, conducting a consistent soft diplomacy on a global scale implies the consistency of policy actorness. Does the European Commission have the capacity, as an actor, to promote the EU's soft diplomacy? Second, what is the effectiveness of 'soft diplomacy' when confronted with 'hard geo-politics'? What more precisely is the influence of exporting values in a conflictual world? Is there not a need for the EU to strengthen its cultural influence with more stringent diplomatic and military tools?

Can the European Commission lead the EU's soft diplomacy?

The Community's external co-operation programmes are managed by the European Commission. In this respect, the Commission may be seen as the 'agent' of the EU's international co-operation policy (even if a clear distinction must be made with respect to the weight of the EC's and the EU's financial aid in the world).[7] But it is precisely this heavy task that has contributed to the Commission's daily management problems including: the multiplication of services in charge of external relations split in four different DGs (Development, External Relations, Trade, Enlargement); the proliferation of legal and financial resources (60 budget lines and about 80 regulations); the lack of staff (at least 1,300 persons are missing in services of external relations according to the Commission). One consequence of this gap between the level of staff and the scope of co-operation programmes is clearly a problem of mismanagement, which manifests itself in the very slow financial execution of co-operation programmes. It takes an average of four years to disburse funds when a decision to launch a project has been taken. The EC aid implementation problem is taken very seriously by the Commission as a real threat to the credibility of the EU vis-à-vis its partners in the world. As Commissioner Poul Nielson argued in a speech he made in Amsterdam in March 2000, 'Reform is important for the Commission as a whole. But reform is a question of do or die for the Commission's external aid' (Nielson 2000).

To remedy the situation, Commissioner Chris Patten decided to launch an important reform of the external relations services in May 2000. One particular reform listed among the Commission's objectives is the transfer of more financial autonomy to the Commission delegations worldwide to facilitate the financial implementation of co-operation programmes. Another main objective is to rein- force the co-ordination between the different programmes by transforming and delegating more power to the Common Service for External Relations which was created in 1998 and staffed with roughly 600 people. The transformation of this Common Service into a 'Co-operation Office' working under the collegial authority of the Commissioners in charge of external affairs occurred in January 2001. The question is now whether those measures will be sufficient to rationalize the management of co-operation programmes. According to an external evalua- tion, the current reform will not be sufficient since one major problem – not addressed by the reform – is that the external relations services are half based on functional criteria and half based on geographical criteria. As a civil servant of the Commission argues, 'Everybody does everything in the Commission. A person who draws the budget for a project is sometimes the same person who writes the speech for a Commissioner'.[8] This claim suggests that the Commission should thoroughly reorganize its services on a functional basis (Bossuyt *et al.* 2000).

The bureaucratic mismanagement of EC co-operation is not only due to the internal structure of the Commission, but also to the institutional constraints which limit the autonomy of the Commission. As Christian Lequesne argues, the Commission remains a semi-independent institution in its relations with the member states (Lequesne 1996). This general statement can be verified in the case of co-operation policy. This is, for example, clearly the case of EU co-operation with the ACP countries. The negotiation of the framework agreements (Lomé Agreements and now Cotonou) is primarily an intergovernmental bargain between ACP states and EU member states. The Commission's role is to offer expertise. The contributions to the European Development Fund are voluntary contributions from the member states and the Commission has no authority over them. Even as regards the day-to-day co-operation and management of the EDF (for example the selection of projects to be financed, etc.) the Commission is assisted by the EDF committee which comprises representatives of the member states in charge of approving – or not – the Commission's project proposals.

Generally speaking, co-operation policy is mainly tied to the member states. As with any first pillar issue, the Commission has both initiative and executive powers, but the member states keep strong powers in the decision-making process both in the legislative and executive phases. First, the member states are the primary actors at the Council and working groups level. There were, for example, 43 meetings of the working group on development policy in 1997. Second, the member states dominate the comitology level since there are roughly 50 comitology committees active in various co-operation programmes. Most of these are 'management' committees, whose task is to assist the Commission in the implementation of those programmes (Pedler and Schaefer 1996).

It is also worth noting that the Amsterdam Treaty has increased the co-decision procedure for co-operation policies. From a democratic point of view, this is certainly relevant since the Parliament will be more deeply involved in the formation of co-operation policies. On the other hand, however, since the member states do not lose any of their influence, the decision-making process may be even more complicated and slow moving than it already is.

'Soft diplomacy'? Limited by 'hard geo-politics': the need for a stronger CFSP?

Now, apart from the bureaucratic problems in the management of EU co-operation, its politicization trend towards a 'soft diplomacy' faces obvious geo-political constraints. It is widely believed that economic sanctions are all the more effective as a policy instrument because they put intermediate pressure on governments before a potential and credible resort to military action. In this respect, the economic sanctions taken by the EU in the first pillar suffer in terms of efficiency from the weakness of a CFSP support in highly conflictual situations. The risk here is that the EU may remain confined within the arena of 'soft diplomacy' which may be adapted to 'soft' conflictual situations where economic sanctions are sufficient to exert an effective pressure on governments. However, in more serious cases of political/military conflict such as mass crimes (Rwanda), civil wars (Sierra Leone, Angola, Congo) or authoritarian regimes resistant to economic pressures (Iraq, Serbia, Nigeria, Sudan), the efficiency of European sanctions has proved to be quite limited (De Wilde d'Estmael 1998). Therefore the objective of 'conflict prevention' set by the Cotonou Agreement as a new objective of EU co-operation with ACP states seems quite unrealistic without a strong CFSP commitment. As a cabinet member of Commissioner Poul Nielson admitted, 'Conflict prevention sounds great in speeches, but in practice, unless involving 500,000 soldiers, we do not know how we will manage'.[9]

In sectors where the politicization of EU co-operation is supposed to bridge the gap between the first and second pillars and to tackle geo-political issues, its progress is all the more disappointing. In Asia for example, the strategy presented by the Commission in 1994 includes a strong EU contribution to regional security including negotiations about arms control and non-proliferation. But it is argued that these objectives are mainly rhetorical given the weak political influence of Europe in Asia (Mahncke 1992). The case of the Middle-East is another classic example of the EU's limited capacity to link economic co-operation with diplomatic influence. The EU provides more than 50 per cent of international aid to the Palestinians (Marin 1998). However, the diplomatic position of the EU, which is reputed to be closer to the Palestinians than the US, has given Israel the incentive to leave the EU out of the Israeli-Palestinian negotiation process. Consequently, the political influence of the EU is commonly recognized as quite limited in the Israeli-Palestinian conflict despite some significant political initiatives such as the appointment of Miguel Moratinos, the former Spanish Ambassador, as a special representative of the EU (Charillon 1998).

Undoubtedly, soft diplomacy is not enough when, apart from economic sanctions with a symbolic effect, the EU is unable to play any significant role in close and violent conflicts such as the Balkan wars of the 1990s. This observation may be generalized: without support from a stronger CFSP, including military potential, the EU's capability to play a major role in conflict-preventing and peace-building operations may remain quite limited in the future. Therefore we believe here that the EU's current soft diplomacy has more to win than to lose if completed by a stronger CFSP which is equipped with a military potential to perform the so-called Petersberg tasks. As suggested by Christopher Hill (soon after the Maastricht Treaty went into force) an effective EU global presence would involve policies covering all pillars in the external relations system (Hill 1993). Contrary to Karen Smith (2000) and other authors, we do not see the 'end of civilian power EU' in this evolution but the strengthening of the EU's external capability. Indeed promoting democratic and human rights values is not necessarily contradictory with the disposing of a military potential to face, in the last resort, the crises of a frequently 'uncivil world' (Pijpers 1998), provided that the latter is not used as a tool for expansion, imperialism or hegemony. It appears quite certain, given the current state of progress with the EU's defence capability, that the EU will for a long time remain far from becoming a military superpower.

Notes

1   From Lomé I in 1975 to Lomé IV in 1989; the latter agreement was signed for 10 years and revised at mid-term in 1995.
2   Council Regulation no. 2698/2000, 27 November 2000, published in the Official Journal, 12 December 2000.
3   Council Regulation no. 443/92, 25 February 1992.
4   EU co-operation with China is still based on a 1985 trade and co-operation agreement where no provisions about democracy and human rights were included. However, since 1995, the EU has established a 'political dialogue' with Chinese authorities where issues such as human rights and democracy are officially discussed. This process is parallel to the EU's support for China's application to the WTO.
5   The question of whether this 'sanction' against Russia was appropriately balanced against the seriousness of human rights abuses in Chechnya remains open. However, judgement on the EU's behaviour must also be seen in the light of the fact that very few Western states (including the US) and multi-lateral donors have envisaged any form of serious sanction against Russia.
6   Council Regulation no. 1257/96, 20 June 1996, published in the Official Journal, 2 July 1996.
7   EC aid managed by the European Commission represents 12 per cent of international financial aid; the weight of the EU (Community and member states' aid) goes beyond 55 per cent.
8   Interview conducted at the Commission in July 2000.
9   Interview conducted at the Commission in July 2000.

References

Bossuyt, J., Corre, G., Laporte, G., Lehtinen, T. and Simon, A. (2000) *Assessing Trends in EC Development Policy, an Independent Review of the European Commission's External Aid Reform Process,* Maastricht: European Centre for Development Policy Management.

Bretherton, C. and Vogler, J. (1999) *The EU as a Global Actor*, London: Routledge.

Bruter, M. (1999) 'Diplomacy Without a State: the External Delegations of the European Commission', *European Journal of Public Policy*, 6: 2.

Charillon, F. (1998) 'La Stratégie Européenne dans le Processus de Paix au Moyen-Orient: Politique Étrangère de Proximité et Diplomatie du Créneau', in Durand, M.F. and Vasconcelos, A. (eds) *La PESC, Ouvrir l'Europe au Monde,* Paris: Presses de Sciences Po.

Cox, A. and Chapman, J. (1999) *The European Community External Co-operation Programmes, Policies, Management and Distribution,* London: Overseas Development Institute.

Cremona, M. (1998) 'The European Union as an International Actor: The Issues of Flexibility and Linkage', *European Foreign Affairs Review*, 3.

De Wilde d'Estmael, T. (1998) *La Dimension Politique des Relations Économiques Extérieures de la Communauté Européenne,* Brussels: Bruylant.

Devuyst, Y. (1995) 'The European Community and the Conclusion of the Uruguay Round', in C. Rhodes and S. Mazey (eds) *The State of the European Union, vol. III : Building a European Polity?*, Boulder: Lynne Rienner/Longman.

Duchêne, F. (1973) 'The EC and the Uncertainties of Interdependence', in M. Kohnstamm and W. Hager (eds) *A Nation Writ Large? Foreign Policy Problems Before the European Community,* London: Macmillan.

Duke, S. (1999) *The Elusive Quest for European Security: From EDC to CFSP,* London: Macmillan.

Durand, M.F. and Vasconcelos, A. (eds) (1998) *La PESC, Ouvrir l'Europe au Monde,* Paris: Presses de Sciences Po.

Durand, M.F, Giordano, P. and Valladao, A. (eds) (2001) *Vers un Accord entre l'Europe et le Mercosur,* Paris: Presses de Sciences Po.

Edwards, G. and Regelsberger, E. (1990) *Europe's Global Links, the European Community and Inter-regional Cooperation,* London: Pinter Publishers.

Edwards, G. and Philippart, E. (1997) 'The Euro-Mediterranean Partnership: Fragmentation and Reconstruction', *European Foreign Affairs Review,* 2.

European Commission (1994) *Communication au Conseil, Vers une Nouvelle Stratégie Asiatique,* COM (94) 314 final, Brussels.

European Commission (1999a) *Communication au Conseil, au Parlement Européen et au Comité Économique et Social sur un Nouveau Partenariat Union Européenne/Amérique Latine à l'Aube du XXIème siècle,* COM (1999) 105 final, Brussels.

European Commission (1999b) *Communication au Conseil et au Parlement Européen, Evaluation et Avenir des Activités Humanitaires de la Communauté,* COM (1999) 468 final, Brussels.

European Commission (2000) *Communication to the Council and the European Parliament: The European Community's Development Policy,* COM (2000) 212 final, Brussels.

European Commission (2001) *Communication Relative au Rôle de l'Union Européenne dans la Promotion des Droits de l'Homme et de la Démocratie dans les Pays-tiers,* COM (2001) 252 final, Brussels.

Gnesotto, N. (1999) *La Puissance et l'Europe*, Paris: Presses de Sciences Po.

Gomez, R. (1998) 'The EU's Mediterranean Policy: Common Foreign Policy by the Back Door?' in J. Peterson and H. Sjursen (eds) *A Common Foreign Policy for Europe?*, London: Routledge.

Gordon, P. (1997) 'Europe's Uncommon Foreign Policy', *International Security*, 22, 3.

Gupta, J. and Ringius L. (2001) ' The EU's Climate Leadership: Reconciling Ambition and Reality', *International Environmental Agreements: Politics, Law and Economics*, 1, 2.

Hendry, I.D., Macleod, I. and Hyett, S. (1996) *The External Relations of the European Communities*, Oxford: Clarendon Press.

Hill, C. (1993) 'The Capability-Expectations Gap, or Conceptualizing Europe's International Role', *Journal of Common Market Studies*, 31, 3.

Hillion, C. (1998) 'Partnership and Co-operation Agreements Between the European Union and the New Independent States of the Ex-Soviet Union', *European Foreign Affairs Review*, 3.

Holm, E. (2001) *The European Anarchy, Europe's Hard Road into High Politics*, Copenhaguen: Copenhaguen Business School Press.

Kirkpatrick, C. and Richards, G.A. (1999) 'Reorienting Interregional Co-operation in the Global Political Economy: Europe's East Asian Policy', *Journal of Common Market Studies*, 37, 4.

Krenzler, H.G. and MacGregor, A. (2000) 'GM Food: the Next Major Transatlantic Trade War?', *European Foreign Affairs Review*, 3.

Lequesne, C. (1996) 'La Commission Européenne Entre Autonomie et Dépendance', *Revue Française de Science Politique*, 46, 3.

MacMahon, J.A. (1998) 'ASEAN and the Asia-Europe Meeting: Strengthening the European Union's Relationship with South-East Asia', *European Foreign Affairs Review*, 3.

Mahncke, D. (1992) 'Relations between Europe and South-East Asia: The Security Dimension', *European Foreign Affairs Review*, 2.

Marin, M. (1998) *The Role of the European Union in the Peace Process and its Future Assistance to the Middle East*, Speech by the Vice-President of the European Commission, 26 January, Brussels.

Nielson, P. (2000) *European Development Policy: How to Join the Mainstream*, speech by the European Commissioner for Development Cooperation and Humanitarian Aid, 27 March 2000, Amsterdam.

Nye, J. (1990) 'Soft power', *Foreign Policy*, 80, 3.

Pedler, R. and Shaefer, G. (eds) (1996) *Shaping European Law and Policy, The Role of Committees and Comitology in the Political Process*, Maastricht: European Institute of Public Administration.

Petiteville, F. (2001) 'La Coopération Économique de l'Union Européenne entre Globalisation et Politisation', *Revue Française de Science Politique*, 51, 3.

Pijpers, A. (1998) 'The Twelve Out-of-Area: A Civilian Power in an Uncivil World?', in G. Edwards, E. Regelsberger and W. Wessels (eds) *European Political Co-operation in the 80s: A Common Foreign Policy for Western Europe?,* Dordrecht: Martinus Nijhoff.

Rhodes, C. (ed) (1998) *The European Union in the World Community*, Boulder: Lynne Rienner.

Sanches, A.A. (1999) *EU Co-operation with Politically Fragile Countries: Lessons from Angola,* Maastricht: European Centre for Development Policy Management.

Scharpf, F. (2000) *Gouverner l'Europe*, Paris: Presses de Sciences Po.

Smith, K. (1998) 'The Use of Political Conditionality in the EU's Relations with Third Countries : How Effective?', *European Foreign Affairs Review*, 3.

Smith, K. (2000) 'The End of Civilian Power EU: A Welcome Demise or a Cause for Concern?', the *International Spectator*, 25, 2.

Smith, M. (1998) 'Does the Flag follow Trade?: "Politicisation" and the Emergence of a European Foreign Policy' in J. Peterson and H. Sjursen (eds) *A Common Foreign Policy for Europe?*, London: Routledge.

Smith, M. and Woolcock, S. (1999) 'European Commercial Policy: a Leadership Role in the New Millennium', *European Foreign Affairs Review*, 4.

Van Dijck, P. and Faber, G. (eds) (2000) *The External Economic Dimension of the European Union,* The Hague: Kluwer Law International.

Visman, E. (1998) *Co-operation with Politically Fragile Countries: Lessons from EU Support to Somalia,* Maastricht: European Centre for Development Policy Management.

Ward, A. (1998) 'Frameworks for Co-operation between the European Union and Third States: A Viable Matrix for Uniform Human Rights Standards?', *European Foreign Affairs Review,* 3.

White, B. (1999) 'The European Challenge to Foreign Policy Analysis', *European Journal of International Relations,* 5, 1.

Whitman, R.G. (1998) *From Civilian Power to Superpower? The International Identity of the European Union,* London: Macmillan.

Winters, A. (2000) 'EU's Preferential Trade Agreements: Objectives and Outcomes', in P. Van Dijck and G. Faber (eds) *The External Economic Dimension of the European Union,* The Hague: Kluwer Law International.

Young, A. (2000) 'The Adaptation of European Foreign Economic Policy: From Rome to Seattle', *Journal of Common Market Studies,* 38, 1.

Zielonka, J. (1998) *Explaining Euro-Paralysis, Why Europe is Unable to Act in International Politics,* Oxford: Macmillan Press.

8 Exporting regulatory standards

The cases of trapping and data protection

Sebastiaan Princen

The California effect in the EU's external relations

The effects of internationalization on domestic regulatory standards in fields such as environmental policy and consumer protection have been the subject of intense debate. On the one hand, it is often feared that internationalization will lead to a steady reduction in the stringency of regulatory standards. Then, it is argued that relatively stringent standards lead to higher costs of production in the countries imposing them, which in turn worsens their competitive position in world markets. As a result, countries will lower their standards in order to retain business or even to attract it, and a 'race to the bottom' may result.

On the other hand, a number of authors have pointed to the opposite effect. Indeed it is argued that internationalization may also lead to a strengthening of regulatory standards. Vogel (1995) has called this the 'California effect', after the US state that has often played a frontrunner's role in raising regulatory standards in the US. A California effect takes place when a country (or a coalition of countries) exports its own (more stringent) standards to, or imposes them upon, one or more of its trading partners through the use of market access. For example, a country may ban or threaten to ban imports of products that do not conform to certain standards. If, in reaction, that country's trading partners raise their regulatory standards in order to maintain market access for their products, then a California effect has taken place.

In his study of the California effect, Vogel (1995: 263–269) points to three factors that he considers to be crucial in producing a California effect. First, the country imposing the trade measure needs to have a big, rich market in order to induce other countries to raise their regulatory standards and retain their market access. In the exporting country an important role is therefore played by export-oriented firms, which have an interest in retaining market access.

Second, the imposition of more stringent standards through trade measures has to be supported by domestic producers, which have an interest in imposing those standards on their foreign competitors. They may form coalitions with public interest groups, such as environmental groups, that are also in favour of more stringent standards. Such coalitions are called 'Baptist-bootlegger coalitions', after the two groups that supported the prohibition in the US, albeit for different reasons.

Third, international integration schemes may promote more stringent standards, when those schemes foresee positive harmonization of regulatory standards between their member states. Then, member states with more stringent standards may try to have their standards accepted as international standards, thus imposing them upon the other member states with less stringent standards.

The conditions for a California effect limit the number of potential sources for such an effect. The vast majority of reported cases were initiated by the US, the EU or the major EU member states. Japan has also initiated harmonization in a limited number of cases, particularly in the field of food standards.

The EU seems to be a promising source of California effects. It represents one of the largest markets in the world and generally has relatively stringent regulatory standards. The EU's external relations would therefore seem to offer fertile ground for a study of the conditions under which a California effect is likely to take place.

In this chapter, I will examine two cases in which the EU threatened to interrupt the import of American and Canadian products because of differing production standards. The first case is the European leghold trap regulation. This regulation sought to ban furs and fur product imports from countries that allowed the use of leghold traps or did not adhere to 'internationally agreed humane trapping standards'. These countries included the US, Canada and the Russian Federation. The second case is the European data protection directive, which precluded transfers of personal information to countries without 'adequate' levels of protection. Again, it was most likely that both the US and Canada failed the directive's adequacy test.

In both cases, the US and Canadian governments adopted more stringent standards in order to avoid an interruption of trade. Thus, the EU was able to instigate a California effect. At the same time, however, the extent to which standards actually went up, and the models that were chosen, differ strongly between the two cases. This chapter examines both cases and discusses the conditions under which the EU was and was not able to 'export its model' in these two policy fields. To that end, it employs a two-level game framework to analyse the occurrence of a California effect.

The California effect and two-level games

A California effect takes place when a country strengthens its regulatory standards as a result of another country's trade measure. Then, (international) trade measures have an impact on (domestic) regulatory processes. Moreover, the adoption of those trade measures is itself the outcome of domestic political processes. Hence, domestic and international politics, as well as their interaction, come together in the California effect.

A theoretical approach that captures this interaction well is Putnam's 'two-level game approach' (Putnam 1988; Evans *et al.* 1993). The central insight of the two-level game approach is that international negotiations take place at two levels: at the international level, negotiators from different countries negotiate with each other over the terms of an agreement; domestically, each negotiator has to negotiate with his or her constituency in order to have an international agreement ratified. These two processes take place simultaneously and influence each other in that the domestic political context determines the range of acceptable international agreements for a country, while developments in the international arena may affect the range of domestically acceptable agreements.

The two levels of negotiation are connected by the concept of a 'win-set'. A win-set is the set of international outcomes that can be ratified by a country (cf. Putnam 1988: 437). In this definition, 'ratification' refers not only to formal ratification procedures in parliaments or similar institutions, but also to 'informal' ratification by powerful domestic actors, such as interest groups. Thus, each country has its own win-set that is determined by domestic political processes. An agreement between two or more countries can only be reached if that agreement can be ratified in (i.e. is acceptable to) all countries involved or, in other words, if the win-sets of the countries involved overlap.

Apart from this domestic influence on international bargaining, events at the international level can also influence domestic politics and thereby the win-sets of the countries involved in international agreements. This is where trade measures come in: by imposing trade measures, a country may change the win-sets of other countries in such ways as to induce them to adopt more stringent standards.

Originally, the two-level game approach was developed in the context of explicit negotiations over formal international agreements. However, its concepts and insights are also useful in analysing regulatory trade measures that do not lead to formal agreements or even negotiations. In those cases, changes in one country's regulatory standards under the influence of another country's regulatory trade measure can also be analysed in terms of a move toward a mutually acceptable 'agreement' on the terms under which the two countries will conduct trade, or: a shift in win-sets.

The shape and size of a country's win-set are defined in a domestic political process. This process can be analysed as a balance of competing interests and ideas. If a trade measure is to affect domestic regulatory policies, it has to change this balance somehow. At the same time, the adoption of the trade measure is itself the result of some political balance in the country imposing it. Consequently, the affected country or countries can in turn try to change that balance and thereby dilute the effects of the trade measure.

The outcome of the domestic political process is determined by the preferences and constraints facing officials and interest groups in a country and the (institutional) relations between them. Attempts to change the domestic political balance can therefore take several forms. First, and most conspicuously in the context of trade measures, they may change the constraints of some political actors, by manipulating export opportunities. Second, the regulatory standard that is promoted by the trade measure may or may not tie in with deeply-held values and perceived problems in the country affected by it. To the extent that it does, it is more likely to lead to a California effect (cf. Schoppa 1993). Third, trade measures may affect the groups and officials that participate in the domestic political process by involving actors in the political debate over a given issue that were previously absent from that debate. This is a special case of what Schoppa (1993) has called 'participation expansion'.

These mechanisms can also be used against the country imposing a regulatory trade measure. A country affected by that measure might threaten to retaliate, refer to international standards or common values or try to involve other political actors in the country imposing the trade measure. Either way, support for the trade measure may be undercut and a California effect may be prevented from occurring.

The European leghold trap regulation and data protection directive are two cases that offer fertile ground for exploring some of these issues and hypotheses. It will be shown that both cases led to a California effect in the US and Canada, but in different ways. The extent to which the EU succeeded in formulating a coherent regulatory model before imposing a trade measure is crucial in explaining these differences.

The European leghold trap regulation[1]

The European measure and the situation in the US and Canada

Trapping is one of the most controversial and emotionally charged animal welfare issues in many Western countries. On the one hand, opponents view trapping as a cruel and inhumane practice that violates basic animal entitlements. On the other hand, trappers see trapping as a legitimate activity, which is part of a valued lifestyle and provides a useful tool for wildlife management. Apart from the debate over trapping per se, a great deal of attention has focused on specific traps and their effects on animal welfare.

In Canada, for instance, programmes to formulate trapping standards were initiated early as the 1950s (Novak 1987). In the 1980s, the Canadian government attempted to formulate similar standards in the International Organization for Standardization (ISO). Animal welfare activists were often highly sceptical of these attempts either because they viewed them as ways to legitimize trapping or because they wanted to end trapping in general.

In 1991, after strong pressure from European and North American animal welfare groups and the European Parliament, the EU adopted a regulation that banned the use of leghold traps, a kind of trap that was argued to be particularly cruel (EC 1991). Moreover, the regulation foresaw a ban on the imports of 13 species of furs from countries that still allowed the use of leghold traps or did not adhere to 'internationally agreed humane trapping standards'. The ban was set to enter into force in 1995.

As 12 of the 13 species covered by the ban were mainly caught in the US and Canada, where leghold traps were still widely used, the ban mainly threatened to affect those two countries. Trapping was not a large industry in either country, but fur exports were extremely important for trappers since the vast majority of furs and fur products were exported. Furthermore, Europe was the main destination for these furs and products (Shieff and Baker 1987). For some animal welfare activists, a European ban would have been an effective instrument to undermine the fur trade and thereby to deal a decisive blow to trapping in Canada and the US.

The exemption for countries that adhered to internationally agreed humane trapping standards referred primarily to the ISO process, which had been underway for some years when the regulation was adopted. At first the adoption of standards in this process seemed the obvious 'way out' for US and Canadian trappers and officials. In subsequent years, however, progress in the ISO process was stifled, mainly by the controversies between delegations from North American and European countries, which took widely different positions on the content of the trapping standards and on trapping in general. In 1994, the process effectively came to a halt when the word 'humane' was deleted from the standard's title and the EU declared that any result would no longer qualify as an exemption under the regulation.

To US and Canadian trappers and wildlife officials, a ban on leghold traps was unacceptable. To begin with, such traps were still widely used in both countries. Moreover, a ban on leghold traps was considered illegitimate, since trappers and wildlife officials associated it with an 'animal rights' position that was aimed at gradually banning trapping and the fur trade altogether. Finally, the authority for regulating traps and trapping in the US and Canada lay with the states and provinces, respectively. As a consequence, agreement among all states and provinces on this controversial issue would have been required, while the adoption of federal standards would have encountered constitutional and political problems.

Working on an agreement

US and Canadian officials started to lobby European officials in the second half of 1994, shortly before the import ban was set to enter into force. The Canadian government requested GATT consultations, the first step toward a GATT dispute resolution panel, while the United States Trade Representative (USTR) started to push for a bilateral solution.

A case before the GATT (or before the WTO after 1995) would in all probability have been decided in favour of the US and Canada, as the European regulation sought to ban furs exclusively on the way the animals had been caught. In this respect, the regulation was similar to the US ban on tuna that had been caught with dolphin-unfriendly methods, which had been the subject of the (in)famous Tuna-Dolphin cases before the GATT in 1991 and 1994 (GATT 1991, 1994).

For the US and Canadian governments, however, resorting to the GATT was not an attractive option. Politically, they would have been in an awkward position, defending leghold traps against a European measure that was supposed to improve animal welfare. Moreover, a GATT/WTO case could have taken several years, during which damage to the fur industry might well occur. In Canada, the situation was compounded by the effects a European import ban would have had on aboriginal trappers, for whom trapping was part of a subsistence lifestyle. Consequently, both governments preferred a negotiated solution.

In the EU, issues of GATT compatibility had been largely absent from the political debate surrounding the adoption of the regulation. However, the Tuna-

Dolphin cases and the conclusion of the agreements on the World Trade Organization in 1994 led to a greater salience of international trade law issues in the EU.

Until 1994, the leghold trap regulation had been a DG XI (Environment) project, and it had been adopted in the Environmental Council of Ministers. However, the efforts of US and Canadian trade officials led to the involvement of DG I (Trade). For European trade officials, losing a GATT/WTO case was not an attractive prospect, and a negotiated solution was by far preferable. For European animal welfare activists, the proposal to work on trapping standards was difficult to reject. After all, the regulation had officially always been presented as an animal welfare and conservationist measure, and not as a means to stop the fur trade. From that point of view, it was difficult to sustain a ban on one particular kind of trap for a limited number of species and reject an approach that would cover more types of traps and a wider variety of species.

As a result, the European Commission postponed the entry into force of the import ban, and in 1995 it started talks on a separate agreement on trapping standards with US, Canadian, and later Russian officials. In these negotiations, the EU delegation was led by officials from both DG I and DG XI, but gradually the locus of decision-making within the EU shifted to the trade officials.

In the US and Canada, domestic support was obtained through regular consultations with provincial officials and representatives of state officials. Some state and provincial wildlife officials were represented on the delegations, alongside federal officials. The negotiations themselves built on previous work done in Canada and in the ISO process. Among US trappers and officials, the idea of adopting trapping standards was more controversial than in Canada, because nationwide standards had not been formulated. However, a rise in US animal welfare activism in the first half of the 1990s, coupled with successful ballot initiatives to ban leghold traps in several states, put pressure on US trappers and officials. The European regulation worked as a catalyst in that it alerted US officials to the growing opposition to trapping.

Therefore, in 1996, US officials started to work on national trapping standards that became known as 'Best Management Practices' (BMPs: IAFWA 1997). The start of this domestic BMP process also increased the willingness of trappers and officials to accept an agreement with the EU, as long as it was in line with the BMPs. This meant, however, that the US was not willing to accept a binding agreement, but was only willing to agree upon a set of voluntary, non-binding standards. Consequently, the US and Canada negotiated separate agreements with the EU.

As a result of these developments, the US and Canadian governments were able to set much of the agenda during talks with the EU. Most of the debates during the negotiations focused on the substantive standards that would be set. For killing traps, this related to the maximum allowable time to animal death or unconsciousness; for restraining traps, it concerned the indicators that would be used to measure an animal's pain and stress while it was caught in a trap. On the insistence of the US and Canadian governments, the agreements would apply not only to the US and Canada, but also to the EU itself. The number of species covered by the agreements was expanded to include several European species as well.

The agreements

In December 1996, a (binding) agreement was reached between the EU and Canada (and Russia). The EP still had to give its opinion on the agreement, but could not block its adoption. The agreement did still have to be approved by the Council of Ministers. In the Environmental Council, however, there was a blocking minority against adopting the agreement. Among the member states, the UK and Austria were the staunchest supporters of the regulation and an import ban, while Germany, Belgium and the Netherlands were also in favour of a stringent agreement.

After the Environment Council again failed to adopt the agreement in June 1997, the Dutch Presidency of the Council reintroduced the proposal in the General Affairs Council, thus completing the shift within the EU from the environmental to the trade arena. In July 1997, the General Affairs Council approved the agreement by a qualified majority of member states, with only the UK and Austria opposing. The agreement was officially adopted in January 1998 (EC 1998a).

The US and the EU presented their (non-binding) agreement later that year. The substantive standards in this agreement were identical to those in the EU-Canadian agreement, but given its non-binding character, most of the implementing provisions were absent from it. Therefore, adoption of the EU-US agreement by the same member states that had approved the EU-Canadian agreement was not self-evident. The German position was particularly significant in this regard, but after the USTR had written a letter indicating the likelihood of a trade dispute if the agreement was not adopted, Germany supported the agreement. It was approved in December 1997 and officially adopted in July 1998 (EC 1998b).

The European Parliament opposed both agreements. Despite its influential role in having the regulation adopted in 1991, it was no longer able to block adoption of the agreements once they had been approved by the General Affairs Council. Canada ratified its agreement in June 1999 and the agreement did not require formal ratification in the US.

As a result of this process, trapping standards in both the US and Canada have become more stringent, although in the US much will depend on the outcome of the BMP process. Moreover, trapping standards should also become more stringent in the EU. By early 2002, however, the European Commission had not yet started a legislative process to implement these trapping standards in the EU. Implementation was hindered by the fact that responsibility for the agreements lay with the newly formed DG Trade (a successor to DG I), while DG Environment (formerly DG XI) had lost most of its interest in the issue.

The European Data Protection Directive[2]

The European Directive and the situation in the US and Canada

Information has become crucial to business and international trade. Part of this information concerns individuals and although the free flow of information may be economically beneficial, it may also threaten the privacy of individuals. Hence, many Western countries have adopted measures to protect personal privacy in relation to personal information, so-called 'data protection'.

In order to harmonize data protection legislation between its member states, the EU adopted a data protection directive in 1995 (EC 1995). The data protection directive showed two characteristics that built on an established European tradition. First, it was comprehensive, covering both the public and private sectors, and including a wide range of data protection principles. Second, it foresaw the creation of independent national data protection authorities, which had to monitor compliance with the legislation in this field and, in some cases, could block or had to approve particular types of data processing.

Moreover, the directive contained a provision that required data protection authorities to block transfers of personal data to third countries without an 'adequate' level of protection. This provision sought to prevent personal information from being transferred to countries with a less stringent data protection regime in order to circumvent the European requirements.

The adequacy of a third country's data protection standards was determined by the European Commission, subject to approval by a regulatory committee of member state representatives (the 'Article 31 Committee'). In addition to the Article 31 Committee, the directive established a working party consisting of representatives from national data protection authorities (the 'Article 29 Working Party'), which was tasked with giving (non-binding) advice on data protection issues, including the level of protection in third countries.

When the European directive was adopted, the US and Canada were among the countries that did not meet the directive's 'adequate level of protection'. Both countries had established fairly comprehensive federal data protection legislation in the public sector. The private sector, however, was covered by a combination of targeted, sectoral legislation and industry self-regulation. This situation was largely mirrored at the level of the states and provinces, which had jurisdiction over sub-national data protection policies in both countries. As a result, the applicable data protection standards differed widely between sectors but generally fell short of the European yardstick (Bennett 1996; Schwartz and Reidenberg 1996).

In addition, the two countries had no independent data protection authorities in the private sector, and relied instead on private litigation. In the US, the Federal Trade Commission (FTC) could monitor compliance with self-regulatory codes under its general authority to monitor 'unfair and deceptive' commercial practices, but until the mid-1990s it had not been very active in the field of data protection.

Therefore, the European directive posed a significant threat to US and Canadian firms that relied on the exchange of personal information in their trade with European firms. Nevertheless, there were some important differences between the US and Canada, which would prove crucial in subsequent developments. First, Canada's public sector Privacy Act was overseen by the office of the Privacy Commissioner of Canada. As a result, Canada had gained considerable experience with independent oversight of data protection legislation, and the Privacy Commissioner formed an institutionalized advocate of data protection policies within the Canadian federal government.

Second, in 1993, the Canadian province of Quebec adopted a comprehensive data protection law covering both the public and private sectors. This law formed a 'European' element within Canada's data protection regime, and it has been claimed that Quebec's legislation 'was drafted with the EU language in mind' (Bennett 1996: 484).

Third, Canadian government officials and business and consumer groups reached consensus on a set of voluntary data protection standards when they adopted the Canadian Standards Association's (CSA) model code for the protection of privacy (CSA 1996). This consensus was politically highly significant in that it could (and would) form the basis for future legislation in this area.

The US did not have such a generally agreed upon set of data protection principles. Much of the debate was dominated by a set of four data protection principles that had been formulated in a 1973 government report (HEW 1973: 41). These four principles would resurface in several reports in the second half of the 1990s. However, this set of principles was much more limited than the sets contained in the European directive and the CSA model code, and some of these four principles themselves remained controversial among US business groups.

Thus, although the statutory and regulatory situation was largely similar in the US and Canada in the mid-1990s, their political contexts differed widely. This was to affect, to a great extent, the way the two countries reacted to the European directive.

The US and the Safe Harbour Agreement

According to Bennett and Raab (1997: 256), the US response to the European directive was a combination of distrust of the EC's possible protectionist motives, resentment about the EC's attitude toward US data protection policies, and scepticism over the EC's willingness and ability to block data transfers. In the years after 1995, however, it became clear to US officials and firms that the directive could indeed pose a threat to transatlantic data flows. Although some officials in the US administration wanted to take a hard line against the EC and treat this as a trade issue, others were wary of the trade dispute that would arise and preferred talks. Success before a WTO panel was unlikely, in any case, as the General Agreement on Trade in Services (GATS) contained an exception for the protection of privacy (see also Princen 2002: 284–287).

During 1997 and 1998, the US Department of Commerce and the EU DG XV (Internal Market) explored the possibilities of reaching an agreement that would satisfy the directive's adequacy requirements. This agreement would contain a set of data protection principles that US firms could choose to adhere to when processing personal information on EU citizens. This, in turn, would qualify for an adequacy finding under the directive. In the second half of 1998, this approach crystallized under the name of the 'Safe Harbour' approach.

In the following years, the specifics of the Safe Harbour Agreement were discussed. Although the issue was also raised in talks between the United States Trade Representative and European trade officials, these negotiations remained confined to the Department of Commerce and DG Internal Market. The European directive came into effect in October 1998, but the national EU data protection authorities agreed to treat data flows to the US favourably during the course of the negotiations.

Several issues were important in the talks between DG Internal Market and the Department of Commerce. First, the set of substantive data protection standards was subject to debate, and this set was refined and adjusted during the process. Second, the enforcement of the agreement proved crucial. The European Commission demanded active oversight by US governmental agencies, whereas the US government wanted to secure as little government interference as possible. Over the summer of 1999, this led to a stronger role for the FTC in enforcing the agreement. The FTC would act on violations of self-regulatory codes under the Safe Harbour Agreement and promised to give priority to complaints under the Safe Harbour Agreement. Third, the US government wanted to obtain adequacy findings for specific industries that were subject to relatively stringent data protection legislation, in particular the financial sector. It proved impossible to reach agreement on this issue, however, and the financial sector was excluded from the agreement in early 2000.

Within the EU, the most important actors in the process, besides DG Internal Market, were the Article 31 Committee and the Article 29 Working Party. The Article 29 Working Party delivered highly critical opinions on the various drafts of the agreement, although it saw some movement forward. These opinions were mostly reflected in the position of the Article 31 Committee, which rejected a series of drafts presented in 1998 and 1999. Within the Committee (and the Working Party), there was a broad division between Northern and Southern member states. To most Northern European member states, the idea of reaching an agreement based on a self-regulatory approach was quite acceptable, while most Southern European countries were more reluctant to endorse this approach.

However, after March 2000, the blocking minority that had existed in the Article 31 Committee started to break down, as it was felt that the EU had obtained the most it could from the US. After some last changes had been made, the Department of Commerce published the final version of the Safe Harbour Agreement in July 2000, and the European Commission adopted its adequacy finding a few days later (Department of Commerce 2000).

Because of the self-regulatory character of the agreement, its eventual impact on US data protection standards depends largely on the degree to which US firms will adopt them. Nevertheless, the agreement's standards are more stringent than those found in most US legislation or self-regulatory codes and, in contrast to existing codes in the US private sector, they are cross-sectoral. Moreover, the enforcement of the standards is more stringent. In addition, the Safe Harbour Agreement may have a number of indirect effects in that it may set the stage for future initiatives and that it may strengthen the positions of supporters of more stringent data protection legislation in the US (see also Shaffer 1999).

Canada and comprehensive data protection legislation

The development of Canadian data protection legislation after 1995 is closely linked to the rise of the Internet and e-commerce. In September 1995, an advisory council consisting mainly of industry representatives recommended the adoption of federal legislation to protect personal information, both online and offline. It argued this was necessary to create sufficient consumer confidence in the new commercial opportunities offered by the Internet (IHAC 1995).

Around that same time the European directive gained the attention of Canadian privacy specialists. In the mid-1990s, officials from Industry Canada (the federal Department of Industry) started to warn about the possible trade effects of the directive and argued the need for domestic legislation that could remedy the situation. As a result, the European directive became an important element in the Canadian government's thinking about data protection legislation.

Contemporary observers of the process also acknowledged this. In a 1996 article, Bennett (1996: 484) claimed that 'the impact of the EU Data Protection Directive on Canada has been a constant underlying theme within the recent debates'. In an article published in 1997, Bennett and Raab (1997: 259) stated that 'concern about the EU Data Protection Directive [was] manifested in the Canadian policy debate from the moment it arrived on the agenda in 1990'.

In May 1996, Industry Canada endorsed the adoption of a legal framework for privacy protection in order to create consumer confidence in electronic commerce. In September of that year, the Minister of Justice announced that Canada would have federal data protection legislation in the private sector by the year 2000. By that time, Canadian business and consumer groups generally supported data protection legislation on the basis of the CSA model code. In addition, there was broad support for the Privacy Commissioner of Canada as the oversight agency. At the same time, these groups differed on the specifics of the legislation, relating both to the need to specify the CSA principles and to the enforcement powers of the Privacy Commissioner.

In September 1998, Industry Canada, supported by the Department of Justice Canada, introduced Bill C-54, which foresaw comprehensive data protection legislation on the basis of the CSA model code. The law would cover both online and offline data processing; the enforcement was given to the Privacy Commissioner of Canada. The debate over the bill related mainly to domestic issues, most importantly the federal authority to adopt legislation that would also cover provincially regulated industries. After some small changes had been made to the text of the bill and it had been reintroduced as Bill C-6 in October 1999, it was adopted as the Personal Information Protection and Electronic Documents Act and received royal assent in April 2000 (Canada 2000).

With the Act, Canada had adopted 'European-style' data protection legislation that was both comprehensive and contained independent oversight. All along the legislative process, officials from Industry Canada had been in contact with officials from DG Internal Market to discuss the adequacy of the proposed law under the European directive. These discussions became gradually more specific as the legislative process proceeded. In May 2000, after the Act had been adopted, the talks became more formal.

In general, the Canadian law was considered to be adequate, but some specific issues remained. These were all issues that could be dealt with within the framework of the Canadian law, however, and the European Commission adopted an adequacy finding in December 2001 (EC 2001).

This case demonstrates a California effect in both the US and Canada. In the US, some strengthening of standards took place because of the Safe Harbour Agreement with the EU. In Canada, a considerable strengthening of standards occurred, and this strengthening was partly a response to the European directive.

Conclusion

Both cases show a California effect, albeit to different extents, in that the US and Canada adopted more stringent regulatory standards as a result of an EU trade measure. Thus, the European measures resulted in a shift in the US and Canadian win-sets. However, the size and shape of the shifts differed between cases and between countries. Moreover, in the leghold trap case, the US and Canada succeeded in imposing some of their own standards on the EU in the process.

In the leghold trap case, the relative importance of fur exports to the EU triggered a response on the part of the US and Canadian governments. In Canada, the potential trade effects were much more targeted than in the US, which increased the political costs associated with the ban for the Canadian government and, consequently, led to a greater willingness on the part of the Canadian government to agree on a binding agreement.

At the same time, values and perceived problems determined much of the substantive outcomes of the process. In both the US and Canada, banning leghold traps would not only have entailed costs for trappers, but the idea of banning traps was associated with an animal rights position that was considered illegitimate among trappers and officials alike. As a result, a ban on leghold traps was hardly feasible in either country.

Trapping standards, on the other hand, were much more acceptable. Canada had a tradition of formulating trapping standards, which it had already sought to internationalize through the ISO process. When, in the US, public pressure to ban leghold traps increased, formulating this type of trapping standard was a logical and attractive solution.

Moreover, these programmes of national trapping standards offered a way out of the trade conflict with the EU. Not only did it offer a way out for US and

Canadian trappers and officials, but equally importantly, it offered a way out for the European Commission, which had become increasingly uncomfortable with the pending import ban.

In the EU, a decisive role was played by trade officials, who had become more aware of GATT/WTO issues during the first half of the 1990s, and who wanted to avoid a trade dispute over an import ban on furs. A separate agreement on trapping standards seemed the most logical compromise between the wish to avoid a trade dispute and the animal welfare considerations of DG Environment and the European Parliament. This case therefore shows a good example of successful participation expansion by countries affected by a trade measure.

Crucially, the failure to formulate a coherent vision on trapping standards on the part of the EU was an important reason why the US and Canadian governments could turn around the process and take over the initiative on this issue. Several factors account for this lack of a coherent vision. First, neither the EU nor its member states had much experience in formulating trapping standards. Consequently, expertise was lacking. Second, there was no clear locus for animal welfare issues within the EU or the European Commission. DG XI/Environment had taken the lead on this issue in the late 1980s, but in fact the issue stood a bit uncomfortably alongside the issues the DG had traditionally dealt with. When some of the main supporters of the regulation left their posts, there was no institutional back-up to secure continuing support. Finally, the leghold trap regulation seems to have been informed by a significant degree of symbolism, and mixed motivations. One part of the animal welfare community wanted to improve animal welfare. Another part wanted to end trapping and the fur trade as such, and saw an import ban as a useful means to that end. As the official arguments for an import ban related to animal welfare and, to a lesser extent, to conservation, it became increasingly more difficult for European officials to support an outright ban on only one type of trap for a limited number of species, while rejecting trapping standards that might improve animal welfare for all traps across a broader range of species.

The case of the European data protection directive shows quite a different process. Here, too, the potential trade effects were important in triggering a response from the US and Canadian governments. In the content of their responses, however, the US and Canadian governments took markedly different routes, each tying in with existing domestic approaches. The US sought to negotiate an agreement with the EU, which later became the Safe Harbour Agreement. This was not self-evident, however, as initially some officials in the US government pushed for a rejection of the EU's demands and a possible trade dispute. During the Safe Harbour talks, the USTR continued to question the GATS-compatibility of the European directive and sought to involve European trade officials in the process.

Yet, unlike in the leghold trap case, within the EU, the negotiations remained confined to a relatively limited group of data protection specialists within DG Internal Market, the Article 29 Working Party, and the Article 31 Committee. Despite the attempts by US officials to raise the issue with European trade officials and at higher political levels, the agreement was eventually negotiated and finalized by this group of specialists.

Several factors explain this remarkable absence of 'participation expansion' in this case. First, EU member states had a strong tradition in data protection regulation, which had largely been incorporated in the European directive. Secondly, there was a clear institutional framework for data protection issues within the EU and its member states, including both DG Internal Market and national data protection authorities. This strongly-knit data protection community ensured not only the expertise needed to conduct the negotiations, but also increased the credibility of the threat to interrupt data transfers if the US did not offer an adequate level of protection. Third, the data protection directive was not likely to violate the WTO Agreements (here: the GATS) and a US case before the WTO was therefore likely to have failed.

The talks between Canada and the EU never reached the stage of formal negotiations, although officials from both sides remained in close contact all along the Canadian legislative process. In Canada, the European directive combined with several domestic developments to create a favourable environment for data protection legislation. Still, here too, the existence of a clear, well-elaborated and broadly-supported body of European data protection standards was an important impetus for the Canadian response.

Thus, the institutional framework within which the EU adopted and implemented the two measures is highly significant for understanding the effects those measures had on the US and Canada. However, the multi-level character of the EU as such does not seem to have made much of a difference. In both cases, member states had to approve the measures and the outcomes of negotiations over bilateral agreements, either through the Council of Ministers or through a regulatory committee. In both cases, the European Parliament was a vocal participant, although more so in the case of leghold traps.

The main difference between the two cases was not formed by the degree of member state or European Parliament participation, but by the degree to which the EU succeeded in formulating a coherent regulatory framework backed up by a coherent institutional framework encompassing both levels. Using a two-level game framework, with the member states as the 'domestic level' of EU politics, presents a useful approach to analysing the dynamics leading to these outcomes.

Notes

1 For this case study, interviews have been conducted with US, Canadian and EU officials, representatives of trappers, and animal welfare groups. A more detailed analysis of this case is reported in Princen (2002).
2 For this case study, interviews have been conducted with US, Canadian and EU officials, trade associations, and consumer and privacy advocacy groups. A more detailed analysis of this case is reported in Princen (2002).

References

Bennett, C. J. (1996) 'Rules of the Road and Level Playing-Fields: The Politics of Data Protection in Canada's Private Sector', *International Review of Administrative Sciences*, 62, 4: 479–491.

Bennett, C. J. and Raab, C. D. (1997) 'The Adequacy of Privacy: The European Union Data Protection Directive and the North American Response', *The Information Society*, 13, 3: 245–263.

Canada (2000) *Personal Information Protection and Electronic Documents Act*, Assented to on 13 April 2000, available on http://www.parl.gc.ca

CSA (1996) *Model Code for the Protection of Personal Information. A National Standard of Canada*, CAN/CSA-Q830-96.

Department of Commerce (2000) *Final Safe Harbour Documents,* 21 July 2000, available on http://www.ita.doc.gov/td/ecom/menu.html

EC (1991) *Council Regulation (EEC) No. 3254/91 Prohibiting the Use of Leghold Traps in the Community and the Introduction into the Community of Pelts and Manufactured Goods of Certain Wild Animal Species Originating in Countries Which Catch Them by Means of Leghold Traps or Trapping Methods Which Do Not Meet International Humane Trapping Standards,* Adopted on 4 November 1991, OJ L 308, 9 November 1991: 1–3.

EC (1995) *Directive 95/46/EC of the European Parliament and of the Council on the Protection of Individuals with Regard to the Processing of Personal Data and on the Free Movement of such Data*, Adopted on 24 October 1995, OJ L 281, 23 November 1995: 31–50.

EC (1998a) *Council Decision 98/142/EC Concerning the Conclusion of an Agreement on International Humane Trapping Standards between the European Community, Canada and the Russian Federation and of an Agreed Minute between Canada and the European Community Concerning the Signing of the Said Agreement*, Adopted on 26 January 1998, OJ L 42, 14 February 1998: 40–57.

EC (1998b) *Council Decision 98/487/EC Concerning the Conclusion of an International Agreement in the Form of an Agreed Minute between the European Community and the United States of America on Humane Trapping Standards*, Adopted on 13 July 1998, OJ L 219, 7 August 1998: 24–37.

EC (2001) *Commission Decision 2002/2/EC Pursuant to Directive 95/46/EC of the European Parliament and of the Council on the Adequate Protection of Personal Data Provided by the Canadian Personal Information Protection and Electronic Documents Act,* Adopted on 20 December, 2001, OJ L 2, 4 January 2002: 13–16.

Evans, P.B., Jacobson, H.K. and Putnam, R.D. (eds) (1993) *Double-Edged Diplomacy. International Bargaining and Domestic Politics*, Berkeley: University of California Press.

GATT (1991) 'United States – Restrictions on Imports of Tuna', Report of the Panel, not adopted, Submitted to the parties on 16 August 1991, *International Legal Materials,* 30: 1594–1623.

GATT (1994) 'United States – Restrictions on Imports of Tuna', Report of the Panel, not adopted, Released in June 1994, *International Legal Materials,* 33: 839–903.

HEW (1973) *Records, Computers and the Rights of Citizens*, Report of the Secretary's Advisory Committee on Automated Personal Data Systems, July 1973, DHEW Publication No. (OS) 73–94.

IAFWA (1997) *Improving Animal Welfare in US Trapping Programs: Process Recommendations and Summaries of Existing Data*, Unpublished report.

IHAC (1995) *Connection, Community, Content: The Challenge of the Information Highway*, September 1995, available on http://strategis.ic.gc.ca

Novak, M. (1987) 'Traps and Trap Research', in M. Novak *et al.* (eds) *Wild Furbearer Management and Conservation in North America*, Toronto: Ontario Trappers Association/Ontario Ministry of Natural Resources.

Princen, S. (2002) *EU Regulation and Transatlantic Trade*, European Monographs Series, The Hague: Kluwer Law International.

Putnam, R. D. (1988) 'Diplomacy and Domestic Politics: the Logic of Two-Level Games', *International Organization*, 42, 3: 427–460.

Schoppa, L.J. (1993) 'Two-Level Games and Bargaining Outcomes: Why Gaiatsu Succeeds in Japan in some Cases but not others', *International Organization*, 47, 3: 353–386.

Schwartz, P.M. and Reidenberg, J.L. (1996) *Data Privacy Law. A Study of United States Data Protection*, Charlottesville, VI: Michie Law Publishers.

Shaffer, G. (1999) 'The Power of EU Collective Action: The Impact of EU Data Privacy Regulation on US Business Practice', *European Law Journal*, 5, 4: 419–437.

Shieff, A. and Baker J. A. (1987) 'Marketing and International Fur Markets', in M. Novak *et al.* (eds) *Wild Furbearer Management and Conservation in North America*, Toronto: Ontario Trappers Association/Ontario Ministry of Natural Resources.

Vogel, D. (1995) *Trading Up. Consumer and Environmental Regulation in a Global Economy*, Cambridge: Harvard University Press.

9 The export of the fight against organized crime policy model and the EU's international actorness

Francesca Longo

The European Union (EU) has developed several types of policies towards third states ranging from economic policy to foreign and security policy. Despite the fact that the EU is not a traditional unitary actor with a stable set of preferences and that the EU's interests, institutional arrangements and intervening actors differ from policy to policy, the EU has promoted its internal policy models towards the external environment. The impact of the EU's internal policy models on its role as an international actor is a growing mainstream in integration studies.

There is a broad consensus among scholars that the European Union has a visible presence in the international community (Ginsberg 1989); there is, however, little consensus on how to theorize about the EU as an international actor. Caporaso and Jupille (1998), in evaluating the international actorness of the EU in the field of environmental international conferences, argue that the resistance of member states to the transfer of full legal power in international negotiations to European institutions impedes the development of the EU's international actorness. The authors define the EU's international actorness by the presence or absence of four variables: acceptance of the EU's competence by member states, legal authority to act, autonomy from the member states and cohesion. This interpretation is strictly connected with the traditional interpretation of 'sovereignty' and considers international actorness as a sum zero game between the EU and its member states.

The definition of international actorness in terms of a 'structured presence' in the international arena appears to be more a fruitful concept for analysing the capability of non-state actors. Allen and Smith (1990) argue that the EU, despite its shortcomings as an institutionalized unified actor, has a significant and salient presence in the international arena resulting from distinctive forms of external behaviour (the objective level) and from other actors' perceptions of the EU's importance in the global system (the subjective level).

From this perspective the export of internal policy models assumes a high value in boosting both levels of the actorness. In fact, the objective level is asserted by the mobilization, at the international level, of the EU's economic and political resources that are engaged in the export activity. The subjective level of actorness results from the perception held by third countries that the EU is a relevant international actor because it plays a leading role in the definition of the rules and practices of international co-operation and dispatches personnel and material resources.

This chapter seeks to analyse this issue by examining the EU's counter transnational crime policy. The aim is to establish whether the EU policy for combating transnational organized crime (TOC) is one of the internal policy models that the EU is exporting to the global system.

The theoretical assumption of this analysis is that the common institutional framework matters. Even if the nature of involved actors, the nature of decision-making processes and the efficiency of the policy instruments depend upon the considered issue and the involved pillar, it is still possible to affirm that institutions, rules and procedures strengthen the EU's capability to promote convergence of interests and to define collective external policy strategies towards external actors.

The EU is far from being a 'single voice' in international negotiations and the capabilities-expectations gap (Hill 1993) is far from being closed. Nevertheless, the neo-realist interpretation of EU external action, which is dominated by the security interests of the member states, should be revisited. The EU institutional context has an effect on the powers and limitations of the member states in at least three ways (Hix 1999): first, through the existence of the European Commission that has formal or informal agenda-setting powers (Nuttall 1997), and in some cases implementation power, and that promotes unitary policy outcomes; second, through the existence of a stable set of formal and informal rules and procedures for the decision-making process which develop a 'habit of working together', thereby limiting member states' autonomy and promoting convergence of competing interests (Bulmer 1991); and finally, through the existence of normative policy outcomes,[1] which bind member states to common policy outcomes. The identification of European external action not as a temporary convergence of member states' interests, but rather as a continuous process of redefinition of member states' interests within existing institutional structures allows us to consider the export of the counter-TOC internal policy model which has 'lock-in effects'. In other words, the internal model affects the way the member states shape their external policy preferences in the field of counter-TOC international co-operation. The result is the formation of a unified position on this issue, stemming from the existence of the internal institutional structures.[2] This unified position gives the EU the ability to present itself as an actor in international negotiations where the co-operation agreements are discussed.

One aim of this chapter is to describe the model of the EU's policy against TOC, which is one of the main policies managed in the framework of the European Union Policy on Justice and Home Affairs (JHA). From the 1980s a policy model characterized by two main distinctive features developed in this field. The first feature is the approximation of the member states' criminal law and criminal procedures. The creation of minimum standards in the definition of those criminal offences that are related to organized crime, the provision of common minimum penalties and the mutual recognition of findings and judicial decisions are the instruments used to attain this goal. The second feature is judicial and police co-operation, which is developed by operational co-operation among judicial authorities and law enforcement agencies, technical co-operation among law enforcement authorities and institutionalized integration.[3]

From the early 1990s the EU began to externalize its policy, and the fight against TOC has been steadily developing. Externalization[4] is defined here as the recognition of the international dimension of the policy to combat transnational organized crime and the consequent insertion of this policy among the variables that influence the structure of the EU's political and security relationships with non-EU states. The externalization of the fight against TOC initiated a second process, whereby the EU's internal counter-TOC policy model is exported to the international system, because the EU, in structuring co-operation with non-EU countries, adopts the same models as those designed for internal co-operation on transnational crime.

The chapter also analyses the three EU international agreements that created a bi-multilateral co-operation mechanism to target TOC between the EU and the applicant Central and Eastern European Countries (CEECs), Cyprus, Russia and the Mediterranean region. This analysis seeks to determine whether the international agreements considered here reproduce forms of the EU internal policy model. It tracks corresponding provisions in the internal model and the international agreements with these external partners.

These agreements with Central and Eastern Europe and the Mediterranean area affect zones where the Union has mainly and consistently focused its external action and which, therefore, are considered truly representative of the EU's external activity.

Some preliminary terminological and conceptual specifications need to be made at the outset.

The first explanation regards the concept of security and the distinction between internal and external security. National and EU measures against organized crime have traditionally been considered to belong to the sphere of internal security, defined as the safeguard of the citizen and his or her goods within the state. The process of externalization of the policy against TOC implies a transformation in the nature of action that guarantees internal security, as defined above, to action which seeks to safeguard external security, or the protection of the state and its political, institutional and territorial structure from both outside military and non-military threats. This distinction, implied in the concept of externalization, is maintained throughout this chapter for heuristic reasons to avoid the risk of losing the explanatory and epistemic value of the concept of security. This difference, however, diminishes when the instrumentation and strategic procedures guaranteeing security are considered. The very broad nature of many of the issues relevant to security makes it difficult to categorize them in such a way as to distinguish clearly between external and internal threats. It is increasingly difficult to identify strategies according to 'internal' or 'external' aspects of security, apart from a limited number of cases that deal only with internal protection (e.g. micro criminality) or external aspects (such as the management of military relations).

The second point that needs to be clarified here relates to the scope of the analysis undertaken. The concept of externalization and the exporting process model are only analysed here with regards to policies that institutionally fall under the third pillar post-Amsterdam. Consequently, a number of issues are considered relevant including: drug traffic; terrorism; international fraud; organized crime and crimes closely connected with this including the traffic in human beings, new slave smuggling and exploitation, economic exploitation of migrants, laundering of criminal proceeds and financial and high-tech crimes.[5] Policies for managing migration are not considered because they fall under the sphere of title IV of the Treaty on European Community (TEC).

The third definition concerns the term transnational crime. The phenomenon of transnational crime cannot be defined as the emergence of a particular criminal group which, regardless of its members' nationality, works on a worldwide scale. Rather, the phenomenon is considered here as a process that determines an increasing structuring of complex and stable links between organized ethnic criminal groups,[6] which maintain their original nature but at the same time align with other ethnic groups to forge a complex network of alliances and interdependence (Williams 1994). From this view point the transnational mafia takes on the form of a network. It connects with national or ethnic groups, and makes fluid relationships, which simplify both the conduct of illegal activities and the build-up of contacts with the outside environment. The latter is usually represented by legal actors.

The co-operative model within the Union

The development of the so-called 'third pillar' among EU member states did not imply that the development of a common European system in the field of internal security would substitute for national provisions. Diversity between EU states' criminal systems has been one of the major dilemmas facing the EU and, perhaps, it will persist for many years to come. Nevertheless, the developing common policy in the JHA field has developed some specific features. Analysing key documents[7] which address the definition of the Union's Justice and Home Affairs policy makes it possible to identify a co-operative model on which the development of co-operation amongst EU member states is based.

The EU's policy for fighting against TOC rests on two 'pillars': the approximation of national criminal laws and criminal procedures and judicial and police co-operation. The first of these two pillars is articulated into two different political strategies. The first strategy consists of the creation of minimum standards in the definition of those criminal offences that are related to organized crime and the provision of common minimum penalties. This activity is essentially based on normative acts[8] which define the constitutive elements of some offences strictly connected with the organized crime and their minimum penalties,[9] and it aims at the approximation of the national criminal systems and the recent move towards the creation of common criminal law (Grasso 1998). In November 2000 the Council introduced a second strategy for implementing the judicial co-operation:

the mutual recognition of findings and judicial decisions. Mutual recognition is a principle already successfully adopted in other sectors of integration, particularly the common market completion phase. It provides a pragmatic tool for judicial co-operation, because it compensates for the slow process of approximation of national criminal legislation, which is still bound to the rule of unanimity. Thus, mutual recognition increases co-operation, even in the presence of different national criminal systems.

The second 'pillar' of the EU fight against TOC is based on the development of a stable system for the exchange of police and judicial information, technical assistance and investigative methods aiming to increase mutual confidence among police and judicial authorities and to facilitate joint investigative activities.

At the moment this system is mainly realized by the creation of networks and co-operation bodies aiming to improve joint collecting and analysis of information and data by means of computerized information exchange systems and transfrontier police co-operative measures. Europol, EUROJUST, the European Task Force of Police Chiefs and the European Police College are bodies where the harmonization of national investigative styles should be realized. Moreover, the Treaty of Nice foresees the possibility for the member states to set up 'Joint Investigative Teams'. A second goal of the police and judicial co-operation is the approximation of different national investigation strategies and equipment. It involves the training of personnel, the standardization of equipment and transmission frequencies and research in the field of investigation techniques and criminology issues.

The export of the JHA policy model and the international actorness of the European Union

The links between co-operation in matters regarding the fight against transnational crime and the Union's foreign policy date back to the origins of the member states' common activity regarding Justice and Home Affairs. The TREVI group, the first forum in which formal co-operation in the field of police action was established, was instituted in 1975 under the auspices of the European Political Cooperation (EPC). Since 1997, however, these connections have evolved into what can be defined as a process of externalization of the internal security policy. The externalization of internal security presupposes the classification of transnational crime as a threat to the integrity of the political, economic and social system of the Union. In this way, the fight against crime has moved from the area of internal public security policies to that of the Union's policy towards third countries. The year 1997 marks the beginning of the externalization process in this analysis, because that is when the high-level group on organized crime[10] produced the Action Plan to Combat Organized Crime.[11] It was then that the need to identify a specific external dimension in the fight against organized crime and to structure a specific field of co-operation with non-EU countries was stressed for the first time. The Presidency Conclusions of the Tampere European Council (EU Presidency 1999),[12] and the joint working document drafted by the Council and the Commission (EU Council 2000), are the key documents that structure an agenda for the EU's external action in the field of JHA policies. These documents identify priorities by determining both the geographic areas and the issues to be considered, the partners towards whom the external action of the Union should mainly be addressed, and the means, tools and structures with which this action must be carried out.

When we consider the modalities of the development of the externalization process of the JHA policy, it appears to be based on the establishment of co-operation agreements with third countries who have also prioritized the fight against TOC. Nevertheless, this process is not developing through the elaboration of any specific models that are bargained and designed case by case. Rather, the EU is adopting the same structure for its external co-operation that it uses in the internal co-operative model.

The three chosen international agreements between the EU and non-EU countries serve as analytical tools which demonstrate that the co-operation model adopted by the EU in the planning of its external relations remains stable in terms of its structural characteristics but varies, according to the partners, in intensity and extension. Intensity is measured by the presence or the absence of these two 'pillars' which characterize the internal model and their normative and technical implementation measures. Extension is measured by the quantity of specific issues involved in the co-operation among those considered relevant for internal JHA co-operation.

Moreover the export of the internal model is proceeding along two different pathways. The first consists of setting and implementing a specific agenda for the JHA's external action. As Malcolm Anderson (Anderson *et al.* 1995: 175) argues, the policy area inherent in JHA is to be found at a level of 'internal security issues with a potentially international dimension' in issue areas such as the exploitation of illegal immigration and the traffic of arms, drugs, nuclear and chemical materials. The strengthening of the external dimension of the policies within the sphere of Justice and Home Affairs implies a transformation from 'internal security issues with a potentially international dimension' to security issues with an international dimension. This transformation is realized by the creation of procedures and institutions that allow for stable and structured forms of co-operation with non EU countries in matters within the competence of the JHA policy.

The second pathway for externalization is represented by the uses of CFSP tools (both political and institutional) for the realization of JHA objectives. Article 38 of the Amsterdam Treaty states that the agreements signed under Article 24 can incorporate subjects that fall under Title VI. Therefore, this article permits the Council to sign agreements with non-EU countries that address JHA issues through CFSP procedures, thus formalizing the possibility for the Union to negotiate and sign international JHA agreements.[13]

The result of this double pathway is the start of a 'cross pillar' institutional approach. It is one that requires the combined use of the instruments and policies of both Title V and Title VI of the TEU.

The first agreement to be considered is the Pre-accession Pact (May 1998) on organized crime between the EU member states and the applicant CEECs and

Cyprus (OJEC n. C 220 15/07/1998), which is one of the first pathways. The Pact was formalized under the provision of Title VI.

The Pre-accession Pact aims to transfer co-operation mechanisms and standards from the EU to the applicant countries to target TOC. The plan provides for a complex model of co-operation based on both the JHA policy pillars. Moreover, it foresees the establishment of evaluation mechanisms that permit a periodic control of the status of co-operation. In particular, the plan insists that the legislation of the CEECs should be structured according to the standards foreseen for the EU member states and that, therefore, they should follow the indications supplied by the legislative decisions inherent in the JHA policy. The following commitments of the candidate countries are to be considered part of the approximation of the criminal law and criminal procedure pillar of the EU's internal model: the ratification of the international conventions recommended by the action plan on organized crime,[14] the application of the OLAF recommendations[15] in matters regarding the fight against money laundering, the adoption of laws compatible with the anti-laundering legislation being developed by the EU,[16] the development of an anti-organized crime legislation based on the basic principles stemming from the JHA legislation, protection programmes for witnesses and for individuals who co-operate with the judicial authorities during enquiries and proceedings,[17] and the ratification of the EU Convention on extradition practices in recognition of the principle '*aut dedere aut iudicare*'.[18]

The Pre-accession Pact provides for judicial and police co-operation, the 'second pillar' of the internal model as well. It foresees: continual forms of information exchange both among law enforcement agencies and judicial authorities;[19] the use of liaison officials and magistrates;[20] common investigations, also by means of setting up joint investigating groups supported by Europol, oriented towards both the solution of specific cases as well as the elaboration of long-term strategies and techniques;[21] CEECs' commitment to respect the indications of the JHA Council's common action on the best practice on mutual legal assistance;[22] and mutual assistance in the training and activity of personnel.[23] The co-operation assumes an institutionalized character. In fact, not only is the adherence of the CEECs and Cyprus to the Europol convention foreseen, but so are stable and institutionalized fora of co-operation[24] and the control and evaluation of the results.[25] The number of issues provided for by the pact is high, giving it a high degree of extension. Co-operation is provided for issues regarding organized crime, crimes connected with drug trafficking, money laundering, corruption, trafficking in human beings and organized illegal immigration.

The text of the pact shows another aspect of the relations between the EU and the CEECs with regards to the fight against organized crime. The CEECs seem to have agreed to reconstruct national law enforcement and public prosecution services according to the model that the JHA policy has identified as efficient in dealing with the threat posed by organized crime. This model, mainly identified in the Action Plan on Organized Crime, is based on principles of centralization and specialization of the judicial and law enforcement services and on the provision for an investigative and procedural model valid only for criminal offences connected with organized crime. In the Pre-accession Pact the CEECs commit themselves to: instituting central judicial and police bodies which have the task of elaborating the national policy against organized crime and of co-ordinating the relevant national operational activities; creating national contact points dedicated exclusively to information exchange on organized crime issues; structuring a network designed to put the magistrates entrusted with the fight against organized crime in contact; organizing integrated and multidisciplinary investigative groups[26] and investigative units specialized in financial crime and in the fight against money laundering.[27] The CEECs, moreover, recognize the validity of the investigative techniques that the JHA policy considers efficient, for example undercover operations, controlled deliveries and electronic surveillance.[28]

The Pre-accession Pact is an instrument of the broader enlargement negotiations. The adoption of the Justice and Home Affairs *acquis* by applicant countries is one of the non-negotiable and most sensitive areas of the enlargement process. Applicant countries are requested to adopt the full JHA *acquis* without the possibility of bargaining on the contents of the rules. This is justified by the need to safeguard the JHA *acquis* and by the need to establish an 'area of freedom, security and justice' throughout the Union. Because compromises or concessions are not possible in the JHA policy, the CEECs' criminal systems are being shaped with the features adopted by the EU.

EU enlargement is not the only variable explaining the transfer of the EU model towards third countries. The export of the JHA model towards CEECs is characterized by the highest degree of intensity and extension, because it covers the same issues considered in the internal policy and provides for the same normative and technical instruments adopted by the member states for their internal co-operation. Nevertheless, the EU is transferring the JHA model towards third countries that are not involved in the pre-accession process.

The 'Common Strategy on Russia' (OJEC L 157, 24–26.1999, pp. 1–9) and the following 'Action Plan Against Organized Crime in Russia' (EU Council 1999) are another result of the second strategy of externalization. In fact, they were adopted in the frame of Title V of the TEU. The aim of both documents is to address the fight against organized crime in the EU-Russia relations and to provide for a common strategy and common instruments for combating organized crime, the laundering of 'dirty money' and trafficking in human beings and drugs. Again, the EU-Russia co-operation in fighting TOC appears to be shaped by the same characteristics as those of the EU internal model. The Common Strategy and the Action Plan establish forms of co-operation based mainly on the 'second pillar' of the JHA policy. In fact, the approximation of criminal law and criminal procedure is not explicitly mentioned in the texts, even though both documents highlight all the necessary measures for structuring the Russian legal system according to a model that simplifies Russian co-operation with the member states. The action plan[29] aims at 'strengthening judicial and law enforcement co-operation' and at helping Russia to develop a 'legislative framework and other means required to provide co-operation to other countries' with aid from the EU. Moreover the EU commits itself to facilitate the adhesion of Russia to the international legislative provisions that discipline the fight against international crime and the criminal offences connected with it. In the follow up meeting of the EU-Russia Troika JHA-Ministers, held in Stockholm on 6 April 2001, it was agreed to establish an EU-Russia working group on judicial co-operation in criminal matters. The working group is entrusted with the task of analysing some basic issues permitting the Russian judicial reform to move towards the EU's standard. In fact this bilateral group should work on common definitions of offences, a common police manual and the establishment of contact points.

Even if these provisions do not directly result in the harmonization of Russian and EU criminal law they will, undoubtedly, increase the compatibility of the EU penal legislation with the Russian system. The ratification of international instruments will establish common minimum standards diminishing diversity.[30] Nevertheless, the Common Strategy and the Action Plan have mainly focused on police and judicial co-operation, which seeks to transfer expertise and training methods. In particular, the Common Action outlines a number of sectors for co-operation with Russia in developing specific investigative techniques with respect to organized crime and the criminal offences connected with it; assistance with training in both the judicial and investigative fields; the development of close and stable co-operation between EUROPOL and the competent Russian authorities; the setting up of channels of contact and information exchange to be realized by means of the creation of a mechanism of constant dialogue between liaison officials; and central contact points. In the follow up to Stockholm officials agreed to 'twin' EU-Russian magistrates and to use the Tacis financing for assisting the Academy of Justice and other relevant training institutes, as well as selected regional courts, as part of a large training and re-training programme.

These provisions aim to push along Russian reforms of the judicial and police system by creating formal and informal working groups which foster ties between European and Russian experts, civil servants, police and magistrates elites. European expertise and the established habit of internal co-operation permit the EU to play the rule-maker role in these groups. The EU is also able to export the European police and judicial model because the Russian police and judicial system, particularly with regard to the fight against organized crime, are in a development phase.

The extension of the Common Action and the Action Plan cover all areas included in the co-operation agreement including: organized crime, corruption, money laundering, drug trafficking, trafficking in human beings, arms and stolen goods trafficking, exploitation of clandestine immigration and illicit economic activity.

The 'Common Strategy on the Mediterranean', approved by the Santa Maria de Feira Council in June 2000 in the legal framework of Title V, establishes the contents, the objectives and the means that characterize the relations between the EU and Mediterranean non-EU countries. It emphasizes JHA co-operation between the EU and signatories of the Barcelona Process. Again, the emphasis is on joint responses to terrorism, organized crime and drug trafficking, which are defined as global challenges to security. This Common Strategy describes a co-operative model with a high degree of extension. It extends co-operation to almost all the sectors in the competence of JHA including terrorism, organized crime, drug trafficking,[31] clandestine immigration organizations, trafficking in human beings[32] and money laundering.[33] The Common Strategy offers assistance for training judiciary personnel and law enforcement officers, who are thus kept up-to-date with information on the community *acquis* regarding organized crime, and offers EU collaboration with the Mediterranean partners in developing national enquiry and judicial systems capable of efficiently combating transnational organized crime and the criminal offences closely connected to it.

As in the case of the common strategy for Russia, the EU offers Mediterranean partners its know-how for facilitating the development of an efficient police and judicial system able to fight against TOC. In doing so, it transfers its investigative and organizational style and techniques. In this case, the main instrument for exporting the internal model is structured co-operation, or the establishment of stable inter-regional dialogues, common bodies and programmes. In addition, the European Commission proposed the creation of a JHA regional co-operation programme (EU Council 2001).

The EU's contribution to structuring JHA policy in the Mediterranean is also a result of the bilateral agreements under the Euro Mediterranean Partnerships.[34] JHA policies feature in a large number of these agreements. The Euro-Med Association Agreement with Lebanon contains commitments on judicial co-operation and respect for the rule of law, and requires parties to respect international rules on money laundering and on combating organized crime and illicit drugs. Eight million Euros has been committed since 2000 for a programme that supports the modernization of the Algerian Police Force, and the Euro Mediterranean Agreement between the EU and Algeria has specific clauses covering co-operation for money laundering, corruption, bank secrecy and drug trafficking. In 2000, the European Commission approved a project for reforming justice in the framework of the MEDA Agreement with Morocco and financed it with 27.6 million Euros.

While attention in the Russian case is focused primarily on the fight against crime and on the necessity to reduce the diversity of juridical and penal systems, the main priorities of Euro-Mediterranean JHA co-operation seem to be the establishment of a common 'dictionary' in the field of law and the development of stable bodies to provide assistance in the training of law enforcement personnel and judges in the Mediterranean region. Official documents and meetings[35] stress the necessity to create a common ground on the significance of some basic principles of the law, such as the 'rule of law', the 'promotion of equal access to justice', the 'independence of the judiciary' and the 'right to legal assistance' in order to promote 'l'emergence d'une culture juridique communne' (European Commission 2001).

Table 9.1 Intensity and extension of JHA co-operation agreements

	Intensity	*Extension*
Pre-accession Pact	Approximation of criminal law and procedures; judicial and police co-operation	Organized crime, drug trafficking, money laundering, corruption, trafficking in human beings, organized illegal immigration
Common strategy on Russia	Judicial and police co-operation	Organized crime, corruption, money laundering, drug trafficking, trafficking in human beings, arms and stolen goods trafficking, exploitation of clandestine immigration, illicit economic activity
Common strategy on Med.	Judicial and police co-operation	Terrorism, organized crime, drug trafficking, exploitation of clandestine immigration, trafficking in human beings, money laundering

Conclusion

The EU's international actorness, defined as the EU's capability to act as an 'international actor' is a controversial issue. One of the focal points of the debate is to identify what the 'EU's external action' is. As Martin Holland (1999) points out, the terms 'EU foreign policy' and the 'EU external relations' do not match. Foreign policy strictly refers to the process of co-operation that has developed since the establishment of EPC, which began in the 1970s and developed through the CFSP up to the most recent European Security and Defence Policy (ESDP). It has been described as 'co-ordination of the foreign policies of member states' (White 1999) or as a 'process of integrating policies and actions of the member states' (Ginsberg 1989).

The broader term 'external relations' refers to the EU's activities towards third countries. It covers a broad area of 'interpillar' and 'cross pillar' actions: foreign policy, common trade, economic aid, development policy, association agreements, economic sanctions, and all forms of the most recent co-operation agreements in which the EU incorporates economic, political, social, cultural and human affairs.[36]

In this perspective the EU anti-crime policy affects the international activity of the European Union on two levels. The first level concerns the foreign policy realm, in which the JHA policy is an integral part of the security guarantees for EU territory and society. The variables that motivate this phenomenon are exogenous and endogenous to the Union's political system.

The first exogenous process regards the transnationalization of organized crime. The discovery that ethnic mafia groups act in a stable way in territories other than their countries of origin or that they interact with other 'ethnic' groups according to a model of co-operation (by, for example, subdividing tasks) has led policy-makers to take notice. Traditionally this phenomenon was only considered to be an internal problem, specific to just a few national political systems. A second exogenous process is the international system's assumption that the phenomenon of transnational crime is a threat to the security of states. The consequent inclusion of the fight against criminal networks in the global security agenda is demonstrated by the fact that the majority of the official documents today include organized crime among the new threats facing states.[37]

The Union's endogenous processes can be identified in the evolution of the European integration process. On the one hand it extends the geographical borders to areas perceived as sources of insecurity because of the weakness of the institutions of the countries that are part of them. On the other hand, it increasingly widens the scope of the policies within its competence and intensifies the systemic constraints on the governance capabilities of the member states, both in the field of sectoral policies and in that of external and security political relations.

The second level concerns the extension of external relations to JHA policy. The fight against transnational crime has changed from an internal policy, seen as the security of the individual on Union territory, into a composite policy, seen as the security of the Union as a political system and relevant to the structuring of external relations. This is particularly the case in areas which expose the EU's vulnerability to transnational criminal networks.

At both levels the EU's external co-operation against transnational crime is structured by agreements which are based on internal policy models. The analysis of the three international agreements considered in this chapter shows that the models vary only in the intensity of co-operation, which in some cases is extensive and in others limited to some specific issues. However, the structure of the co-operation (since TREVI at Amsterdam) is based on the model that has characterized the co-operation on JHA issues between the member states.

In this perspective, the EU exports endogenous policy models to the outside world, and influences both the structuring of global co-operative processes which target transnational crime and the restructuring of national police and judicial and law enforcement systems in some countries, such as the CEECs, which are undergoing political and institutional reconstructions.

By considering 'international actorness' as a structured presence, it could be argued that JHA co-operation between the EU and third countries, which consolidates internal policy models, is playing an important role in providing incentives and opportunities for EU international presence. First, JHA policy represents an additional variable that increases the contents of the EU's external relations' agenda, thereby broadening the issue-domains of international activity. In this case, JHA co-operation boosts the objective level of EU actorness, asserted by the mobilization of EU economic and political resources engaged in the export activity.

Second, the possession of economic and political resources – experience, knowledge and consolidated institutional structures – permits the EU to play a leading role in the definition of the shapes and models used for international co-operation in the fight against transnational crime. In this case, the export of the internal JHA model reinforces the subjective level of actorness by expanding the source of the EU's perceived relevance in the international arena.

Notes

1 The official label of the normative policy outcomes varies from pillar to pillar. In the case of the first pillar the main normative instruments are directives and decisions. In the case of the second pillar they are common strategies, joint action and common positions. In the case of the third pillar they are common positions, framework decisions and decisions.
2 Here an institution is intended as the formal or informal procedures, norms, rules and bodies that are active in the policy (Pierson 1996).
3 For a deeper analysis of this model see Longo (2002).
4 The term 'externalization' has been introduced into EU theoretical analysis by Schmitter (1971). He developed an 'externalization hypothesis' in order to explain the importance of the external environment in creating common institutions and the role of interaction between Member States and the international system in stimulating closer integration of those states. In this chapter the term is used with a different meaning.
5 This list of issues is taken from the provisions of Title VI of the Treaty on European Union and from all the other documents relevant to the JHA policy.
6 The study of organized crime is often based on the classification of criminal groups on the basis of their geographical origins, rather than on the nature of the illicit activity. On this point see Albanese (1989), and Mcillwain (1999).
7 These documents are the Action Plan Against Organized Crime (OJEC C 97 pp. 1–18), the Conclusions of the Tampere European Council (15–16 October 1999) and the following Action Plan, and the new action plan valid until 2005, titled 'The Prevention and Control of Organized Crime: a European Union strategy for the beginning of the New Millennium' (OJEC, C 124, 3 May 2000: 1–33).
8 The 'framework decisions', Art. 34.b TUE
9 Some examples include: common action making it a criminal offence to participate in a criminal organization in the EU member states, common action on corruption in the private sector and one on money laundering, the identification, tracing, freezing, seizing and confiscation of instrumentalities and the proceeds from crime.
10 The 'HLG on International Crime' was instituted by the European Council of Dublin in December 1996.
11 The 'Action Plan to combat organized crime' was subsequently approved by the European Council of Amsterdam in June 1997 (OJEC C 251, 15-8-1997). This is the document on which the development of Union policy on this question is based. For an analysis of the 'Action Plan' see Longo and Strano (1999).
12 5–16 October 1999. For the complete texts of the Presidency conclusions relating to the meetings of the European Councils see the site: http://ue.eu.int/presid/conclusions.htm
13 From a formal point of view, the agreements are signed by the EC, not by the EU. The latter in fact does not have juridical status and consequently cannot sign international agreements. On the occasion of the signing of international documents regarding issues within the competence of the CFSP or the JHA, the signatories for the European Union are the EC and the member states.
14 See Principle no.2 of the Pre-accession Pact.
15 OLAF: European anti-Fraud Office, which belongs to the European Commission.
16 See Principle no. 13 of the Pre-accession Pact.
17 See Principle no. 7 of the Pre-accession Pact.
18 See Principle no.10 of the Pre-accession Pact.
19 See Principles nos. 3 and 4 of the Pre-accession Pact.

20 See Principle no. 13 of the Pre-accession Pact.
21 See Principles nos. 5 and 6 of the Pre-accession Pact.
22 See Principle no. 9 of the Pre-accession Pact.
23 See Principle no. 6 of the Pre-accession Pact.
24 This is the case with the regular consultation mechanism on the fight against corruption provided for by Principle no. 12 between the competent authorities of third countries and the European Commission and the European Council.
25 This is the case of the evaluation group on the co-operation status provided for by Principle no. 15.
26 See Principle nos. 3 and 5 of the Pre-accession Pact.
27 See Principle no.13 of the Pre-accession Pact.
28 See Principle no. 6 of the Pre-accession Pact.
29 In April 2000, the EU-Russia Co-operation Council endorsed a Joint Action Plan to fight organized crime.
30 In the framework of the Central European Initiative (CEI), the CEI conference of the Ministers of Justice adopted the 'Trieste Declaration' on judicial co-operation and legislative harmonization, which commits them to promote harmonization of criminal law and criminal procedures. Even if the Russian Federation is not a member of the CEI, it participated at the Trieste conference as a guest of the Presidency.
31 Part III, point 13 and point 22 of the Common Strategy.
32 Part III, point 22 of the Common Strategy.
33 Part III, point 22 of the Common Strategy.
34 The MEDA bilateral agreements and the Euro Mediterranean Bilateral Association Agreement are the principal financial instruments of the European Union for the implementation of the Euro-Mediterranean Partnership. In both cases the agreements offer technical and financial support measures to accompany the reform of economic and social structures in the Mediterranean partners.
35 An *ad hoc* meeting of senior officials was held in Montpellier in June 2001 for launching a stable dialogue on JHA policy among 27 Euro-Mediterranean partners and a conference on 'access to justice' was held in Uppsala in April 2001. For their preparatory papers and conclusions see the Monthly Calendars of the Barcelona process, European Commission, DG External Relations (unit F.1).
36 Euro-Mediterranean Partnership, EU-Russia co-operation, and the Cotonou Agreement are some examples.
37 See, for example, the NATO 'Washington Declaration' and the OSCE 'Charter for European Security'.

References

Albanese, J. (1989) *Organized Crime in America*, 3rd edn, Cincinnati: Anderson Pub. Company.

Allen, D. and Smith, M. (1990) 'Western Europe's Presence in the Contemporary International Arena', *Review of International Studies*, 16, 1: 19–37.

Anderson, M., den Boer, M., Cullen, P., Gilmore, W., Raab, C. and Walker, N. (1995) *Policing the European Union*, Clarendon Press: Oxford.

Bulmer, S. (1991) 'Analysing European Political Co-operation: the Case for two-tier Analysis', in M. Holland, (ed.) *The Future of European Political Co-operation: Essays on Theory and Practice,* London: Macmillan.

Caporaso, J. and Jupille, J. (1998) 'States, Agency and Rules: the EU in Global Environmental Politics', in C. Rhodes (ed.), *The European Union in the World Community*, Boulder: Lynne Rienner.

European Commission, External Relation DG (2001) *La Formation des Praticiens du Droit dans l'Espace Euro-Méditerranéen comme Element de Contribution a l'Etat de Droit*, Monthly Calendars of the Barcelona process, Brussels.

EU Council (1999) Document no. 13009/1/99, Brussels.

EU Council (2000) *European Union Priorities and Policy Objectives for External Relations in the Field of Justice and Home Affairs*, Document no. 7653/00, Brussels.

EU Council (2001) *Report from the Council to the European Council on the Implementation of the Common Strategy in the Mediterranean Region*, Press release, no. 9124/01, Brussels.

EU Presidency (1999) *Enhanced and More Coherent External Action of the Union in the Field of Justice and Home Affairs*, SI(99) 762 – Annexe SN 3664/99.

Ginsberg, R. (1989) 'Narrowing the Capability-Expectation Gap', *Journal of Common Market Studies,* 37, 3: 429–454.

Grasso, G. (1998) 'La Formazione di un Diritto Penale dell'Unione Europea', in G. Grasso (ed.) *Prospettive di un Diritto Penale Europeo*, Milan: Giuffrè.

Hill, C. (1993) 'The Capability-Expectations Gap, or Conceptualizing Europe's International Role', *Journal of Common Market Studies,* 31, 3: 305–328.

Hix, S. (1999) *The Political System of the European Union*, London: MacMillan Press.

Holland, M. (1999) 'The Common Foreign and Security Policy', in L. Cram, M. Dinan and N. Nugent (eds) *Developments in the European Union*, London: MacMillan.

Longo, F. (2002) 'Shaping the Political Model of the EU Policy for Combating Transnational Organized Crime', in F. Longo (ed.) *The European Union and the Challenge of Transnational Organized Crime. Towards a Common Police and Judicial Approach,* Milan: Giuffrè.

Longo, F. and Strano, A. (1999) *Criminalità senza Frontiere. Le Istituzioni Internazionali di Lotta alla Criminalità Internazionale*, Catania: Bonnano.

Mcillwain, J. S. (1999) 'Organized Crime: a Social Network Approach', *Crime, Law and Social Change,* 4: 301–323.

Nuttall, S. (1997) 'The Commission and the Foreign Policy-Making', in G. Edwards and D. Spence (eds) *The European Commission*, 2nd edn, London: Catermill.

Pierson, P. (1996) 'The Path to European Integration: an Historical Institutionalist Perspective', *Comparative Political Studies,* 29: 95–146.

Schmitter, P.C. (1971) 'A Revisited Theory of European Integration' in L.N. Lindberg and J.A. Scheingold (eds) *Regional Integration: Theory and Research*, Cambridge: Cambridge University Press.

White, B. (1999) 'European Challenge to Foreign Policy Analysis', *European Journal of International Relations,* 5, 1: 37–66.

Williams, P. (1994) *Transnational Criminal Organisations: Strategic Alliances,* Washington Quarterly: Ridgway Center's Publications.

10 A challenge for the commons
EU[1] fisheries management in international arenas[α]

Marta A. Ballesteros

We have only one globe with which to experiment.

(Ostrom *et al.* 1999)

Introduction

The European Union (EU) has established major institutional changes that shape the way member states manage their common pool resources (CPRs). Contrary to the worldwide tendency to decentralize or share control over the management of natural resources, the EU is moving towards a centralized system to govern highly diverse ecological phenomena. Currently, however, little or no systematic attention has been paid to the role of the EU as a common pool resource manager and its outcomes in international and local arenas. What impact does the EU have in CPR management? Do current theories and approaches adequately explain it? What does this imply about the larger role that the EU plays in the world?

Fisheries resources have, among CPRs, a prominent international dimension. The scope of fisheries arenas in which the EU is involved ranges from bilateral agreements to regional and international organizations. Understanding how the EU affects world fisheries management requires two analytical levels: first, the EU is an actor that changes the patterns of interaction in the international arena; second, the EU is itself an arena in which multiple actors shape its international role. This essay identifies the main changes arising from the EU's international presence and examines how its role is shaped internally. Analysing those changes and their observable political effects will highlight how the EU affects world fisheries management.

Using the Institutional Analysis and Development Framework (IAD), we analyse the impact of the EU in world fisheries management. This chapter is organized as follows. The first section covers the analytical framework, and the second briefly describes the international dimension of fisheries. The third section analyses the EU's policy instrument for fisheries management, the Common Fisheries Policy. Finally, we draw a picture of the EU's international role in fisheries management. The conclusion discusses challenges for the EU.

The theoretical framework

The Institutional Analysis and Development (IAD) framework provides meta-theoretical tools to guide the diagnosis of institutions and their effects on policy outcomes. It directs the study of institutions by identifying key variables that jointly affect patterns of interaction in *action arenas* (Ostrom *et al.* 1994) defined as 'the social space[s] within [which] individuals interact-exchange goods and services, solve problems, dominate one other, or fight' (Ostrom 1998: 68). Action arenas 'include an *action situation* and the *actors* in that situation' (Ostrom 1999a: 41). The structure of an *action situation* is identified according to various situational variables such as the types of participants, their positions, actions, information and outcomes. Preferences, resources, information processing capabilities and selection criteria characterize actors. Action situation and actors then form the action arenas, which are shaped broadly by attributes of the physical world, attributes of the larger community and the different rules, or institutions, used in each setting (Kiser and Ostrom 1982).[2] They jointly affect 'the types of actions that individuals can take, the benefits and costs of these actions and resulting outcomes and the likely outcomes achieved' (Ostrom 1999a: 50).

We find the IAD to be a useful framework for examining the international role of the EU in CPRs management due to its unique focus on multiple levels of institutions, as well as the factors that shape institutional outcomes. In fact, 'since the late 1980s, the IAD has been used as the language to develop a theory of common-pool resources' (Ostrom 1999a: 59), focusing primarily on CPR management on a small-scale.[3] Over the last decade this research advanced efforts both to link theoretical approaches in international and local arenas, and to analyse institutional responses to global dilemmas such as climate change (McGinnis and Ostrom 1992, 1996; Keohane and Ostrom 1995).[4]

The questions posed in this chapter reiterate the relevance of the IAD's variable set. The attributes of the physical world (international fisheries), attributes of the larger community and a priori rules do not change with the EU's incorporation in fisheries management. What changes is that the EU redefines the structure of the situation externally with its presence as an international actor. On the other hand, the EU shapes its international role internally, as an arena in which member states – prior international actors in fisheries matters themselves – interact with the European institutions to conform to that role.

The EU presents a big puzzle in terms of scale, arena and scope of activities. Neither a state nor an international organization, the EU involves: i) differential patterns of internal and international co-operation and conflict; ii) a multi-level system of governance not captured by either international anarchy or national sovereignty.

Why are those aspects relevant? Noonan (1998) has from a comparative perspective analysed the institutional effectiveness of the EU's Common Fisheries Policy (CFP) and the South Pacific Forum Fisheries Agency (FFA). Two main problems constrain that comparison: i) the EU is not an international organization – it is more a supra-national entity of governance, with economic, political and social realms that go far beyond fisheries; ii) if we just focus on fisheries, the EU is attempting to manage not only fisheries stocks but also distribution of quotas and access control. EU fisheries policy also covers structural policies, market, employment and so on. None of the other fisheries bodies[5] do that. Furthermore, the EU is itself a member of those fisheries bodies. The particular features of the EU are relevant in terms of shaping institutional outcomes. Examining this relationship in the framework of existing theories could provide a more comprehensive approach both theoretically and empirically.

As a starting point, it is important to identify what kind of institutional situation we are dealing with. Briefly, we have an actor (the EU) managing a common pool resource (fisheries) in the international sphere. From a general perspective, the EU altered the structure of the situation, the number and heterogeneity of actors involved and their incentives, the decision-making process and even the markets. Clearly, this is a first step in understanding how the EU affects world fisheries management. Therefore, the purpose of the following institutional analysis is twofold. First, it seeks to identify the main changes in the international arena derived from the EU's presence. Second, it examines how the EU's role in that arena is shaped internally. Prior to this analysis, the IAD framework points out the importance of defining the characteristics of fisheries as CPRs, given their relevance for understanding institutional choices to govern these resources (Ostrom *et al.* 1994).

Common pool resources

Common pool resources[6] refer to a 'natural or man-made resource system from which it is difficult to exclude or limit users once the resource is provided, and one person's consumption of resource units makes those units unavailable to others' (Ostrom 1999b: 497).[7] The oceanic ecosystems, from which fish are harvested, are a CPR. For centuries, the number of fishermen in the oceans was significantly less than the productive capacity of the resource. However, technological developments in the twentieth century led to an increase in both the number of fishermen and fishing capacities. When the quantity of fish withdrawn from an ocean ecosystem threatens the sustainable yield, collapse or depletion of the resource is the likely outcome. In fact, that is the case with many fish stocks in the world's oceans.

The attributes of CPRs and the kind of incentives that they generate for resource users help explain the depletion of fisheries stocks. Overappropriation and free riding are at the core of CPR problems. The subtractability[8] of the resource, together with overuse, leads to the exploitation of the CPR beyond optimal or safe yield. Subtractability implies, for instance, that the fish caught by a fisherman are no longer available for other fishermen. In addition, 'the fish in the sea are valueless to the fisherman, because there is no assurance that they will be there tomorrow if they are left behind today' (Gordon 1954: 135). When the CPR is a renewable resource, such as fisheries, that process could lead to the destruction of the resource itself (Keohane and Ostrom 1995: 13). Free riding problems arise due to the difficulty of exclusion. In CPRs 'users free ride when they harvest from or dump pollutants into the resource independently, and take only their own costs and benefits into account' (Ostrom *et al.* 2002: 19).[9]

The CPR characteristics imply that unless there are some kind of rules governing access and use, individuals will have incentives to overuse the resource – as has been the case with many world fisheries. As a result, some scholars have argued that individuals are unable to manage a CPR, and are somehow trapped through these incentives into the 'tragedy of the commons' (Hardin 1968). The predicted outcome is the depletion of the resource itself by users. (The main policy recommendations derived from such assumptions are privatization or control by an external agency.)

Studies using the IAD framework, however, have taken a different approach to understanding how best to govern shared resources (Ostrom 1990) and how CPR problems can be overcome. As a result, empirical evidence strongly supports the conclusion that 'overuse and destruction of CPRs is not a determinant and inescapable outcome when multiple users face a commons dilemma' (Ostrom 1999a: 495). By examining in detail the action arenas of various CPR situations around the world, the IAD studies have helped identify various attributes of institutional arrangements, as well as the actors and physical settings that are more likely to be associated with the successful governance of CPRs. For instance, among these institutional attributes are clearly defined boundaries and rules that are appropriate to local supply and demand conditions, which are often associated with successful governance (Ostrom 1990). Where such local institutions exist, they are more successful when nested within larger-level institutions. The size of the resource and the number and heterogeneity of actors are, among the other physical or actor attributes, known to shape CPR outcomes. However, most of the attributes of effective CPR institutions have been identified by studies of small-scale CPR governance, rather than large-scale regimes like the EU. How then do we analyse the role of the EU in managing a large-scale CPR resource such as fisheries? In the following sections we use the IAD to further evaluate the structure of the action situation affecting EU fisheries as a common pool resource.

Fisheries management: the international dimension

Fisheries management on a large scale has been absent throughout history. This can be attributed to two complementary sources: an abundance of fish in the seemingly endless oceans, and a convergence of opinion around the notion that oceans were an open access resource to be used by all to the exclusion of none. Degradation and potential destruction are the likely outcomes when a CPR is left to an open access regime (Ostrom *et al.* 1999: 279).

The extension of the Exclusive Economic Zones (EEZs) of coastal states to 200 miles in the 1970s[10] limited the doctrine of the freedom of the seas. This redefinition of boundaries led to a new allocation of resources and the possibility of exclusion, transforming some international CPRs into national ones. Although an enormous part of marine stocks falls under EEZ areas (Soroos 1988: 15), the necessity of international co-operation in fisheries management

is still relevant and somehow reinforced. Peterson (1993: 10) offers three explanations that support this argument: straddling[11] and migrating stocks, and that
developing countries lack the administrative capacity to address the problem. In
addition, we argue that distant water fleets were driven out of numerous fisheries grounds, putting pressure on the high seas that remain open access, at the
EEZs' borders, and on developing countries to open access to their now exclusive areas.

This process of 'regulating the sea' could be analysed as a reactive response
to both the evolution of world fisheries stocks and conflicts among users.
Although the situation pointed to the necessity of reducing fishing effort and
devising institutional mechanisms to govern ocean fisheries, the clear distributional effects of any fisheries regulation slowed down the process. Attempts to
promote international collaboration were strongly affected by individual states'
conflicting interests. For instance, Peterson (1993: 7) identifies four domestic
patterns that yielded severe reluctance to adjust fishing capacities: i) privately-
owned distant water fleets exerting pressure on their governments to retain or
expand fishing opportunities; ii) governments with state-owned distant water
fleets; iii) developing countries' view of fisheries as a new opportunity for
industrial development; iv) pressures from coastal fleets looking for governmental protection measures against competition from distant water fleets.
Moreover, even when states agree to co-operate under a particular fisheries
body, conflicts arise leading to individual or collective withdrawal from the
organization, and even to serious confrontations using gunboat diplomacy (see
Baden 1996).

Today the massive effort of global management – articulated under the
International Law of the Sea Treaty and further developments – is combined with
a series of *ad hoc* arrangements at the regional level, through fisheries bodies that
widely vary in their properties and success. All of them constitute institutional
arrangements to govern CPRs, or the oceanic ecosystems from which fish is harvested. They try to regulate the access and use of the resource, and their outcomes
can be evaluated by analysing the institutional settings that they devised (see
Peterson 1993; Hanna 1998; Noonan 1998). The attempts to overcome free riding
and overfishing are their underlying goals. In a progressive way, the international
community has devised mechanisms to limit the use of the resource in the oceans'
fisheries that remain open access[12] or to prosecute 'flags of convenience' practices. Furthermore, fisheries bodies such as NAFO have reinforced their binding
capacities.

However, despite the growing development of international fisheries management and the redistribution of resources under exclusive coastal states, the overall
situation of fisheries stocks in the world is somehow discouraging (Hanna
1998[13]). In addition to the classical problems identified in the literature, Wilson
(Wilson *et al.* 1994, 2002) points out that scientific uncertainty has a key role in
this situation. Finally issues such as biodiversity, ecosystem health, or food security are receiving growing attention, bringing more complexity to fisheries
governance (Hanna 1998: 258).

Current EU members, as individual states, participated in international fisheries management according to their own interest, being members of different fisheries bodies, having divergent concerns about fisheries areas. To illustrate this point Table 10.1 (p. 186) depicts membership of member states in fisheries bodies, and Table 10.2 (p. 187) shows their participation in major international fisheries agreements. However, since the EU assumed exclusive competencies in fisheries matters (see below) fisheries management has changed. It has changed not only for member states, but also for the international community. The following section analyses three main changes in both international and European arenas.

The EU: changes in the action arena of world fisheries management

The European integration process is characterized by a re-allocation of authority. An extensive literature and research agenda has analysed that process, focusing on multi-level governance (Hooghe and Marks 2001), multi-level European problem solving (Scharpf 1999, 2001) or the integration outcomes in national policy-making (Héritier 2001). What seems clear across those fields is that co-operation in the EU is highly nested in institutions that severely limit the exit options of member states (Gehring, cited in Börzel 2000:6).

How does this affect the structure of the situation in international fisheries management? Fisheries policy is an EU exclusive competence, which implies that the EU replaces some member states in fisheries bodies. However, the EU *represents* the 15 member states, including those land-locked states that were previously absent from fisheries arenas. Replacement by the EU also precludes the opt-out option of individual member states from fisheries bodies. It seems clear that the EU's economic power redefines the asymmetries among states involved in international fisheries; but there is also a redefinition of traditional strategic alliances among states. In addition, the broader international agenda of the EU, including environmental leadership, trade and aid development policies, affects fisheries issues.

How is the structure of the situation defined in the European action arena? Fisheries fall under the EU's 'first pillar', referring to issues that are covered directly by the EC Treaty. As with other policies in the first pillar (see introduction to this volume), the fisheries policy allocates authority at different levels in the four branches of the CFP. The EU has exclusive powers regarding conservation, management and markets, although some powers are shared with the member states, or are still under their competence, as in structural policy and control. The institutional interplay and joint decision-making process (see below) determine the positions held by the EU in international forums. Moreover, the fact that both the EU and the individual 15 member states are present in international agreements under the framework of the International Law of the Sea reflects the distribution of competences regarding not only fisheries matters but also other related issues.

One of the main struggles in the analysis of the EU is linked with the nature of actors that participate in the European and international arenas. We could categorize the EU as a collective actor of corporate actors. States have been studied in international relationships as collective entities, designed as the agents for complex publics, with interactive behaviours formed in both intricate and unpredictable domestic processes (Young 1995: 31–32; McGinnis and Ostrom 1996: 471). These complex domestic processes are exacerbated by the distribution of authority between the EU and the member states, concerning aspects of sovereignty at the very end.

The EU visibly changes the number of actors involved in international fisheries management but this change is twofold. In the international arena, the number of actors is reduced since the 15 member states fall under the umbrella of the EU elected delegate in fisheries matters, which speaks with one voice. But in the European arena the number of actors increases, because the 15 member states are joined by the European institutions (the Commission, the Council, the Parliament and the Court of Justice, etc.). The nature of the actors involved has also changed. Institutions like the European Commission or the Council of Ministers became new spaces to deal with conflict and co-operation.

The increased number of actors involved in fisheries policies is linked to the heterogeneity of actors, in terms of preferences, capabilities and so on. At a minimum, the EU reduces heterogeneity in the international arena internalizing it through its domestic process. In an idealized situation, the EU interacts with other international actors as a single body, characterized by its 'unitary' capabilities, that is interest, information and so on. But the effects of heterogeneities inside the EU cannot be ignored, since these are at the core of the EU's international actorness. Once Pandora's Box opens, the degree of homogeneity/heterogeneity of the EU is related to the issue of concern. In terms of fishery policy, heterogeneity crosses all dimensions from the divergence in member states' fisheries interests to the position of the Commission or the Council in international negotiations.

The EU's fisheries management: the Common Fisheries Policy (CFP)

The institutional structure of the CFP places the management of fisheries resources at the European level, creating a highly centralized system. The CFP is organized in four policy areas – resources, structural policy, market, and external policy – and has an asymmetric allocation of competences among member states and European institutions (see above).

Inside the EU, the fisheries policy relies on the joint mode of decision-making (Scharpf 1999, 2001). The joint-decision mode is characterized by the strong role of the Commission and reinforced by its legislative initiative. Although the veto positions of member states have been reduced by the translation of policy arenas under the qualified majority decision rules, 'at the end of the legislative process, European policies still depend on the support of a large majority of the weighted votes of member governments in the Council' (Scharpf 2001: 8: see also Figure 10.1).

The general puzzle of EU's fisheries management has two clear dimensions – internal and external – although both are interdependent. Furthermore, the policy instrument designed to deal with the two dimensions is the same: the Common

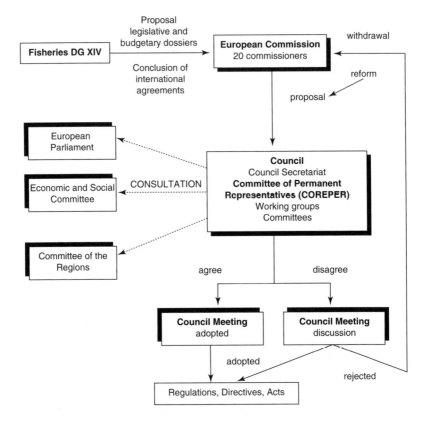

Figure 10.1 Decision-making process in the fisheries policy
Source: Mahou (2001:12); consultation depends on the character of the proposal.

Fisheries Policy (CFP). Nevertheless, the EU seems to be developing diverse orientations to its internal and external fisheries policies,[14] each based on different
institutional arrangements.[15]

The CFP, a critical review

The CFP has attracted vigorous critique among scholars from biological to economic and social fields (Crean and Symes 1994; Sandberg 1994; Noonan 1998;
Bailly and Collet 1999; Payne 2000; Grieve 2001; Imeson and Van den Bergh,
2002).[16] The main criticisms vary in emphasis and focus. The failure of conservation measures, manifested by the resource situation in the EU's waters, and the
failure of structural policies, blamed on subsidized overfishing through the EU
and national governments' aid schemes, are both cited. So is the centralization of
fisheries management leading to lack of flexibility and adaptation, lack of capacity for monitoring, sanctioning and enforcing the policy measures and lack of

compliance. Moreover, the EU itself has recognized the failures of its fisheries policy (European Commission 2000, 2001).

Most of those criticisms point to the foundations of fisheries management in the EU. The institutional setting that governs fisheries management was the result of complex and conflictive negotiations among member states (see below). The common policy was created as a result of that process rather than as a sustainable management of resources, so as to ensure their long-term economic viability. In other words, the mechanism devised to manage fisheries in Europe was the answer to the overall political process. It was never designed to overcome the problems associated with CPRs.

The internal fisheries policy

There are three main puzzles in the EU's internal fisheries management. First, to cope with vastly heterogeneous fishing sectors across the EU – from Spain or Denmark to Luxembourg – policies must take into account the highly diverse institutional backgrounds in the member states which are anchored in a national basis. Second, to manage fisheries resources, policy-makers must take into account highly diverse ecological ecosystems, from the Baltic to the Mediterranean Sea. And third, such a centralized policy, founded in the EU's treaties, has to incorporate a range of interests from the freedom of markets to the principle of equity.

The institutional arrangement governing the internal fisheries resources derives from the creation of the EU's common policy. Lequesne (1999) identifies three historical conditions for the CFP: i) the impact of EU enlargements;[17] ii) the international debate over declining resources; iii) and the vindications of the EEZs. Based on the Treaty of Rome (1957) and born under the Agricultural Policy, the first EU fisheries measures focused on market and structural aspects of fisheries policy.[18] In 1976, member states followed the worldwide movement to extend their rights to a 200-mile fishing zone off the coastal areas.[19] Negotiations to regulate a common system of access and catches began, but it was not until 1983 that the CFP came into existence[20] (see Payne 2000).

The core principles of the CFP were established in the 1983 regulation: i) equal access principle based on the principle of non-discrimination; ii) a partial derogation which limits the access of foreign boats to sensitive inshore fisheries in a coastal band of 6–12 miles; iii) the principle of relative stability, which ensured states the same proportion of a stocks' quota each year (Payne 2000: 306); iv) the EU's exclusive policy authority for marine fisheries;[21] v) the member states' competence on monitoring and enforcement.

Those core principles – after three decades, one major reform,[22] and over 300 pieces of primary and secondary legislation – are still unchanged.[23] Under the internal institutional arrangement actors make decisions about fishing technology or higher levels of quotas, but the core rules of the game have been settled. For instance, the member states have exclusive competences in policy implementation and control and the Commission has not been able – despite its many proposals –

to achieve more competencies in that area. Whenever the failures in the internal CFP are affected by the status quo of institutional arrangements, the conservation of the resource is likely to be at stake.

Under this institutional arrangement, the asymmetric distribution of competencies and the implementation and monitoring capacity of the member states, given their heterogeneous institutional background, aggravates conflicts. The discretionary margin of member states is relatively high, and they tend to act independently in the design of their national policies and structural aids to the fishing sector. Acting independently – on the framework established by the CFP – there is much room for states to free ride under the political pressure of their domestic fisheries sectors.

The external fisheries policy: shaping the international role of the EU

The main puzzles of the EU's external fisheries management are how it participates in the international community – in global or regional management efforts – and how it ensures its fishing sector access to other national or international fisheries.

How is the external fisheries voice of the EU shaped? The European Commission – on behalf of the EU – negotiates fisheries agreements with third countries and participates in various fisheries bodies. The Commission acts under an explicit mandate of the Council. Member states, the Presidency of the Council and the members of the Fisheries Commission in the European Parliament ensure that the Commission's acts are adjusted to that mandate. Before any fisheries body meeting there is an internal meeting between the member states concerned and the representatives of the Council. The Council takes the basic decisions which incorporate fisheries bodies' recommendations into Community law. And finally, international agreements are signed for both the EU and the member states, reflecting its exclusive and shared competences.

Since the external policy is a branch of the CFP, it could be argued that the same analysis of the internal fisheries policy is applicable. However, in contrast to the internal dimension, the external institutional arrangement is shaped by interaction with other actors in the international arena, although the institutional decision-making at the European arena also accounts for a dynamism of force. Actors' choices are shaped in a different way in the external fisheries policy. Member states cannot act independently, since they are 'forced' to agree on a unique position to defend in international forums. Also, there is no room to develop individual member state bilateral agreements with third states, and no option to join a new fisheries body independently. Contrary to the internal dimension – where almost all member states agree that they want to continue fishing – there is no clear agreement on the external fisheries policy. As noted in Table 10.1 (p. 186), this is the case because there are divergent areas of interest. In addition, the distributional effects of the policy are not settled and its priority in the EU international agenda regarding other issues is relatively low. The non-renewal of the EU-Morocco fisheries agreement (which ended in 1999) illustrates this.

Under this institutional arrangement, the relevant member states try to pressure other states using trade-offs. The Commission looks for its own institutional consolidation using a proactive role in international arenas. Interdependence among actors and issue-linkage ensure that member states without a strong external fisheries interest will not be alien to this process. Also, the fisheries sector capacity to lobby its own government or European institutions is reduced. Last but not least, the image of the EU in fisheries management matters for its legitimacy in other international areas.

The EU role in international fisheries management

The EU is one of the major world fishing powers and the largest market for processed products and aquaculture. Such characteristics imply that the impact of its performance in the international arena is crucial. The EU choices for a conservation/predation approach to international management are aggravated by the worldwide state of fisheries resources. Until now, even in a common policy the EU's international role is an ongoing process, which shapes its own institutional development. For example, the EU agreed in 1998 simultaneously to ratify the UN Agreement on Straddling and Highly Migratory Fish Stocks with the ratification of all the member states. This decision was shown when three member states (see Table 10.2 (p.187)) deposited the ratification document individually and later had to withdraw it. This was a big step in the consolidation of the EU, but a little step in terms of conservation since the treaty had yet to be ratified by the EU.

The external branch of the EU's fisheries policy is composed of bilateral agreements with third countries, participation in regional and international fisheries organizations and international agreements within the framework of the Law of the Sea.

There are three types of bilateral agreements: i) reciprocal agreements provide fishing rights in third country waters in return for the equivalent access to EU waters, involving mainly shared fisheries; ii) bilateral agreements provide fishing rights in return for financial compensation and/or market access (mainly with African, Caribbean and Pacific countries (ACP)); and iii) second generation agreements, such as joint enterprises and joint ventures, based on financial assistance, tariff reductions and transference of know-how (only with Argentina).[24]

The performance of the EU under those agreements has been strongly criticized especially in relation to developing countries in what some called, until recent years, a disguised form of neo-colonialism (Bailly and Collet 1999: 1). However, the EU is changing its approach to bilateral agreements. The arguments for that change are mainly economic. Bilateral agreements accounted for 28.5 per cent of the CFP budget in 2000 (an average of 270 million Euros from 1992–2000). Both the budgetary impact and the heterogeneous distribution of beneficiaries among the member states were at the core of this debate. Another powerful argument can be made about the balance between the fisheries policy and the development policy of the EU, since most of those agreements are signed with ACP countries.[25] Although the changing tendencies in bilateral agreements are not guided by conservational criteria, it seems that the movement from a 'pay and fish tendency' to a greater involvement in the development of local industry and fisheries management could have some positive effects on the resource.

The EU's involvement in regional and international fisheries organizations has been growing in recent years. In 2000 the EU was a contracting party in ten regional fisheries organizations,[26] with the prospects of joining another four. The EU financial contribution to those fisheries bodies ranged between 480,000 Euros to ICCAT and 28,000 Euros to NAFO (average 1992–1993).

The performance of the EU in fisheries bodies also fluctuates. For example, the conflictive relationships in NAFO during the 1980s have evolved – with infamous crisis – and the EU now has an instrumental role in improving and strengthening that organization (Hedley 2000: 45; Grieve 2001: 27). In this case the driving forces of change are different from those identified for bilateral agreements and are more closely linked to patterns of institutional learning. In the very beginning, the EU acted as a substitute for the member states in fisheries bodies. For the member states, the change was more than a shift from international to the European level decision-making. They lost the power of numbers in the fisheries body negotiations, because the EU has only one vote to represent the disparity of its member states. However, they gained a priori because the EU is a more powerful actor. Problems arose with the EU's inability to articulate its political power, but recent developments show that the capacity of this power is growing.[27] In the broader range of international agreements under the International Law of the Sea, the EU is showing an incipient, although limited, leadership, as we showed above.[28]

This position regarding fisheries conservation is directly linked with the EU's leadership in environmental issues. The EU has been scrutinized in both of these policy sectors. However, the impact of 'green' pressure is affecting fisheries. The EU faces the same international community in international fisheries management that it is trying to push into environmental agreements. International compromises such as the 1992 Earth Summit in Rio called for an EU conservation approach in fisheries management. As Sjursen (1999: 8) has pointed out, '[t]here are indications of a tendency to link the EU's international role to certain general ideas and values in international politics'.

Conclusions

The major challenge for the EU, as a system of multi-level governance, is to make institutional arrangements at the local, regional, national, European and international levels coherent, nested, and mutually reinforcing. Nonetheless, the EU is an ongoing process built upon highly heterogeneous institutional backgrounds.

Borrowing from the IAD framework, we showed that understanding how the EU affects world fisheries management requires two analytical levels. At the first level, the EU is an actor that changes the patterns of interaction in the international arena; second, the EU is itself an arena in which multiple actors shape its international role. At the international level, the changes in the structure of the situation point to a new, powerful but learning actor. Institutional mechanisms governing international fisheries were untransformed by the EU's presence. It had to adapt to the rules devised in fisheries bodies, or to the regulations created by the international community. However, its broad international agenda, its leadership in environmental matters and its own learning process are changing the EU's role in fisheries from a beginning that tried simply to represent the divergent interest of the member states to a more global and proactive approach in fisheries management.

On the other hand, the EU is an arena in which multiple actors shape its international role. The analysis of the policy instrument designed for fisheries management stresses the links but also the differences between the internal and the external policies. In fact, the institutional arrangements that govern both dimensions account for their contrary orientations: the internal status quo versus the external dynamism put resource management in different puzzles.

The complexity and variety of fields related to our analysis create some big puzzles and remaining questions. Further research will require an in-depth and comparative analysis of the EU's participation at regional levels, measurement of its institutional effectiveness in resources' conservation, and even a detailed comparison with previous member states' role in the international fishing community.

There is no doubt that the EU's role in international fisheries management is crucial, both for the future of resources and fishing communities and for its own institutional consolidation. Examining its performance presents real challenges to theoretical analysis. But instead of looking for an *ad hoc* framework focused on the EU's particular features, current theories provide powerful tools for studying and comparing the EU's management of CPR. This essay framed the analysis as a first step towards understanding the EU's role as a CPR manager. In addition to the theoretical relevance, the practical implications concern the future of natural resources worldwide.

Table 10.1 EU and member states' participation in international fisheries (for notes see p. 189)

Country	Membership in Regional and International Fisheries bodies[1]	Bilateral agreements: Southern[2] and Northern	Vessels under bilateral agreements (total by area)[3]	Vessels in international waters
Austria	EIFAC			
Belgium	EIFAC, ICES	Northern	62	Atlantic Ocean
Denmark	NAFO, IWC, IBSFC, ICES, NASCO, NEAFC	Northern	865	North Sea and Baltic Sea, Atlantic Ocean and Greenland
Finland	EIFAC, IWC, IBSFC, ICES,	Northern	22	Baltic Sea and Bothnian Sea
France	NAFO, APFIC, CECAF, EIFAC, GFCM, IOTC, WECAFC, CCAMLR, IWC, ICCAT, ICES, SPC, IATTC	Southern, Northern	S: (tuna); N: 43	Atlantic, Pacific and Indian Oceans
Germany	NAFO, EIFAC, CCAMLR, IWC, IBSFC, ICES	Northern	158	Atlantic Ocean
Greece	EIFAC, GFCM, ICES*	Southern	S: n.s;	Mediterranean Sea, Atlantic Ocean
Ireland	EIFAC, IWC, ICES	Northern	3	Atlantic Ocean
Italy	CECAF, EIFAC, GFCM, CCAMLR, IWC, ICCAT, ICES	Southern	S: 11;	Adriatic and Mediterranean Seas
Luxembourg				
Netherlands	CECAF, EIFAC, WECAFC, CCAMLR**, IWC, ICES	Southern, Northern	S: n.s; N: 185.	Atlantic Ocean
Portugal	NAFO, CECAF*, EIFAC, ICCAT, ICES	Southern, Northern	S: 38; N: 8	Atlantic Ocean
Spain	NAFO, CECAF, EIFAC, GFCM, WECAFC, CCAMLR, IWC, ICCAT, ICES	Southern, Northern	S: 725; N: 22	Atlantic, Pacific and Indian Oceans, Mediterranean Sea
Sweden	EIFAC, CCAMLR, IWC, ISBFC, ICES	Northern	126	Atlantic Ocean
UK	APFIC, CECAF*, CIFA*, EIFAC, IOTC, WECAFC, CCAMLR, IWC, ICCAT, ICES	Southern, Northern	S: n.s; N: 432.	Atlantic Ocean

Table 10.2 EU and member states' participation in major international fisheries agreements (for notes see p. 189)

Country	United Nations Convention on the Law of the Sea (in force as from 16.XI. 1994)			Agreement relating to the implementation of Part XI of the Convention (in force as from 28.VI. 1996)		Agreement for the implementation of the Convention relating to the conservation and management of straddling and highly migratory stocks (in force as from 11. XII. 2001)		
	S	Declaration/ Statement	Ratification	S	Ratification	S	Declaration/ Statement	Ratification
Austria	✓	✓	14 July 1995	✓	14 July 1995	✓		
Belgium	✓	✓	13 November 1998	✓	13 Noember. 1998	✓		
Denmark	✓	✓	–	✓	–	✓		
Finland	✓	✓	21 June 1996	✓	21 June 1996	✓		
France	✓	✓	11 April 1996	✓	11 April 1996	✓	✓	
Germany	✓	✓	14 October 1996 (accession)	✓	14 October 1996	✓		
Greece	✓	✓	21 July 1995	✓	21 July 1995	✓		
Ireland	✓	✓	21 June 1996	✓	21 June 1996	✓		
Italy	✓	✓	13 January 1995	✓	14 January 1995	✓		4 March 1999[1] (withdraw)
Luxembourg	✓	✓	5 October 2000	✓	5 October 1995	✓		5 October 1995 (withdraw)
Netherlands	✓	✓	28 June 1996	✓	28 June 1996	✓	✓	
Portugal	✓	✓	3 November 1997	✓	3 November 1997	✓		
Spain	✓	✓	15 January 1997	✓	15 January 1997	✓		
Sweden	✓	✓	25 June 1996	✓	25 June 1996	✓		
UK	✓	✓	25 July 1997 (accession)	✓	25 July 1997	✓		10 December 2001 (partial withdrawal)[2]
European Union[3]	✓	Yes	Formal Confirmation 1 April 1998	✓	1 April 1998	✓	✓	

Notes

1 We use European Union in a whole sense, as an inclusive reference to the European Economic Community, the European Community, and the European Union. It should be noted, however, that only the European Community has legal standing in the international arena.

α The author acknowledges the Workshop in Political Theory and Policy Analysis at Indiana University for the opportunity to develop this research. Useful comments by Elinor Ostrom, Michel McGinnis, Amy Poteete and the editors on earlier drafts are deeply appreciated. I owe a particular debt to Tanya Heikkila for her comments and editing skills and to Ramon Máiz for all his support throughout my career.

2 'The framework links the characteristics of a physical world (such as *fisheries*) with those of the general cultural setting (the *local* communities and *fishermen* that use the *fisheries*); the specific rules that affect the incentives individuals face in particular situations (how *fish* can be harvested, utilized and maintained); the outcomes of these interactions (regeneration or *depletion*); and the evaluative criteria applied to these patterns and outcomes (efficiency, equity, sustainability)' (Ostrom 1994: 34; the examples provided have been adapted from forest to fisheries). [Present author's italics]

3 For a comprehensive and updated review of the CPR literature see Ostrom *et al.* 2002.

4 Moreover, multiple theories and models operate under the IAD framework, including game theory, local public economy theory or international development studies.

5 We use fisheries bodies as a general concept to refer to either Regional Fisheries Organizations or International Fisheries Organizations.

6 It is important to discern between *common property resources*, which implies a kind of management arrangement and *common pool resources*, a term referring to the characteristics of the resource (see Ostrom *et al.* 2002: 17).

7 Examples of common pool resources are irrigation systems, forests, or the Internet.

8 Also referred to as rivalry or jointness of supply.

9 Thus, overappropriation is a form of free riding. I thank Elinor Ostrom for this clarification.

10 Around 1973, 17 countries had asserted jurisdictions to 200 miles (Soroos 1988: 14). The International Law of the Sea – completed in 1982, in force in 1994 – provided legality to this de facto process, recognizing the coastal state's sovereign rights in its EEZ with respect to natural resources and certain economic activities.

11 The issue of one state's fishing practice causing stress on species of fish whose territory spans the boundaries of more than one state (straddling stocks) provided impetus for affected states to begin co-ordinating their fishery co-operation.

12 See agreements in Table 2 and footnote 28.

13 Hanna (1998) provides an excellent overview of the state of ocean fishery resources in its biological, economic, management and equity dimensions.

14 Most countries present that dichotomy regarding fisheries matters. For instance, Canada has been resisting the imposition of international fishing standards within the 200-mile exclusion zones, even though it strongly supports international standards on the high seas.

15 Set of rules which determine the access and use of the resource, attributes monitoring and enforcing functions to specific actors and so on.

16 Those critics normally do not discern different patterns of interaction between internal and external fisheries policies.

17 For a discussion of the UK, Ireland, Denmark, and Norway applications to join the EU see Payne (2000). The accession of Spain and Portugal in 1986 doubled the number of EU fishermen and consumption increased by half. Issues related to the Baltic arose with the accession of Finland and Sweden in 1995.

18 Community regulations 2141/70 and 2142/70.

19 Council resolution of 3 November 1976 (OJ C 105, 7.5.1981).
20 Regulation ECC 170/83 (OJ 27.1.83). It is viewed as the core of the CFP and although it has been amended many times, its essential fundamentals remain (Lequesne, 1999: 3).
21 See also community case law Kramer (1976), ECR 1981 n. 1045.
22 The next reform is forthcoming at the end of this year. It will be a good opportunity to test our arguments.
23 See Scharpf (1999, 2001) for explanations of deadlock or status quo under the joint-decision-making model.
24 The EU concluded 23 of these fishing agreements in 2000.
25 For each Euro paid as financial compensation for fishing rights, the EU obtains 3 Euros in turnover; see IFREMER (1999).
26 Namely ICCAT, NASCO, NEAFC, NAFO, IBSFC, CECAF, WECAFC, GFCM, IOTC, and CCAMRL.
27 In the ongoing fisheries organization that will manage the Central West Pacific Ocean resources, there was a reluctance to allow the participation of member states. It was the pressure of the European Commission under United Nations and particularly under the FAO that allowed the EU to enter as a contracting party.
28 Among them, the Code of Conduct for Responsible Fishing, Plan Action of FAO to curb Illegal, Unreported and Unregulated fishing, Consultation on the Management of Fishing Capacity, Shark Fisheries and Incidental Catch of Seabirds in Longline Fisheries, adoption Plans of Action; see also Table 10.2.

Notes to Tables

Table 10.1, p. 186

Source: Columns 3, 4 and 5: IFREMER 1999, excluding tuna. *Observers; ** Party of the convention but not Members of the Commission; n.s: not significant.
Acronyms: APFIC: Indo-Pacific Fisheries Commission Agreement; CCAMLR: Commission for the Conservation of Antarctic Marine Living Resources; CECAF: Fishery Committee for the Eastern Central Atlantic; EIFAC: European Inland Fisheries Advisory Committee; GFCM: General Fisheries Commission for the Mediterranean; IBSFC: International Baltic Sea Fishery Commission; ICCAT: International Commission for the Conservation of Atlantic Tunas; ICES: International Council for the Exploration of the Sea; IOCT: Indian Ocean Tuna Commission; IWC: International Whaling Commission; NAFO: North Atlantic Fisheries Organization; NASCO: North Atlantic Salmon Conservation Organization; NEAF: Northeast Atlantic Fisheries Commission; SPC: Secretariat of the Pacific Community; CAFC: Western Central Atlantic Fishery Commission.

1 Membership covers: previous membership before the EU became a member of those fisheries bodies; membership in representation of overseas territories out of the Treaty of Rome; actual membership in organizations that still do not recognize the EU as a member. ICES is an international forum of scientific discussion.
2 Southern agreements include 8 African EEZs (including Morocco, with which bilateral agreement ended in 1999 without renovation after 2 years of negotiations). Northern agreements include: Baltic Sea, Norwegian EEZ, Greenland, Faeroe Islands and Iceland. In 1998 29 EU vessels were under joint venture or joint enterprise with Argentina (Germany: 2; Italy: 1; UK: 2; Spain: 24).
3 Average 93/97. For countries with nil returns the data provided correspond to 1998 (Finland, Ireland, Spain and Sweden).

Table 10.2, p. 187

S: signature
Source: United Nations, International Law of the Sea (www.un.org).
1   See EU as an actor in International Fisheries Management for further explanation.
2   Ratified on behalf of overseas territories to which the EC treaties do not apply (see above).
3   We recall that only the European Community has international legal capacity.

References

Baden, J. (1996) 'Democracies Don't Fight – Except Over Fish', Editorial opinion in www.free-eco.org.

Bailly, D. and Collet, S. (1999) 'An Ethical Approach to Re-Think the Present and the Future of the Common Fisheries Policy in the European Union', Presented at the 'Workshop on the Workshop 2', Workshop in Political Theory and Policy Analysis, Indiana University, Bloomington, 9–10 June 1999.

Börzel, T. A. (2000) 'EU Infringement Proceedings as a Proxy for Non-Compliance', Working Paper, Max-Planck-Project on Commons Goods, manuscript draft.

Crean, K. and Symes, D. (1994) 'Social Objectives, Social Research and the Recalibration of Management Policies in Fisheries: The Case of the European Union', Presented at 'Improving the Link between Fisheries Science and Management: Biological, Social and Economic Considerations' 82nd Statutory Meeting of the ICES, St. John's, Newfoundland, Canada, 22–30 September.

European Commission (2000) *Report from the Commission to the Council and the European Parliament on the Application of the Community System for Fisheries and Aquaculture in 1996–1998*, COM, 15 final.

European Commission (2001) *Green Paper on the Future of the Common Fisheries Policy*, 135 final, Brussels, 20 March 2001.

Gordon, H. S. (1954) 'The Economic Theory of a Common Property Resource: The Fishery', *Journal of Political Economy*, 62: 124–142.

Grieve, C. (2001) *Reviewing the Common Fisheries Policy. EU Fisheries Management for the 21-Century,* IEPP, London.

Hanna, S. (1998) 'Strengthening Governance of Ocean Fishery Resources' in R. Constanza and F. Andrade (eds) *Ecological Economics and Sustainable Governance of the Oceans,* Lisbon: Silvas.

Hardin, G. (1968) 'The Tragedy of the Commons', *Science*, 162: 1243–1248.

Hedley, C. (2000) 'International Relations and the Common Fisheries Policy: The Legal Framework' in A. Hatcher and D. Tingley (ed.) *International Relations and the Common Fisheries Policy*, Proceedings of the fourth Concerted Action Workshop on economics and the Common Fisheries Policy. Bergen, Norway, 26–28 October 2000: CEMARE.

Héritier, A. (2001) *Differential Europe. The European Union Impact on National Policymaking,* Oxford: Rowman and Littlefield Publishers.

Hooghe, L. and Marks, G. (2001) *Multi-level Governance and European Integration*, Oxford: Rowman and Littlefield Publishers.

IFREMER/CEMARE/CEP (1999) 'Evaluation of the Fishing Agreements concluded by the European Community'. Summary in: www.europa.eu.int

Imeson, R. J. and Van den Bergh, J. C. J. M. (2002) 'Managing the Fisheries: Linking Old and New Ideas', forthcoming, Manuscript sent by the authors.

Keohane, R. O. and Ostrom, E. (eds) (1995) *Local Commons and Global Interdependence. Heterogeneity and Cooperation in Two Domains,* London: Sage.

Kiser, L. L. and Ostrom, E. (1982) 'The Three Worlds of Action: A Metatheoretical Synthesis of Institutional Approaches', in E. Ostrom (ed.) *Strategies of Political Inquiry,* Beverly Hills: Sage.

Lequesne, C. (1999) 'Quand l'Union Européenne Gouverne les Poisons: Pourquoi une Politique Commune de la Pêche?', *Les Études du Ceri,* 61, December.

Mahou, X. M. (2001) 'The Reform of the Common Fisheries Policy: Renationalisation or Europeanisation of the Decision-Making Process?', Paper presented to ECPR Joint Sessions of Workshops, Grenoble, 5–11 April.

McGinnis, M. and Ostrom, E. (1992) 'Institutional Analysis and Global Climate Change: Design Principles for Robust International Regimes' in M. Rice, J. Snow and H. Jacobson (eds.) *Global Climate Change: Social and Economic Research Issues*: 45–85, Proceedings of a Conference Held at Argonne National Laboratory, Chicago, Illinois, 11–13 February 1992.

McGinnis, M. and Ostrom, E. (1996) 'Design Principles for Local and Global Commons' in O. R Young, (ed.) *The International Political Economy and International Institutions,* 2nd edn, Cheltenham: Elgar: 465–493.

Noonan, D. S. (1998) 'International Fisheries Management Institutions: Europe and the South Pacific' in J. A. Baden and D. S. Noonan (eds) *Managing the Commons,* Bloomington: Indiana University Press: 165–177.

Ostrom, E. (1990) *Governing the Commons: The Evolution of Institutions for Collective Action,* New York: Cambridge University Press.

Ostrom, E. (1994) 'Institutional Analysis, Design Principles and Threats to Sustainable Community Governance and Management of Commons', in R. S. Pomeroy (ed.) *Community Management and Common Property of Coastal Fisheries in Asia and the Pacific,* International Center for Living Aquatic Resources Management (ICLARM): 34–50.

Ostrom, E. (1998) 'The Institutional Analysis and Development Approach' in E. Tusk Loehman and M. D. Kilgour (eds) *Designing Institutions for Environmental and Resource Management,* Northampton: Edward Elgar: 68–90.

Ostrom, E. (1999a) 'Institutional Rational Choice: An Assessment of the Institutional Analysis and Development Framework', in P. Sabatier (ed.) *Theories of the Policy Process,* Boulder: Westview Press: 35–71.

Ostrom, E. (1999b), 'Coping with Tragedies of the Commons' in *Annual Reviews of Political Science,* 2: 493–535.

Ostrom, E., Gadner, R. and Walker, J (1994) *Rules, Games, & Common-Pool Resources,* Ann Arbor: University of Michigan Press.

Ostrom, E., Burguer, J., Field, C. B, Norgaard, R. B., and Policansky, D. (1999) 'Revisiting the Commons: Local Lessons, Global Challenges', *Science,* 284, April: 278–282.

Ostrom *et al.* (2002) *The Drama of the Commons,* Washington: National Academy Press.

Payne, D. C. (2000) 'Policy-making in Nested Institutions: Explaining the Conservation Failure of the EU's Common Fisheries Policy', *Journal of Common Market Studies*, 38, 2: 303–324.

Peterson, M. J. (1993) 'International Fisheries Management' in P. Haas, R. O. Keohane and M. A. Levy (eds) (1993) *Institutions for the Earth: Sources of Effective International Environment Protection*, Cambridge: MIT Press.

Sandberg, A. (1994) 'Community Fish or Fishing Communities?', Paper given at EU/AIR Programme Workshop: Social Issues and the Socio-Economic Paradigm in Fisheries Management: Framing the Research Agenda. Brussels, 5–6 May.

Scharpf, F. W. (1999) *Gobernar en Europa ¿eficaz y democráticamente?*, Madrid: Alianza Editorial.

Scharpf, F. W. (2001) 'What Have We Learned? Problem-Solving of the Multi-level European Polity', MPIfG Working Paper, 1–4 July.

Sjursen, H. (1999) 'The Common Foreign and Security Policy: an Emerging New Voice in International Politics?', ARENA Working Papers, 99, 34.

Soroos, M. S. (1988) 'The International Commons: A Historical Perspective', *Environmental Review,* 12, 1: 22

Wilson, J. *et al.* (1994) 'Chaos, Complexity and Community Management of Fisheries', *Marine Policy,* 18, 4: 291–305.

Wilson, J. (2002) 'Scientific Uncertainty, Complex Systems and the Design of Common Pool Institutions', in E. Ostrom (ed.) *The Drama of the Commons*, Washington: National Academy Press: 327–359.

Young, O. (1995) 'The Problem of Scale in Human/ Environment Relationships', in R. O. Keohane and E. Ostrom (eds) *Local Commons and Global Interdependence*, London: Sage.

Part IV

Conclusion

11 Understanding the EU's external relations

The move from actors to processes

Sebastiaan Princen and Michèle Knodt

The previous ten chapters have discussed a range of issues and perspectives concerning the EU's external relations. In this concluding chapter, we will draw together the arguments presented in those chapters and link them to the questions we formulated in the introductory chapter. That way, we hope to offer more insight into the way the EU operates in its external relations, and the opportunities and difficulties the EU's external relations pose for political science theory.

To begin with, we will bring together the main conclusions of the three parts of this study. First, we will discuss the process that leads to co-operation in the EU's external relations in the first place, and the ways in which this process is affected by the EU's characteristics. Then, we will examine how the EU's characteristics affect the way the EU operates externally, once it has decided to do so. Third, we will draw some conclusions about the effects the EU has on other countries and the international arena. Finally, we will bring together the threads from these three parts in order to arrive at a more general perspective on the EU as an international actor.

After these conclusions, we will turn to the issue of theorizing the EU's external relations. We will make an argument in three steps. To begin with, we will argue that it is difficult to apply existing theories to the EU as an actor. However, these theories apply much more readily to processes in the EU's external relations. Moreover, we will argue that this may in turn lead to a critical re-examination of the assumptions underlying existing theory and an improved understanding of political processes in traditional states and international organizations.

The EU as an external actor: main conclusions

The chapters in this book have been divided into three parts, which reflect the three main claims for uniqueness of the EU:

- the extent to which the EU member states co-operate externally;
- the EU's internal decision-making process on its external policies;
- the effects the EU has on other actors or the international system as a whole.

In this section, we will formulate the main conclusions relating to each of these three claims. These conclusions form the basis for the theoretical exercise in the next section, but are also of interest in themselves.

The EU as an incomplete actor? The decision to co-operate externally

The EU differs from traditional states not only in that its external policies are contested substantively, but also in that the very decision to act externally often has to be taken anew in new policy areas. In most states, external competencies rest firmly with the national government. Even though domestic actors may differ as to the substance of the external policies and whether the state should act on a specific issue in the first place, there is no doubt that if the state is going to act, it will be through the national government.

In the EU, by contrast, the member states are important rivals for the EU as actors in the international arena. Only a few policy areas clearly belong to the EU's exclusive competence, the common commercial policy perhaps being the best example. Even in that policy area, however, there has been a battle among member states and between member states and the European Commission about the extent of the EU competencies. In 1994, this led to the European Court of Justice ruling against exclusive EU competence in important areas of trade in services, but in the Nice Treaty EU competence in these areas has been strengthened again.

In other policy areas, the EU has had to share competencies with its member states, while in still others the member states have retained the lead. These intergovernmental policy areas include most conspicuously those relating to foreign and defence policies, and to justice and home affairs. As a result, the EU seems to be an incomplete actor in the international arena, lacking several foreign policy competencies that have traditionally formed the core of states' external policies.

The three chapters in Part I specifically address the decision to co-operate externally. Taking a neo-classical realist approach, Rynning analyses the ways in which the EU's foreign and security policies could evolve. In his analysis, two capacities of international actors are crucial: the capacity to formulate a coherent vision, and the capacity to mobilize resources, including armed forces. Strong states have both capacities and form so-called 'strategic actors', the US being the best example. As the EU lacks a strategic vision, development into a strategic actor seems unlikely. However, it has gradually succeeded in building up an institutional framework that is capable of mobilizing resources, which would make it a 'civilian actor'. At times, member states may be able to agree on the strategic vision for a specific crisis and some may join (military) forces, leading to a 'directorate' in which a few member states act on behalf of a shared vision. In many ways, Rynning's analysis runs along the lines of classic neo-realist theory in international relations. In doing so, it shows how the EU is likely to evolve, and in which ways it will remain constrained in its external relations.

Sjursen takes a different approach, arguing that neo-realism and its rationalist heirs may rely on fundamentally flawed or incomplete assumptions. Rather than taking fixed state interests as her point of departure, she seeks to show how the existence of the EU and an EU framework for decision-making on foreign and security policies may affect the way EU member states formulate and justify their foreign policies. This may lead to a significant 'Europeanization' of the member states' external policies, in that these member states may take some set of common, European norms as their point of reference in formulating and carrying out their foreign policies.

Both Rynning and Sjursen discuss foreign and security policies under the EU's second pillar. Young's contribution, by contrast, focuses on policies under the first EU pillar, in which the EU has a range of competencies, and EU actors, such as the European Commission, play a much greater role. In an expanded two-level game approach, Young shows that the EU has to share its external competencies with its member states in many policy areas under the first pillar. Contrary to what might be expected, however, this need not impede the EU's capacity to act in the international arena. First, mixed competence offers the opportunity for the EU to act without first having to come to one common position among the member states, which may actually facilitate participation by the EU. Second, although the de facto unanimity that results from mixed competence may prevent the EU from taking the initiative in international negotiations, this is only the case to the extent that the EU has less ambitious internal policies than the ones that are discussed internationally. If the EU has agreed on more ambitious policies internally, it will be able to play an active role, even if unanimity among its member states is required.

What do these contributions tell us about the decision to co-operate externally within the EU? To begin with, the contributions reinforce the notion that the EU's external competencies and external co-operation between member states are hotly contested. Under the second pillar, this has received ample attention from scholars and the media, mainly in relation to important international crises and milestones in the development of a common foreign and security policy framework. Yet, as Young shows, many of these controversies are also inherent in policies under the first pillar.

Therefore, the differences between pillars seem to be a matter of degree rather than a matter of principle. This is reinforced by the insight that decisions to co-operate cannot be divided into a simple 'yes or no'. There are various modes of co-operation between full co-operation and no co-operation, as both Rynning and Young show. These modes differ crucially on the relation between EU actors and member states. The EU actors include most importantly the European Commission and the Council of Ministers (which, of course, is composed of member state representatives itself), but also the European Parliament and the European Court of Justice, depending on the specific policy area at stake.

Under full co-operation, EU actors play the most important role, and there is no room for independent member state action in the international arena. Under no co-operation, there is no room for independent EU action, while the member states retain all their room of manoeuvre. In between, member states can give up various degrees of independent action in favour of the EU. They can do so, for instance, by only leaving certain decisions in a policy area to the EU, by leaving decisions to the EU while keeping the responsibility for implementation and/or enforcement, or by retaining member state competencies alongside EU competencies. Each type of co-operation results in a specific division of tasks and competencies between the EU and its member states.

Further, even if no or few formal competencies are transferred to the EU, the mere existence of the EU may lead to a degree of co-ordination between member states that could be labelled 'co-operation' under or even within the EU. This line of argument is supported by Sjursen's analysis of the development of the EU's external policies. The existence of a common frame of reference may effect changes in member states' behaviour, in that the behaviour of member states will conform more closely to a common standard. Then, external policies of EU member states may become more coherent among themselves without any involvement by EU actors.

If this line of argument is accepted, the EU may play a role in a wider range of issues than is usually acknowledged: 'EU action' could be construed more broadly as 'co-ordinated action by EU member states', either through and by EU actors and institutions or not (cf. Allen and Smith 1990: 21–22). Whether or not this is a useful extension depends on whether or not the EU is seen to constrain or guide member state action, even outside EU institutions per se. Sjursen would probably argue 'yes'; Rynning would lean toward 'no'.

Although these arguments usually arise in the context of the second pillar's foreign and security policies, they may also be relevant in the context of the first pillar. In general, an interesting question is whether dynamics in the second (and, possibly the third) pillar differ fundamentally from those in the first pillar. Young shows that the relations between EU actors and EU member states can take various forms in different policy areas under the first pillar, too. This observation may well extend to the broader definition of co-ordination discussed above. In first pillar policies, the existence of the EU may also exert a considerable influence on the external policies of the EU member states. As a result, member state actions may be more coherent and co-ordinated than they would have been without the existence of the EU, even if the member states retain independent competencies.

This points toward opportunities for fruitful exchange between analyses of these two pillars. Research that is based on common notions and that draws on experiences under all pillars would bridge the gap that currently exists between scholars working on issues under the first pillar and those who are working on issues of foreign and security policies. The viability of such a cross-fertilization does not depend on an actual identity between developments under these pillars. As the contributions in the first part show, developments in either pillar are not likely to show a uniform picture. This does not necessarily preclude the use of similar concepts and theories. Rather, it may provide for a useful variation on key variables in a theory, which makes it theoretically even more interesting to apply similar concepts and insights across pillars.

The EU as a fragmented actor? Decision-making on the EU's external policies

Once the EU operates externally, its decision-making procedures differ distinctly from those in traditional states. First, the EU allows for a strong member states' role in decision-making, through the Council of Ministers and a plethora of regulatory and other committees. Second, the EU's multi-pillar structure is also a distinctive feature of the way the EU's external relations are organized. This multi-pillar structure does not only lead to differences in the role the EU plays in various policy areas, but also to peculiar dynamics that arise out of the interactions between pillars. The contributions in Part II of this book deal with these issues of multi-level and multi-pillar decision-making. In so doing, they take various approaches as their points of departure.

Mörth's analysis focuses on the way issues are brought under one pillar or the other through a process of 'framing' by the actors involved. Her example of defence equipment is a case in point, as it combines military, foreign policy, technological and economic aspects. The first two fall under the second EU pillar, whereas the technological and economic aspects come under the first pillar. As a consequence, the European Commission could use the technological and economic aspects to draw the whole issue of defence equipment into its field of competence. This process of 'drawing' an issue into some political arena is the outcome of activities by political actors to frame an issue as belonging to one or another arena.

In the issue of sanctions discussed by Buchet de Neuilly, the interaction between pillars is part of the institutional framework governing sanctions. This framework places the political decision to install sanctions in the second pillar, while leaving the implementing decisions on which trade is to be affected to the first pillar. This segmentation allows for a considerable disparity between outcomes under the two pillars, as the example of sanctions against Serbia shows. A firm political stance in the second pillar decision-making process was followed by much weaker implementing decisions under the first pillar. Buchet de Neuilly explains this disparity by pointing to structural differences between these two sub-fields, which led to different outcomes, even if the same member states were involved.

A similar example of 'saying one thing and doing another' is highlighted by Papadimitriou, in his analysis of the agreements between the EU and Central and East European Countries (CEECs). Although EU and member state officials were quick to emphasize the importance of supporting the CEECs, the position eventually taken by the EU in the negotiations was much less generous. Using a rational choice approach, Papadimitrou explains this discrepancy by analysing the negotiations between the EU and CEECs in the context of parallel negotiations within the EU and in the international arena. The EU's pay-offs in its negotiations with the CEECs were strongly affected by those parallel negotiations, since the outcomes of the negotiations with the CEECs would also affect the outcomes in the parallel negotiations.

Both Buchet de Neuilly and Papadimitriou offer a way out of the apparent contradiction in the EU's position on the same issue. In Papadimitriou's analysis, there is no contradiction, since the EU's position is consistent and rational across all relevant games taken together. Buchet de Neuilly points toward differences between political arenas within the EU that yield different outcomes.

What does the EU's multi-level and multi-pillar character imply about the EU's external relations? To begin with, the EU's multi-pillar and multi-level character adds a degree of complexity to the EU's decision-making on external policies. In multi-level processes, the added level of the EU means that some actors have to play an additional game. This raises the number of interactions between actors. The same is true for issues that are decided in more than one pillar. Moreover, when political processes in different arenas arc coupled, the additional level or pillar increases the number and complexity of possible outcomes and interest configurations among actors.

At the same time, the multiplicity of levels and pillars does not just shape political processes as an exogenous force. Multiple levels and pillars also offer opportunities for actors to choose arenas and to exploit the possibilities inherent in the differences between levels and pillars. That way, they can actively make use of the implications multiplicity has for outcomes and interest configurations. The extent to which political processes take place at multiple levels and in multiple pillars is also partly determined by the way actors deal with these possibilities. As a result, the multiplicity of levels and pillars is often as much an outcome of political processes as it is shaping those processes.

The EU as an impotent actor? The effects of the EU in the international arena

If the EU is a unique or distinct actor, it could be expected to have different effects on other countries or the international system as a whole than do traditional states. The four chapters in Part III of this book specifically examine these effects by analysing the way the EU seeks to 'export' models to other countries or the international arena at large.

Petiteville focuses on the use of economic co-operation arrangements as a means to export European values. This use of economic instruments, which he calls 'soft diplomacy', is contrasted with the 'hard diplomacy' of military intervention. His chapter seeks to show that, and how the EU has evolved as a soft power. At the same time, it acknowledges the limitations inherent in such an approach, given the lack of military means at the disposal of the EU.

Princen's analysis also concerns the use of economic means, but this time in transatlantic relations. He shows how the use of trade measures by the EU led to the adoption of more stringent standards in the US and Canada in the fields of trapping and the protection of personal information. However, the outcomes of these processes depended crucially on the EU's capacity to formulate a coherent vision internally and on the way this vision related to the existing political debates in the US and Canada.

Longo's discussion of the EU's external policies in the field of justice and home affairs also demonstrates how the EU has been able to export its model of police and judicial co-operation to CEECs, Russia and Mediterranean countries. In each case, the EU was able to reach an agreement that included judicial and police co-operation modelled after the EU's internal framework for co-operation. Yet, although the principles were the same, the intensity of the co-operation differed.

Ballesteros, finally, discusses the EU's external fisheries policies and the way they affect the effectiveness of fisheries management. She argues that the existence of the EU has transformed both the internal and external political arenas in this policy area. Within the EU, it has led to a centralization, while externally it has reduced the number of actors in Regional Fisheries Organizations. However, the internal centralization has arguably led to reduced effectiveness in fisheries management, while the changes in the external political arenas have improved fisheries management.

Ballesteros' point about changing external political arenas presents an important general observation in this regard. The reduction of the number of actors in the international arena, and the pooling of resources at the European level are probably a prerequisite for the kind of economic diplomacy that is central to Petiteville's, Princen's and Longo's analyses.

These three contributions, in turn, offer guidance as to what determines the EU's effects in the international arena. Two factors seem crucial for the EU to be able to export its models to other countries or the international arena. First, the EU needs to formulate a coherent vision internally. The ability to do so does not seem to be affected by the EU's internal structure per se. Princen shows how the EU was able to formulate a coherent vision in one case but not in another, even though internal decision-making structures were similar. The issues of police and judicial co-operation that Longo examines primarily fall under the third pillar, and partly under the second: exactly the two pillars in which decision-making is most intergovernmental.

Rather, consensus on the part of member states is important. This consensus can be wrought by common interests, as is probably the case when it comes to police and judicial co-operation or by a common tradition of dealing with issues. Such a common tradition, or the lack of it, may explain many of the differences found by Princen in his two policy areas. The existence of a common set of values relating to human rights underlies many of the policies Petiteville discusses.

Second, the EU needs to have the means to carry out its vision. These means differ from those of traditional states, and the EU is more of a 'soft power' than such states. As the contributions in Part III demonstrate, this need not be problematic in policy areas that are closely connected to economic and trade relations. However, it limits the EU's capability to play a role in issues that have a military dimension. In these issues, the EU has to rely on its economic force and its political profile. Hence, the formulation of a coherent and appealing political vision may even be more important for the EU than for traditional states.

The EU as a searching actor: links between the three questions

In this book, the questions of whether or not to act externally, how to act externally, and the effects of these actions have been treated as distinct. The contributions clearly show, however, that they are closely linked in many ways. Moreover, these links run in both directions, leading to reverse dynamics between processes in the various parts.

For example, as Longo argues, exporting an EU set of norms may reinforce the EU's international 'actorness', both externally and internally. The EU may raise its profile as an international actor, both toward third countries and among 'domestic' European actors, by showing its effectiveness in the international arena.

This may even be used as a deliberate strategy to strengthen the EU as an international actor, in particular where the exported norms or standards can be presented as distinctly 'European'. This has not only been the case in the area of police and judicial policies, but also in the protection of personal information and the export of human rights. Thus, the questions of Part III seem closely connected to those of Part I: the effects of the EU as an international actor are partly determined by the decision to act externally in the first place, but at the same time, the external effects may have a decisive impact on the EU's international actorness and thereby the extent of the EU's external competencies and responsibilities.

Similar interactions can also be observed between the questions discussed in Parts I and II. Rather than presenting two discrete decisions (first, whether or not to act externally and second, how to act externally), the political processes underlying these two questions will often interact. In many cases, the two decisions will be taken at the same time: by deciding how to act, it is also decided whether or not to act. Therefore, in deciding how to act, political actors within the EU also determine the extent of the EU's external policies and the level of co-operation between member states on external issues. For member states that oppose EU action in the international arena in a specific policy area, decision-making on how to act offers new opportunities to reduce the EU's role.

These interactions can also be observed in traditional states. However, in the EU, they may gain a specific edge because of the inherent contestability of the EU's international role. The EU may well be typified as an actor in search of a role, and this search is likely to affect the whole policy process, from issues of external competencies, via decisions on specific actions, to the effects these actions have on third countries and the international system.

Theorizing the EU's external relations

In the previous section, we discussed the main findings of the ten contributions to this book. In this section, we will turn to the issue of theorizing the EU and the extent to which existing theory is applicable to the EU's external relations.

For the purposes of this discussion, a theory can usefully be seen as a set of related hypotheses that apply to a range of social phenomena. The range of social phenomena the theory applies to is its domain; a theory does not pretend to apply to anything outside its domain. If it is argued that existing theories are not applicable to the EU's external relations, it is in fact stated that the EU's external relations fall outside the domain of existing theories.

This begs the question of how the domain of a theory is defined. As we will try to show in this section, the EU's external relations indeed fall outside the domain of existing theory if the domain is defined in terms of attributes of international actors. Many political science theories are formulated in such a way that they seem to presuppose the existence of traditional states. As a consequence, the EU does not fit well into their conceptual frameworks.

Still, although the EU may defy classification when traditional concepts are used to pin down its 'nature', the processes that are important in shaping the EU's external relations seem much less alien to existing theory. By reformulating existing theories in such a way that they no longer rely on a concept of traditional states, their underlying logic may well be applicable to the EU's external relations, as well. Thus, it may be useful to move away from the question: 'what are the EU's external relations?' to the question: 'what political processes take place in the EU's external relations?'

In addition, studying the EU's external relations may shed more light on political processes in traditional states and international organizations and thereby contribute to political science theory. A move away from actors to processes may therefore be key both to integrating the EU in existing theory and opening up new avenues in political science theory.

To clarify these points, we will first discuss attempts to conceptualize the EU as an international actor. Then, we will show why a focus on processes is more likely to be fruitful. Finally, we will argue that such an approach is also likely to yield additional insights in the study of 'traditional' actors.

Looking for the nature of the beast: the elusive character of the EU

Claims about the uniqueness of the EU tend to focus on the EU as an actor and its attributes. The attributes that seem to set the EU apart typically relate to the degree of coherence in its policy-making process, either horizontally (between policy areas) or vertically (between the EU and member state levels). Indeed, in both respects, the EU does not appear to be comparable to traditional states and international organizations.

Traditional states are much more centralized and possess some form of hierarchy between domestic political actors. As a result, they have stronger ways of integrating policies, which makes them capable of formulating and carrying out a foreign policy. International organizations, on the other hand, are typically highly decentralized, relying exclusively on the authority handed over by their members and on the explicit assent of those members. As a result, international organizations hardly have any autonomy from their members, which are themselves states.

The EU seems to fall between these two extremes. Member states still retain autonomy in their external relations and dominate the EU's decision-making processes, but their influence has been constrained by EU-level actors and by the strong institutional framework that shapes interactions between member states. The extent to which member states have been constrained differs markedly between pillars.

Therefore, EU policies are much less centralized and coherent than those of states. Europe does not always speak with one voice and when it does, member states often dominate the process of formulating that voice. At the same time, the EU's (external) policies encompass a much wider range of issues and policy areas than those of any other international organization and, in some of those areas, the EU has gained a degree of autonomy in its external dealings that is unmatched by any international organization. Since states and international organizations are usually dealt with as separate types of institutions, in which different types of processes are important, existing theory seems to be incapable of dealing with the EU.

Rather, as was discussed in the introduction, European governance possesses some distinctive characteristics. It is a polycentric system, which is split into multiple, overlapping arenas that are characterized by loose coupling. Moreover, the organizing principle of political relations is consensual, relying heavily on interaction and communication between its entities.

The chapters in this book bear out many of these distinct attributes. This is particularly true of the contributions in the first part. For instance, Young analyses mixed competencies, which are typical of the EU's external relations in a number of policy areas, while Rynning shows why the EU is unlikely to become a strategic actor. The same applies to contributions in the other parts. Thus, decision-making on sanctions, as analysed by Buchet de Neuilly, shows a mix of decision-making modes that is typical of the EU's ambiguity. Similarly, the fact that the EU has competence in economic policies but lacks such competence in defence issues underlies Mörth's analysis of framing processes. Papadimitriou's multi-level negotiations are compounded by the additional level formed by the EU, as are the processes examined by Princen. The EU fisheries policies that are central to Ballesteros' chapter are themselves the outcome of relations and policies between member states that are typical of the EU.

Hence, it is not surprising that scholars have found it difficult to pin down the EU in traditional terms. It does not fit well into typologies of states and international organizations. Treating the EU as a 'case in between' does not solve this theoretical problem – rather, it compounds it, since arguing that the EU has attributes of both states and international organizations means one has to integrate the quite different and sometimes contradictory notions and implications that flow from existing theory on these two types of actors.

Moving from actors to processes: the familiar character of the EU

As was argued above, the studies presented in this book bear out many of the EU's unique attributes. At the same time, the processes they discuss are often familiar to observers of traditional states and international organizations. This can be demonstrated most clearly by taking the examples of multi-pillar processes and multi-level processes.

When it comes to multi-pillar processes, the specific ways in which competencies are divided between pillars and the involvement of certain types of actors in those pillars are distinct. However, the concepts used for analysing the political processes that determine the outcomes of multi-pillar decision-making seem directly applicable to traditional states. Mörth uses the concept of 'framing' to analyse interactions between the first and second pillars in policies on defence equipment. Framing is not unique to the EU, however, but is probably part and parcel of any battle between political actors that have distinct areas of competence and want to reach beyond their own remit. Defence equipment issues in general combine economic, technological, military and foreign policy dimensions, which in most states are divided between several agencies. Framing an issue in terms of one dimension or another will then be an important strategy for those agencies if they want to exert influence in the decision-making process.

An analysis in terms of structural differences between sub-fields, which Buchet de Neuilly applies in his analysis of sanctions policies against Serbia, may also yield useful hypotheses for related processes, both within states and between international organizations. Within states, structural differences between policy areas and policy networks may lead to quite different outcomes over a given issue. The process of 'forum shopping' between international organizations in order to obtain a desired outcome is an example in the international arena.

A similar logic seems to apply to multi-level processes. Papadimitriou's analysis in terms of nested games on multiple levels is equally well applicable to the external relations of traditional states and negotiations within international organizations. The EU presents an additional level in this type of analysis, but the analysis of the underlying processes remains the same. The EU may therefore add to the possible number of configurations of pay-offs in the multiple games, but this is only one among a multitude of factors that determine these configurations.

A special case of these multi-level games is formed by Putnam's two-level game approach, which has gained considerable popularity over the last decade and has been applied to the EU as well as to traditional states. In applying the two-level game approach, several authors have argued for an extension to three levels in the case of the EU (e.g. Patterson 1997; Collinson 1999). Such an extension would probably not affect the underlying hypotheses and processes to be studied, although it would complicate the analysis.

Yet it can be argued that extending the two-level game approach to three levels when the EU's external relations are dealt with is not self-evident. In fact, it restricts the levels in the two- (or more-) level game approach to interactions involving state actors, whereas the logic of the approach lends itself to a much wider application.

To begin with, even in traditional two-level games, additional levels can often be discerned. For instance, in a country that has a coalition government so that ratification in parliament has to take place by a number of parties, the political processes within these parties can be analysed as a third level. Similarly, in terms of informal ratification, interest groups often have to negotiate a position among their members, which would constitute an additional level as well. Therefore, the number of levels to be discerned is not fixed but depends on assumptions about decision-making processes, even in traditional states.

Likewise, in federal states, sub-federal governments may play roles similar to those played by member states in the EU, depending on the issue at stake. For instance, in Canada, some observers have characterized the relations between provinces and the federal government as 'federal-provincial diplomacy' (Tuohy 1992: 35), while in some policy areas, US states rather than the federal government have authority. Although foreign and international trade policies usually rest with the federal government, these sub-federal governments may become relevant when an issue also has other, for example regulatory, aspects. In some cases, it would therefore also be useful to apply a three-level game analysis to federal states, which makes the distinction with the EU less black and white.

This is by no means meant to deny the relevance of differences between the EU and federal states. The involvement of member states in EU decision-making is much greater than that of states or provinces in decision-making at the federal US or Canadian level. The roles played by the European Commission and the European Parliament are also different from those played by governments and parliaments in federal states. In applying a theory to a specific case or issue, it is crucial to take account of these differences.

At the same time, this analysis does not point to a need to treat the EU's external relations as a three-level game as opposed to all other states' external relations, which should then be seen as two-level games. The differences between federal states like the US and Canada on the one hand, and the EU on the other, are more subtle and more diverse than that. Indiscriminately applying a three-level game approach to the EU seems to imply a state-centred approach that is not implied by the two-level game approach per se. Rather than using a three-level game approach to the EU's external relations in general, the usefulness of the approach should therefore be examined in each case separately – not just in the EU, but also in cases involving other states.

Thus moving from the EU's attributes as an actor to the characteristics of political processes within the EU may offer a way to integrate theories of the EU's external relations in existing theory. In doing so, theories often need to be reformulated to shift their focus from actors to processes. As White (1999) has shown in regard to foreign policy analysis, many theoretical concepts in international relations seem to imply the existence of traditional states, but their underlying hypotheses do not require the existence of traditional states. By reformulating these theories, their insights can also be applied to the EU's external relations. Thus, applying existing theory to the EU's external relations invites a critical examination of the assumptions underlying those theories and a reformulation that focuses more on processes than on the specific actors those theories are applied to.

Applying the EU to other actors: the EU's external relations as a source of inspiration in political science theory

The analogies between traditional states and international organizations on the one hand and the EU on the other point to ways to integrate EU studies in existing theory. At the same time, they also imply that the results of analyses in the EU context may yield relevant insights for the study of traditional states and international organizations. In the introduction, this was called 'the EU's external relations as a laboratory'.

The idea behind this notion is that the EU's external relations exemplify many processes that also exist in traditional states and international organizations, but in stronger ways. As a consequence, the EU's external relations offer ways to focus more strongly on these processes or to highlight them, which in turn can be useful when analysing similar processes in traditional states and international organizations.

Thus, analysing framing processes in the context of the EU's external relations may yield insights and hypotheses that are relevant in analysing similar processes in, for instance, national administrations. Likewise, analysing EU-member state relations in international regulatory policies may highlight the existence of similar processes between the federal government and sub-federal governments in federal states.

Of course, much of the EU's use in this regard depends on the extent to which the EU does actually exemplify tendencies that are also apparent in traditional states and international organizations. In relation to international organizations, the EU's significance in this regard has been justified by arguing that the EU's reliance on non-military means reflected a general tendency in the international system away from military and coercive methods to non-military and diplomatic means (e.g. Smith 1994). As a result, the international arena would generally show more 'EU-like' qualities.

Such claims are extremely vulnerable to changes in the international political tide. After 11 September 2001, in particular, security issues and military means seem to have gained a new significance in international relations, while multilateral approaches seem to have lost credibility. Still, in a number of policy areas, mainly those related to trade and regulatory policies, there is a discernable trend toward greater international co-operation. The higher these policy areas are on the international list of priorities, the more significant the European experience may be in understanding international developments and developments in traditional states.

Study of the EU's external relations may then lead to a redefinition of existing theories, clarifying their underlying assumptions, and to new insights in the way traditional actors behave internationally. In both these ways, the EU's external relations are likely to lead to progress in our understanding of international politics and in political science theory generally.

References

Allen, D. and Smith M. (1990) 'Western Europe's Presence in the Contemporary International Arena', *Review of International Studies*, 16:19–37.

Collinson, S. (1999) '"Issue-Systems," "Multi-Level Games" and the Analysis of the EU's External Commercial and Associated Policies: A Research Agenda'. *Journal of European Public Policy*, 6, 2: 206–224.

Patterson, L.A. (1997) 'Agricultural Policy Reform in the European Community: A Three-Level Game Analysis', *International Organization,* 51, 1: 135–165.

Smith, M. (1994) 'The European Union, Foreign Economic Policy and the Changing World Arena', *Journal of European Public Policy*, 1, 2: 283–302.

Tuohy, C.J. (1992) *Policy and Politics in Canada. Institutionalized Ambivalence,* Philadelphia: Temple University Press.

White, B. (1999) 'The European Challenge to Foreign Policy Analysis', *European Journal of International Relations,* 5, 1: 37–66.

Index